2019

China PPP Market Transparency Report

PPP Research Center
Shanghai University of Finance and Economics

Shanghai University of Finance and Economics Press

2019

China PPP Market Transparency Report

Client

Asian Development Bank (ADB)

Consultants

Liu Xiaochuan

Professor and Dean of the China Public Finance Institute,
Shanghai University of Finance and Economics

Ko Wang

Professor and Dean's Chair of Real Estate and Infrastructure
Johns Hopkings Carey Business School

Project Members

Fang Fang　**Zong Qingqing**　**Shen Yanyan**

Abstract

PPPs is the acronym for Public-Private Partnerships. At present, China's PPP model is not only a means of market-oriented investment and financing by government, but also has become a comprehensive and systematic market and social reform for the provision of public infrastructure and services. Therefore, all stakeholders (both internal and external) have high expectations for the further development and implementation of PPP, hoping it could play a key role in leading the reform of public finance system and assisting the public sector in deepening reform. In this context, standardized arrangements for the management of PPP projects are particularly important. In particular, the timely and complete information disclosure of PPP projects is the basis for standardized management of PPP projects. From 2017, a number of documents issued by the Ministry of Finance have made provisions concerning the information disclosure of PPP projects. In particular, the *Interim Measures for Administration of Information Disclosure for Public-Private Partnership Integrated Information Platform* (Cai Jin [2017] No. 1) released in early 2017 specified all the requirements for information disclosure of PPP projects. When it came to 2018, the removal of PPP projects from management database became a key mission in PPP management. In specific, more than 2 000 PPP projects that failed to meet the management specifications were cleaned and removed from management database, while many new projects were added to the database as well. From the beginning of 2019, as more PPP projects came to the implementation stage, how to effectively promote the disclosure in due time of PPP projects became increasingly important. Meanwhile, the public had higher and higher requirements for the quality of PPP project information disclosed. On March 31, 2020, the Ministry of Finance released the *Guideline for PPP Project Performance Management*, proposing a complete appraisal system for PPP performance. While clarifying who to take accountability, the document has also incorporated truthfulness, openness, transparency and quality into specific assessment rules.

In this context, the Research Group of PPP Research Center at Shanghai University of Finance and Economics, following the evaluation of the information disclosure of PPP projects in the past two years, carried out a detailed assessment on the latest status as of December 31, 2019. The Research Group assessed in detail the information disclosure work of 9 398 projects included into the management database as of the end of 2019, and compiled a set of "2019 China PPP Market Transparency Index", which incorporates 75 index fields and is divided into transparency index of immediate disclosure, transparency index of disclosure in due time, and transparency sub-indexes at each stage, i.e. identification, preparation, procurement, and implementation. Regarding the synthesis of indexes, the Research Group adopted an approach combining analytic hierarchy process (AHP) and expert scoring: for specific indexes under sub-indexes, different scores were set according to the importance determined by selected experts; and for the synthesis of sub-indexes, the Research Group adopted AHP, a method commonly used in the compilation of similar indexes, thus guaranteeing the reliability of the index preparation method. In the end, through the statistical analysis of final results, the Research Group obtained the following findings:

First, the overall national PPP market transparency index 2019 was 76.19, a slight improvement from 2018. As of December 31, 2019, the overall national PPP market transparency index recorded 76.19 (out of 100, the same below), an increase of about 1 point from 75.25 in 2018. In specific, the transparency index of immediate disclosure was 79.14, an increase of 1.5 points from last year (77.61), while the transparency index of disclosure in due time was 71.57, almost the same as last year (71.55). Further analysis on heterogeneity shows no obvious difference in the transparency scores between industries or between demonstration and non-demonstration projects; while time of project initiation had significant impacts on the score, as the later a project is initiated, the more transparent it is regarded.

Second, change in the evaluation object was an important cause for the cross-phase differences in the PPP market transparency indexes in 2019 from 2018. First, the substantial increase in the proportion of projects entering the implementation phase led to a decrease in the transparency in 2019. Second, by decomposing the effects generated by withdrawal, inventory and new increase, we found that projects with low transparency scores that were withdrawn or remained in the database improved their information disclosure work. On the other hand, newly increased projects scored slightly higher than inventory projects. These factors jointly contributed to a higher PPP market transparency score in 2019.

Third, larger differences between provinces were presented in the PPP market transparency index. The transparency indexes of most provinces were between 70–80 — they formed up the second group. The top five provinces, all scoring more than 80 points, constituted the first group. The last six provincial-level regions all recorded a PPP market transparency score of less than 70 points, belonging to the third group. In specific, the top five in transparency ranking were Gansu (81.97), Hebei (81.29), Jilin (80.52), Shandong (80.2) and Yunnan (80.17). By comparing with last year's ranking, we found that the provinces that made the greatest progress in PPP project information disclosure were Jiangsu (77.69) and Guangdong (77.20). Both of them rose by 17 places from the previous year to No.9 and No.12, respectively.

Fourth, more than half of the cities scored higher than 2018, and the rest showed decline. The Research Group selected 46 cities that managed a relatively large number of PPP projects (>50 projects in the management database) for more detailed analysis. Comparison with the indexes in 2018 shows that some cities above the prefecture level scored significantly higher in 2019 than in 2018. Among them, the largest increase was delivered by Aksu of Xinjiang, the 2019 overall score of which increased by 15.39 points compared to 2018; and followed by Dongguan of Guangdong, with increase of 13.62 points from 2018. However, it can also be found that the indexes of many cities above the prefecture level decreased in 2019 from 2018, especially Qiannan of Guizhou and Haikou of Hainan. They recorded the largest decline from 2018 by 13.10 and 12 points, respectively. The five cities of the highest PPP market transparency index in 2019 were: Aksu of Xinjiang (82.81), Dongguan of Guangdong (82.48), Rizhao of Shandong (82.06), Weifang of Shandong (81.79), and Jining of Shandong (81.62).

Fifth, PPP intermediaries showed minor cross-phase differences in information disclosure, with their transparency indexes positively related to qualifications and business volumes. We made an analysis on the status quo of information disclosure by PPP intermediaries. The main findings are as follows: the average transparency index of intermediaries was 75.20. In secondary indexes, projects engaged by intermediaries scored relatively high in terms of information disclosure, but some of them delivered less satisfactory performance in active information disclosure, with a further decrease in willingness from last year. Further analysis also found that intermediaries' transparency indexes showed a clear positive correlation with the number of PPP projects they were engaged in and how long they had been operating.

During the preparation of this Report and the analysis behind it, the Research Group has also reached some policy recommendations for the further improvement of the information disclosure of PPP projects, such as to add the appraisal of the disclosure timeliness, to improve the management over the disclosure of "inapplicable" information and temporary major events, to reinforce the supervision and inspection of the disclosure of key information in PPP projects, to further clarify the accountability and specific division of labor in information disclosure, etc. We hope to further enhance the information transparency in the PPP market by refining the system of PPP information disclosure and standardized management, thereby facilitating the better and more sustainable development of the entire PPP market.

Contents

1

Introduction

1.1 Basic Concept and Operating Procedure of PPP

1.1.1 PPP Definitions

Definitions of Public-Private Partnerships (PPPs) differ from international organizations and different governments, however they generally involve the use of private capital and in some cases, other forms of social capital in the investment and operation of infrastructure and public utility projects. The Asian Development Bank describes PPPs as a range of possible relationships among public and private sectors in the context of infrastructure and other services. The United Nations Development Programme, also refers to the partnership between government, for-profit companies and non-for-profit organizations regarding certain infrastructure and services projects. Typically, government does not transfer the project responsibility wholly to the private sector. Instead, the parties involved in the cooperation share responsibility and financing risks. The European Commission refers it to the partnership between public sector and private sector, with the aim of providing public projects or services traditionally provided by public sector. The World Bank also provides a definition of PPPs as long-term contracts between the private sector and a government entity regarding the provision of public infrastructure assets or services, in which the private sector bears material risks and management and delivery responsibility. The Chinese government has adopted a specific definition for the PPP model incorporating a long-term benefit and risk sharing partnership established by the government through franchising, reasonable pricing, financial subsidies and other agreed revenue sharing rules disclosed in advance, to introduce social capital to the investment and operation of public infrastructure projects such as urban utility, thus enhancing capacity of supplying public goods and services and improving supply efficiency. The main difference between the Chinese government definition and those by other international organizations and governments relates to the use of the word "social capital" in addition to the word "private capital". In China, social capital covers private capital, foreign capital, state-owned enterprise capital, etc.

For the purposes of this Report, PPP refers to the provision of public products or services (usually infrastructure and public services) through a co-operative partnership between government and social capital. The government generally follows a competitive tendering model to select a social capital partner with optimal investment, financing, operation and management capabilities. The partnership is contracted so that the social capital partner provides public infrastructure and services and the government pays consideration to the social capital partner based on the performance and delivery evaluation of the contracted public infrastructure and/or services. Specifically, in this PPP model, the social capital partner can take charge of project design, construction, operation and maintenance of the infrastructure and the delivery of services as well as assuming commercial and financial risks, for a commensurate investment return (within a contract which clearly specifies the delivery obligations of the social capital partner). The government in turn supervises the quality and pricing of public services and infrastructure, protects the interests of consumers to ensure the maximization of public interests, and bears policy and legal risks. PPPs worldwide have evolved to cover most public infrastructure and/or service areas, including transportation, energy, water conservancy, water utilities and other economic infrastructure, as well as technology, environmental protection, education, culture, sports, health, tourism, social welfare and other social infrastructure.

1.1.2 PPP Operating Procedure

The *Guidelines for the Public-Private Partnerships Model* issued by the Ministry of Finance on November 2014 stipulate the operating standards for the life cycle of PPP projects, incorporating the stages of design, financing, construction, operation, maintenance, and termination & transfer. The operating procedure can be divided into five stages: identification, preparation, procurement, implementation and transfer of project, as shown in Figure 1–1. The guidelines for the administration of information disclosure of PPP projects in the *Interim Measures for Administration of Information Disclosure for Public-Private Partnership Integrated Information Platform* (Cai Jin [2017] No. 1, referred to as "No. 1 Document" in the Report) issued by the Ministry of Finance in early 2017 are also provided separately in accordance with these five stages. Defining the five project delivery stages is also an important intermediate step in the development of the PPP market transparency index.

Figure 1–1 Operating Procedure of PPP Projects

On this basis, in November 2017, the Ministry of Finance issued the *Circular on Regulating Project Database of the National PPP Integrated Information Platform* (Cai Ban Jin [2017] No. 92), which further optimizes the process management of PPP projects by implementing classification management, classifying the project database into Project Reserve List and Project Management Database according to the stage of the project. Projects in the Project Reserve List shall focus on project incubation and promotion; while those in the Project Management Database are subject to strict supervision and life cycle management. Compared with the five-stage division above, the Project Reserve List corresponds to the identification phase, and incorporates the candidate projects to which local government departments have the intention to apply the PPP model, but due to the fact that the value-for-money evaluation and the financial affordability assessment have not yet been completed, they cannot be called PPP projects in the strict sense; the Project Management Database covers the stages of preparation, procurement, implementation, and transfer, and incorporates the PPP projects subject to life cycle management in accordance with related management measures.

1.2 Concept of PPP Market Transparency

Information transparency refers to the degree of information disclosure of a market, company or project. For the purposes of this Report, transparency of PPP market refers to the degree of information disclosure of PPP projects by responsible parties (competent authorities, government-authorized partners, corporate partners, intermediaries, etc.). In theory, information disclosure across the PPP market also covers the disclosure of project management methods, policy documents, and the information of all project participants. For example, the existing PPP expert database, institution library, etc. also contains mass data, but due to data availability and other reasons, the PPP market information transparency in this Report refers only to the degree of information disclosure of PPP projects, and transparency indexes of all kinds are compiled on this basis. Horizontally, we constructed transparency indexes by province, city, and industry. Vertically, our indexes were divided into overall transparency index, immediate disclosure index, disclosure in due time index, and phased index. Besides PPP projects, this Report has also incorporated the information transparency of PPP intermediaries, which is introduced in a separate chapter.

PPP is a market-oriented market-based public infrastructure and services mechanism which requires the management means and service capabilities that are compatible with marketization which requires transparency for the PPP market to deliver real value for money. PPP information disclosure in China has improved over the last three years following the systematic promotion of the PPP Integrated Information Platform. It has become an essential tool for local governments to strengthen project management, promote project connection, and facilitate project implementation. At present, China is accelerating the disclosure of PPP project information and government service information, with an aim to continuously improving PPP management transparency.

In particular, in January 2017, the Finance Department of the Ministry of Finance issued the No. 1 Document, i.e. the *Interim Measures for Administration of Information Disclosure for Public-Private Partnership Integrated Information Platform* (Cai Jin [2017] No. 1). This No.1 Document further clarifies the responsible parties of the PPP project information disclosure, details disclosure content, time limit and methods to ensure timely and full disclosure of key information such as the basic information, implementation program, evaluation and assessment report, procurement documents, project contracts and other information of the PPP projects to be included in the database. It also requires disclosure priority of demonstration projects to ensure that projects operate in a transparent manner, strengthen government supervision and social supervision, and promote project implementation. PPP projects that more completely meet the information disclosure requirements of the No. 1 Document are projects which will be assessed as projects with high information transparency, and where projects fail to disclose the information as required by the No. 1 Document, they will be assessed as projects with low information transparency. Moreover, in order to ensure the objectiveness and fairness of the assessment, all relevant information beyond the scope of the No. 1 Document is not included in the assessment scope in this Report. The reason is that data used by the Research Group comes from the Integrated Information Platform of the China Public Private Partnerships Center, which was designed mainly based on capturing the information disclosure requirements detailed in the No. 1 Document.

1.3 Necessity and Significance of PPP Information Disclosure

First, improve business environment and encourage private capital to participate in public services. PPPs by nature are generally long term with the social capital providers (including private capital providers) often investing large sums of money over extended time period before any returns can be realized. Successful PPPs rely in part on the integrity of Government and the equity of the partnership arrangements. Therefore, improving the market transparency of the PPP processes can support greater participation in PPP projects, encourage competition which drives value and has the potential to create a fairer and more equal market environment. At the same time, improved PPP market transparency will also help support the partnering spirit between the government and enterprises, assist to eradicate corruption, and maintain a clean and efficient government image.

Second, promote social harmony and enhance public awareness and confidence. The adoption of PPP for the provision of public infrastructure and services is closely aligned to the interests of the public. PPP projects are usually infrastructure, goods and services provided for the general public, and therefore, the construction, operation and quality of which directly affects them. Additionally, PPP projects are ultimately paid either by taxpayers through taxation or by taxpayers directly as the end users. Therefore, strengthening the disclosure of PPP information will help the public to understand and supervise the PPP market and PPP projects in a more convenient manner, facilitate the understanding and cooperation of the public, and create a harmonious atmosphere for the progress of related work.

Third, improve supply efficiency and enhance performance management over public goods. PPP projects are mostly applied to infrastructure and other public goods and services. They are generally characterized by detailed information, frequently technical in nature and with complex pricing structures. Strengthening information disclosure will help professionals in various fields make scientific and rigorous appraisal concerning issues such as pricing benchmarks, financial affordability, and charging standards in PPP projects, thus realizing the scientific pricing of public goods and services. At the same time, higher PPP market transparency alleviates information asymmetry during the construction and operation of public goods, removes insider trading, realizes the maintenance and appreciation of state-owned assets, and safeguards the rights and interests of taxpayers and consumers. Finally, sound information disclosure will also help resolve local debt and financial risks.

Fourth, raise governance level and build a new public management model. PPP is a market-oriented and socialized management model for the provision of public goods and services. It aims to, via reforms and innovations, break monopolies, introduce competition mechanisms, utilize market's professional and innovation capabilities, enrich public goods and services and improve the provision quality of public goods and services, to satisfy the growing demands of people for diverse public goods and services. Therefore, it is of great practical significance to improving governance and building a new public management model. Early in the 1980s and 1990s, China began to experiment with public-private partnerships in the field of infrastructure construction. However, due to the absence of institutional construction, the projects faced "variation and distortion". To solve such problems, in this round of PPP promotion, the competent department of the industry started with institutional construction by formulating a system in line with the concept of "top-level design + supporting policies + operating guidelines", covering the life cycle of PPP. Adequate information disclosure is an integral part of the system, where competent authorities could take PPP information disclosure as a means to urging local governments and all relevant parties to participate in PPP projects in a more regulated manner, thereby jointly promoting the continuous improvement of the new management model.

Fifth, promote PPP development and propel the comprehensive deepening of reform process. Promoting PPPs in the provision of public infrastructure and services is an important factor in the delivery of reform. It is also an important measure for advancing structural reform at the supply side, and an important means for implementing innovation-driven development and developing the new economy. Driving the development of PPP market fully reflects the core spirit of law-based governance, giving play to the decisive role of market in the allocation of resources, and better exerting the function of the government. The development of PPP market has promoted reform of the administrative system, the financial system, and the investment & financing systems. Therefore, the standardized development of PPP market brought about by improving its transparency is also of great value to other reforms. At present, China's PPP market is in a leading position in terms of disclosure work among similar government affairs, and even in the whole world. In-depth assessment, analysis and summary of achievements and experience in PPP market's information disclosure work can provide reference value for other reforms.

Sixth, build up national image and demonstrate national confidence in political system. Many countries use PPPs for the delivery of infrastructure and services, as attracted the participation of multiple international organizations. After years of exploration and consideration of options, China has formed its own model and style of PPP projects, and has made innovations in many aspects of PPP models. Accordingly, the summary and analysis on the information transparency of PPP market is important in the shaping of an open and efficient image of the Chinese government as well as increasing its influence and participation in the international PPP market. Moreover, as infrastructure is also an important component of the Belt and Road Initiative, promoting PPP standardization through information disclosure helps China's PPP model to spread in the countries and regions along the Belt and Road, demonstrating China's soft power while exporting products and technologies.

1.4 Development of PPP Information Disclosure in China

Since the initiation of PPP projects in 2013, as deployed by the CPC Central Committee and the State Council, the Ministry of Finance has successively issued the *Interim Measures for Administration of Information Disclosure for Public-Private Partnership Integrated Information Platform* (Cai Jin [2017] No. 1), the *Circular on Regulating Project Database of the National PPP Integrated Information Platform* (Cai Ban Jin [2017] No. 92) and the *Circular on Further Regulating the Project Information Management of the National PPP Integrated Information Platform* (Cai Zheng Qi Han [2018] No. 2), among other documents. And the Ministry of Finance is responsible for planning and implementing the PPP reform and promoting the information disclosure of PPP projects.

I. The National PPP Integrated Information Platform has been established. In 2015, under the guidance of the national "Internet+" action plan, the Ministry of Finance established the PPP Integrated Information Platform — a PPP information network covering all regions of the country and 19 sectors, penetrating all aspects of project implementation, and serving all market players. First, a channel for the collection and management of PPP project information that runs through the finance departments of "state-province-city-county" at all levels has been built up. Second, two platforms — information disclosure and online management, have been set up to publish PPP policies and regulations, news, share knowledge, and enable information tracking & management; and three functions: project management, transaction matchmaking, and information service are offered. Finally, four core application databases, i.e. Project Database, Expert Library, Institution Library and Data Bank are built: Project Database is used to collect and manage key information of PPP projects across the country; Expert Library and Institution Library are designed for the collection and management of the information on experts, consulting agencies, private capital, financial institutions and other parties involved; Data Bank collects and manages PPP related policies and regulations, work updates, guidebooks, training materials and best practices.

II. An information disclosure mechanism has been set up. It clarifies the accountability for information disclosure of PPP projects, the information to be disclosed and specific requirements at each stage, makes regulations for the management of Expert Library and Institution Library, and publishes requirements for information disclosure by PPP experts and consulting organizations.

III. The PPP information disclosure system has been innovated. The information on the addition and removal of PPP projects is disclosed on a monthly basis, and overall PPP project information statistics and release are carried out on a quarterly basis. PPP policies and work updates are published through multiple channels, including the "PPP column" on the official website of the Ministry of Finance, the Chinese and English websites of the China Public Private Partnerships Center (CPPPC), the WeChat public account "China PPP Center", the mobile application "China PPP Map" and other online media. So far, a PPP project information disclosure model featuring regularity, comprehensiveness and multiple approaches has been established in China.

Thanks to the care, support and joint efforts of all stakeholders, PPP information disclosure has achieved positive results. Project Database, Institution Library and Expert Library are gaining greater social influence and recognition, and have become useful tools for strengthening project management, advancing project connection, and promoting project implementation. The Project Database Quarterly Report is regarded as the “CSI 300 Index” in the PPP market. Financial institutions have even opened up a “green channel” for the credit support granted to demonstration projects that have done a better job in information disclosure. According to statistics, as of the end of December 2019, the PPP Integrated Information Platform included 9 440 projects in Project Management Database and 2 922 on Project Reserve List. 497 experts from a variety of fields such as policy, law, finance, consulting, industry, and academia were included into the Expert Library, making it a “professional think tank” that serves PPP development. Websites, WeChat accounts, etc. have become the authoritative publishing platforms for PPP news. On March 31, 2020, the Ministry of Finance released the *Guideline for PPP Project Performance Management*, proposing a complete appraisal system for PPP performance. While clarifying who to take accountability, the document has also incorporated truthfulness, openness, transparency and quality into specific assessment rules. The Guideline is expected to more accurately and effectively improve the quality of information disclosure.

PPP information disclosure has played a positive role in the China’s PPP development. The Procuring Infrastructure Public-Private Partnerships 2018 released by the World Bank has evaluated the PPP policies and regulations in 135 economies from four dimensions: preparation of PPPs, procurement of PPPs, PPP contract management and unsolicited proposals (USPs) for PPPs. The report noted that China has established a basic PPP institutional framework, standardized the operation methods on key stages such as the value-for-money evaluation report and the financial affordability assessment report, and formulated a system for publicizing important information such as procurement documents and project progress, thus having created a favorable policy environment. In specific, China scored 82 points in Procurement of PPPs (average score of high-income economies, 77; average score of upper-middle-income economies, 64), ranking among the top in the world; 76 points in Contract Management (average score of high-income economies, 58; average score of upper-middle-income economies, 57); 61 points in Preparation (average score of high-income economies, 63; average score of upper-middle-income economies, 48); 54 points in USP (average score of high-income economies, 66; average score of upper-middle-income economies, 63).

The achievements and experience gained in disclosing PPP market information needs summary. At the same time, it is also necessary to analyze the content waiting for further improvement. The purpose of this Report is to summarize the disclosure work of the PPP market and analyze its strengths and deficiencies through index preparation. The rigorous and fair assessment on market transparency depends on scientific assessment methods. As for this Report, such a principle is articulated by the design of the PPP market transparency index system and index preparation methods, which is the topic of the next chapter.

1.5 Overview of PPP Information Disclosure in China①

Pursuant to the *Circular on Regulating the Operation of the Public-Private Partnership (PPP) Integrated Information Platform* (Cai Jin [2015] No.166), the Ministry of Finance has developed the Public-Private Partnership (PPP) Integrated Information Platform and Project Library. The assessment of PPP project information disclosure in this Report is based on the data available on the Information Platform. In this section, with reference to such data, an overview of the PPP market in China is provided below.

1.5.1 Overview and Stages Distribution in National Project Management Database

As of the end of 2019, the Project Management Database included a total of 9 440 projects, an increase of 786, or 9.1% over the same period last year; the investment value totaled RMB 14.4 trillion, growing by RMB 1.2 trillion, or 9.1% year-on-year; these projects covered 31 provinces and Xinjiang Production and Construction Corps, and 19 industries. A total of 6 330 projects were implemented, with an investment value of RMB 9.9 trillion, and an implementation rate of 67.1%, rising by 12.9 percentage points from the end of 2018. A total of 3 708 projects with an investment value of RMB 5.6 trillion were started, representing an operating rate of 58.6%, 10.9 percentage points higher than that at the end of 2018. 1 409, 1 701, and 6 330 projects in the Project Management Database were at preparation, procurement, and implementation phases respectively, with investment values of RMB 2.0 trillion, RMB 2.5 trillion, and RMB 9.9 trillion, respectively, as shown in Figure 1–2. There are no projects in the transfer stage.

① The data in this section mainly come from the Annual Report of National PPP Integrated Information Platform — Project Management Database 2019 released by the China Public Private Partnerships Center. Due to missing data, sampling deadline and other reasons, the samples included in index compilation in the following paragraphs do not completely correspond to the samples in this section.

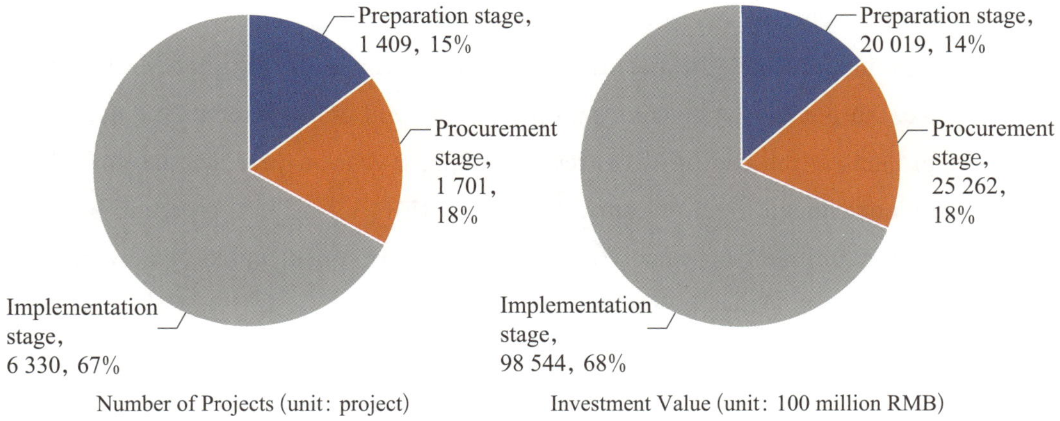

Figure 1–2 Management Database Projects in Each Stage in 2019

In 2019, the PPP market's focus shifted from quantity and speed to quality. Throughout the year, 1 434 new projects were included in the Project Management Database, a year-on-year decrease of 2 640 or 64.8%. They contributed to an investment value of RMB 2.2 trillion, dropping by RMB 3.6 trillion or 62.1% year-on-year. The number and investment value of new projects varied from months, as shown in Figure 1–3. 648 projects were removed from the Database, involving an investment value of RMB 802.3 billion. Due to the change in investment value caused by the structural adjustment to inventory projects in the Management Database, the difference obtained from the investment value of newly-increased projects minus that of the removed projects

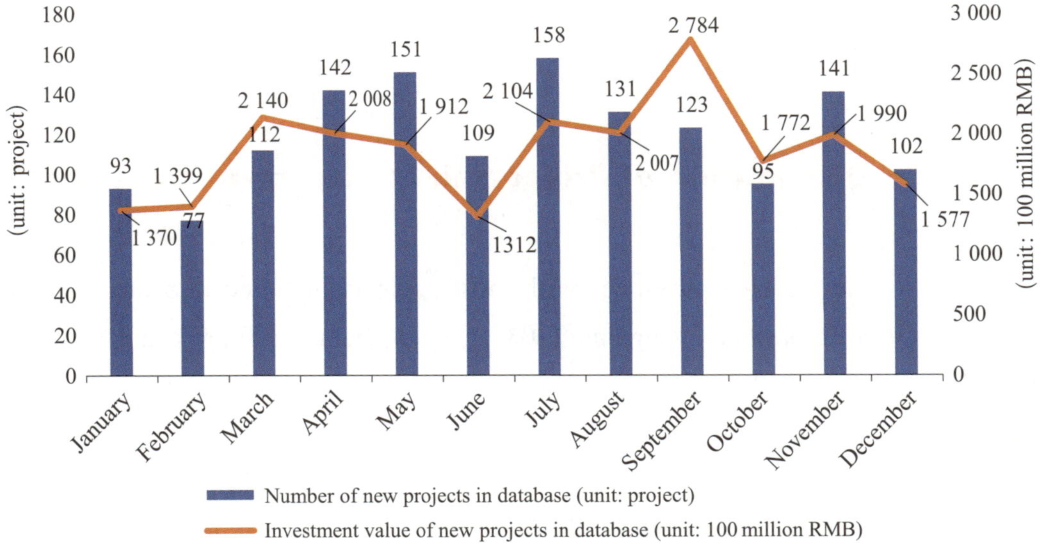

Figure 1–3 Distribution of 1 434 Newly-included Projects in 2019 by Month

was not the same as the net investment value increased.

Throughout the year, the net increase of projects in the Project Management Database (i.e. the number of inventory projects at the end of 2019 minus the number of inventory projects at the end of 2018) recorded 786, a year-on-year decrease of 731 or 48.2%. They contributed to an investment value of RMB 1.2 trillion, dropping by RMB 1.2 trillion or 50.0% year-on-year. The number and investment value of new projects varied from months, as shown in Figure 1–4.

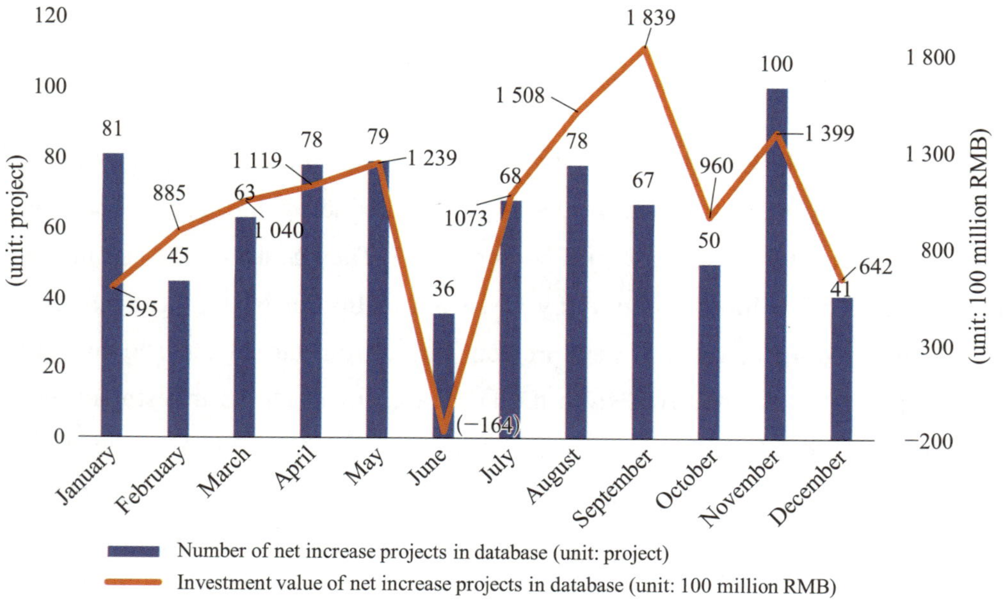

Figure 1–4 Monthly Net Increase in the Number and Investment Value of Projects in Management Database

1.5.2 Distribution of Projects in Management Database by Region

In 2019, the top five provinces with most projects included into the Database were Henan (143 projects), Guangdong (103 projects), Jiangxi (80 projects), Shandong (including Qingdao, 80 projects), and Shanxi (75 projects); the top five provinces in terms of investment value of newly-increased projects were Henan (RMB 224.3 billion), Sichuan (RMB 179.7 billion), Guizhou (RMB 175.2 billion), Tianjin (RMB 151.1 billion), and Chongqing (RMB 150.7 billion). See Figure 1–5 for the number and investment value of new projects in the Database by region in 2019.

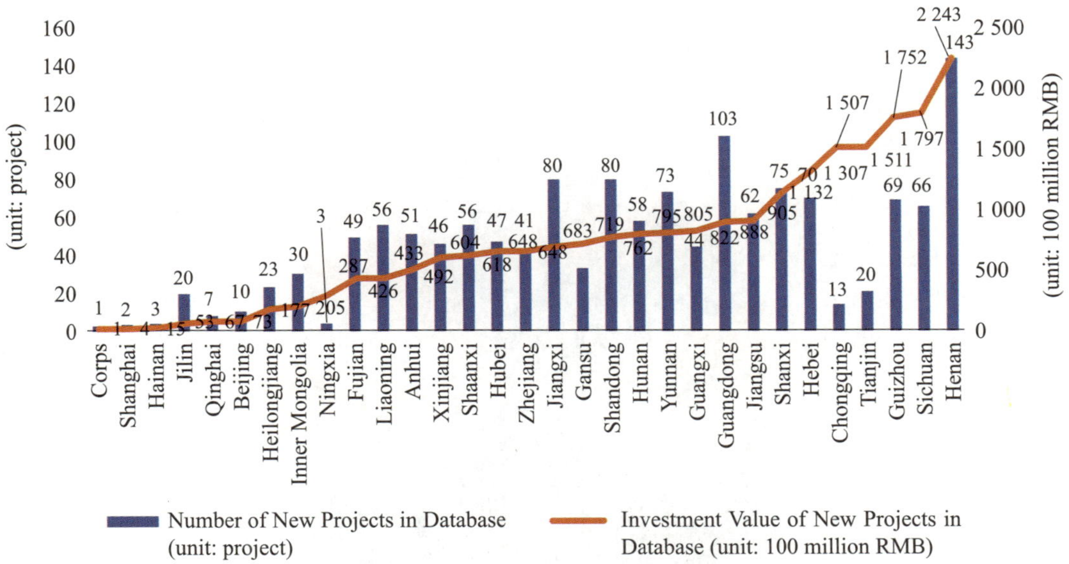

Note: "Corps" refers to the Xinjiang Production and Construction Corps, the same below.

Figure 1–5 Number and Investment Value of Projects in Management Database by Region in 2019

In terms of the total number of projects in the Database, the top five provinces were Shandong (including Qingdao) with 768 projects, Henan 753, Sichuan 559, Guangdong 519, and Guizhou 516, together accounting for 33.0% of the total. Sorted by the total investment value, the top five were Guizhou with RMB 1.2 trillion, Yunnan RMB 1.1 trillion, Sichuan RMB 1.0 trillion, Zhejiang RMB 976.7 billion, and Henan RMB 966.4 billion, accounting for 36.8% of the total. By region, the number and investment value of total projects in the Management Database at the end of 2019 are shown in Figures 1–6 and Figure 1–7.

1.5.3 Distribution of Projects in Management Database by Industry

In 2019, the top five industries with most new projects included to the Management Database were Municipal Engineering (629 projects), Transportation (174 projects), Ecological Construction and Environmental Protection (130 projects), Comprehensive Urban Development (95 projects) and Education (62 projects); and the top five industries in terms of the investment value of newly-increased projects were Transportation (RMB 863.3 billion), Municipal Engineering (RMB 529.8 billion), Comprehensive Urban Development (RMB 277.9 billion), Ecological Construction and Environmental Protection (RMB 147.1 billion) and Forestry (RMB 74.9 billion). See Figure 1–8 for the number and investment value of new projects in the database by region in 2019.

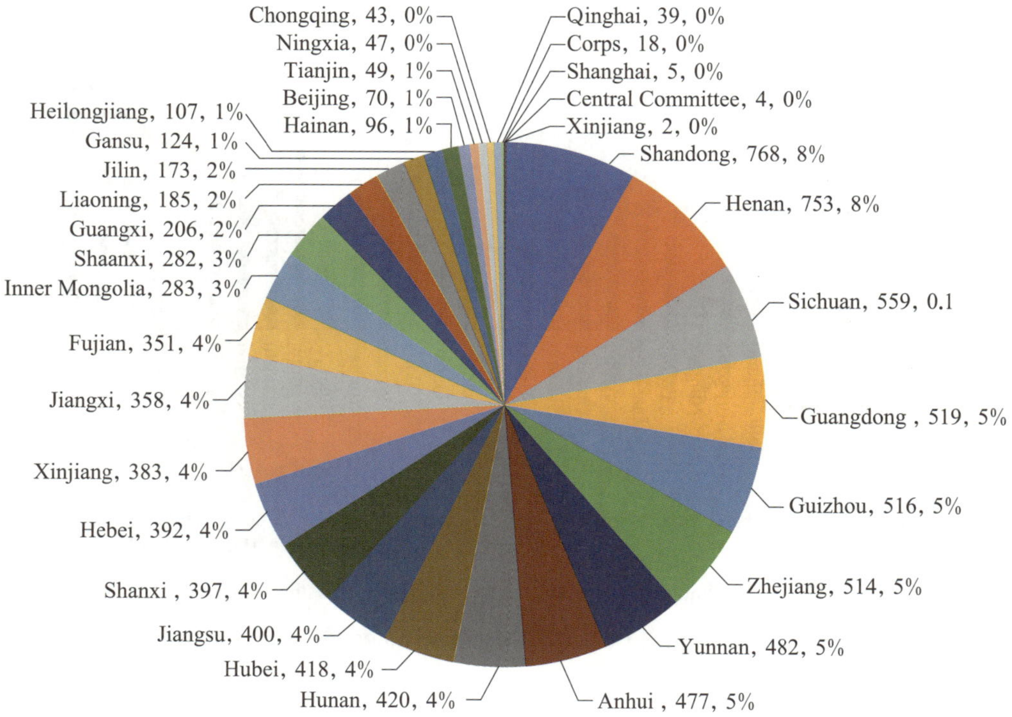

Note: "Central Commitee" refers to projects directly under the central Chinese government, the same below.

Figure 1–6 Number of Projects in Management Database at the End of 2019 by Region

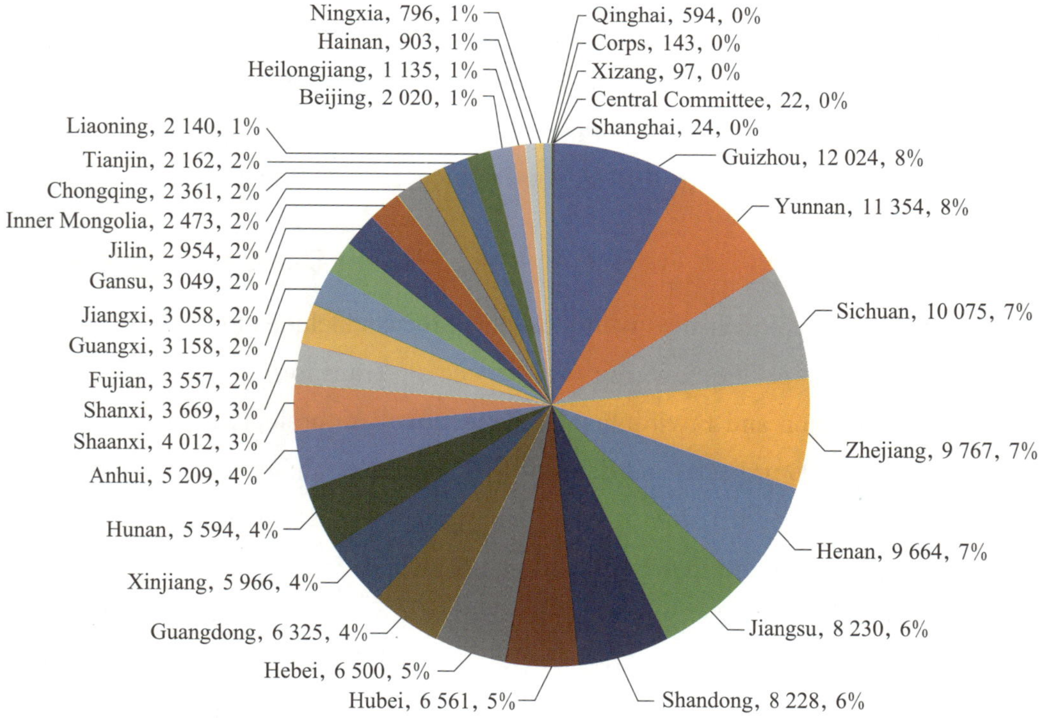

Figure 1–7 Investment Value of Projects in Management Database at the End of 2019 by Region

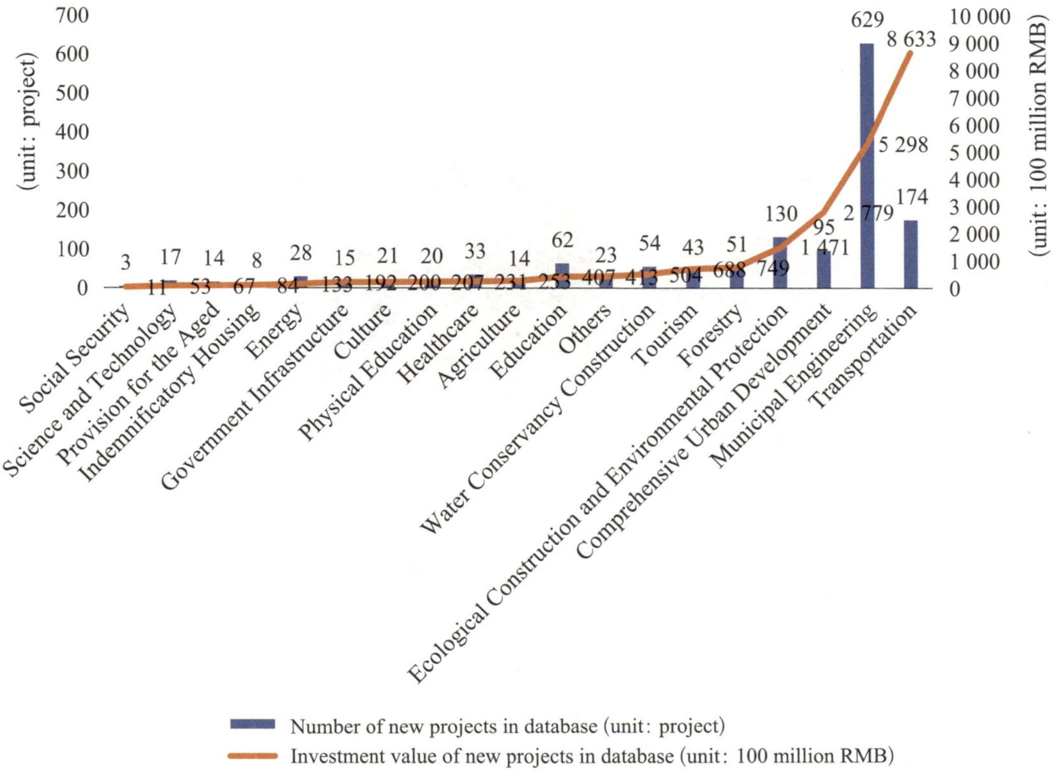

Figure 1–8 Number and Investment Value of Projects in Management Database by Industry in 2019

By the end of December 2019, the cumulative number and investment value of PPP projects in the Management Database by industry are shown in Figure 1–9 and Figure 1–10. In specific, the top five industries with most projects in the Management Database were Municipal Engineering (3 793 projects), Transportation (1 317 projects), Ecological Construction and Environmental Protection (924 projects), Comprehensive Urban Development (611 projects) and Education (447 projects), together accounting for 75.2% of the total; and the top five industries in terms of the investment value of projects were Transportation (RMB 4.6 trillion), Municipal Engineering (RMB 4.2 trillion), Comprehensive Urban Development (RMB 2 trillion), Ecological Construction and Environmental Protection (RMB 998.8 billion) and Tourism (RMB 466.6 billion), accounting for 84.2% of the total.

1.5.4 Project Signing and Implementation

In 2019, 1 639 projects in the Management Database with an investment value of

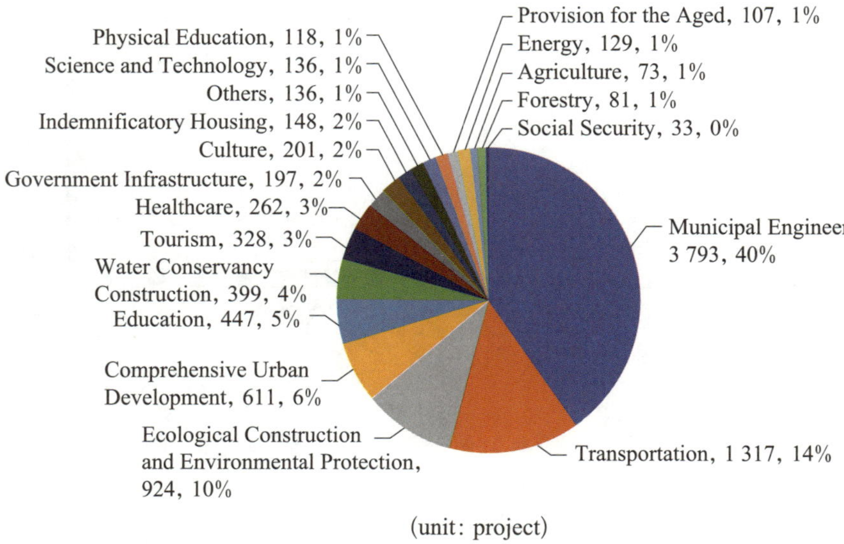

Figure 1–9 Number of Projects in Management Database at the End of 2019 by Industry

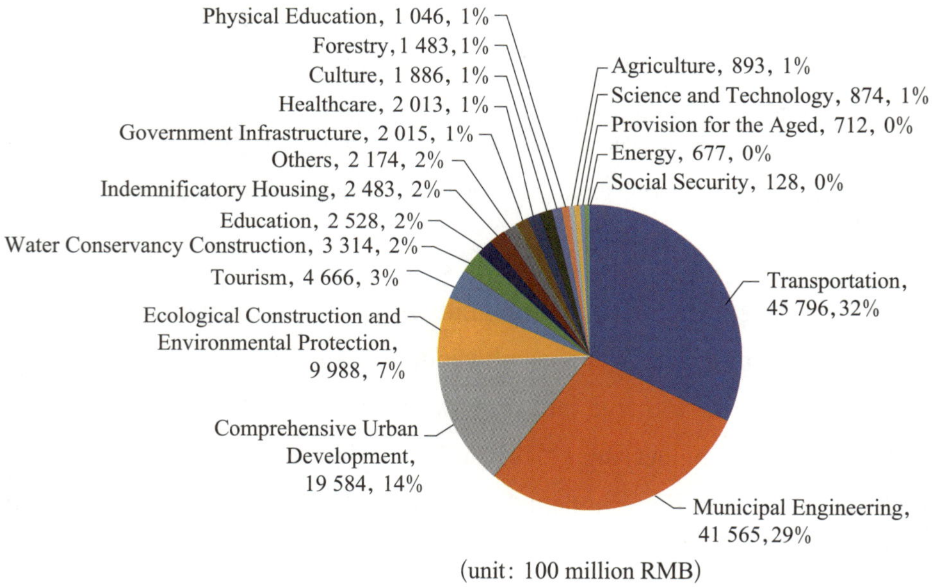

Figure 1–10 Investment Value of Projects in Management Database at the End of 2019 by Industry

RMB 2.7 trillion were implemented — 323 less in number and RMB 58.4 billion or 2.3% more in value than the same in 2018.

As of the end of 2019, the implementation rate was 67.1%, representing a year-on-year increase of 12.9 percentage points. The change in the implementation rate of Management Database projects from the end of December 2018 to the end of December 2019 is shown in Figure 1–11.

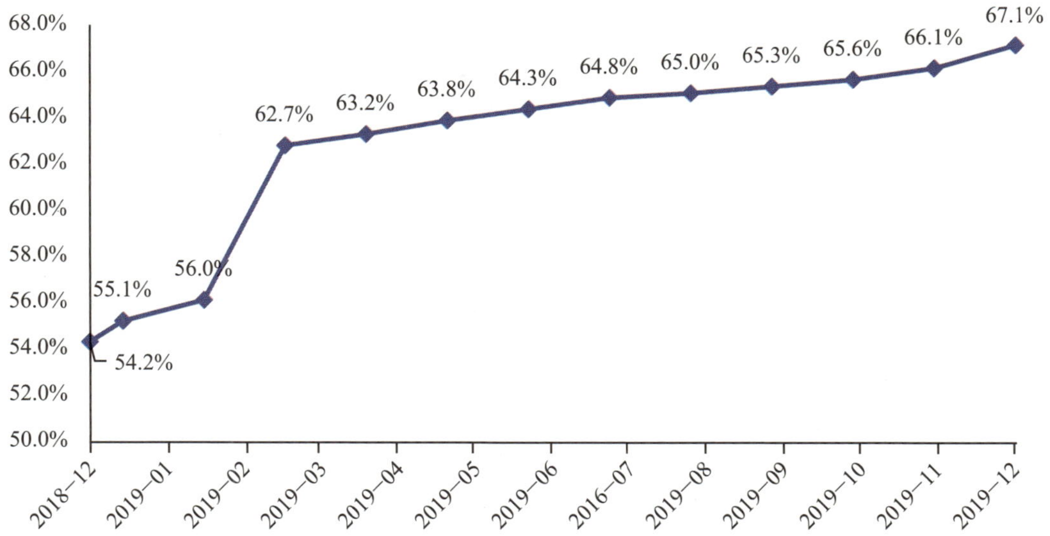

Figure 1–11 Change in the Implementation Rate of Management Database Projects from the End of December 2018 to the End of December 2019

1.5.5 Projects started saw significant increase in investment value

In 2019, 1 471 projects were started, an increase of 393 over 2018, with an investment value of RMB 2.4 trillion, growing by 876.8 billion or 56.4% over the previous year. As of the end of 2019, totally 3, 708 projects with an investment value of RMB 5.6 trillion in the Management Database were started, accounting for 58.6% and 56.7% of the implemented projects respectively.

Operating rate, refers to the ratio of the number of projects started to the number of projects implemented. As of the end of 2019, the operating rate was 58.6%, up 10.9 percentage points from the end of 2018. The change in the operating rate of Management Database projects from the end of December 2018 to the end of December 2019 is shown in Figure 1–12.

1.5.6 Proportion of viability gap funding projects increased steadily

Divided by the three return mechanisms, in 2019 alone there were 3 user-pays projects with an investment value of RMB 314.2 billion, accounting for 25.9% of the total investment value delivered by new projects (net) in the database; 697 viability gap funding (that is, payment by both government and market) projects with an investment value of RMB 992.5 billion, accounting for 81.8% of the total; and 86 government-pays

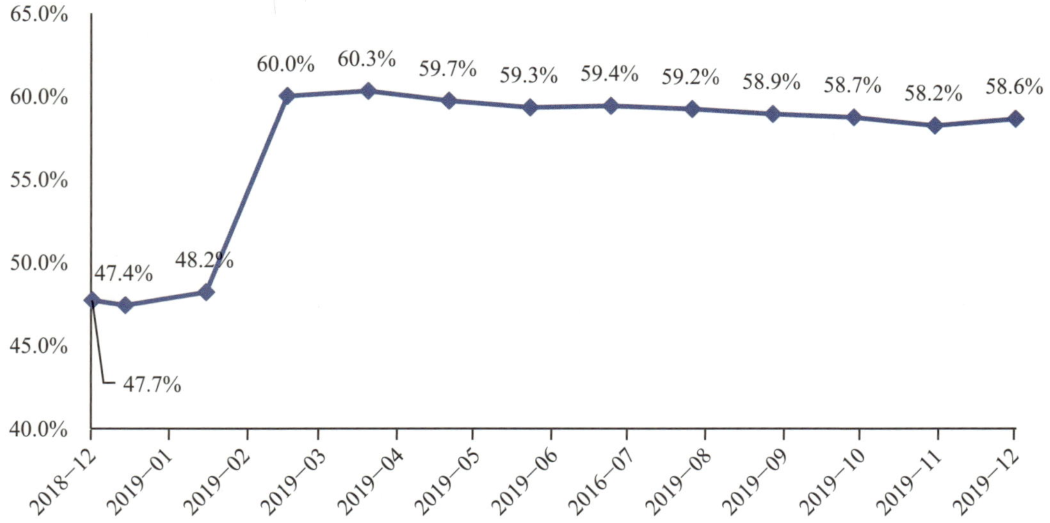

Figure 1–12 Change in the Operating Rate from December 2018 to December 2019

projects, with a net decrease of RMB 93.2 billion in investment value, accounting for –7.7% of the total.

As of the end of 2019, there were a total of 629 user-pays projects with an investment value of RMB 1.4 trillion, accounting for 6.7% and 9.6% of the total in the Management Database respectively; 5 418 viability gap funding projects with an investment value of RMB 9.7 trillion, accounting for 57.4% and 67.1% of the total; and 3 393 government-pays projects with an investment value of RMB 3.3 trillion, accounting for 35.9% and 23.2% of the total, as shown in Figure 1–13 and Figure 1–14.

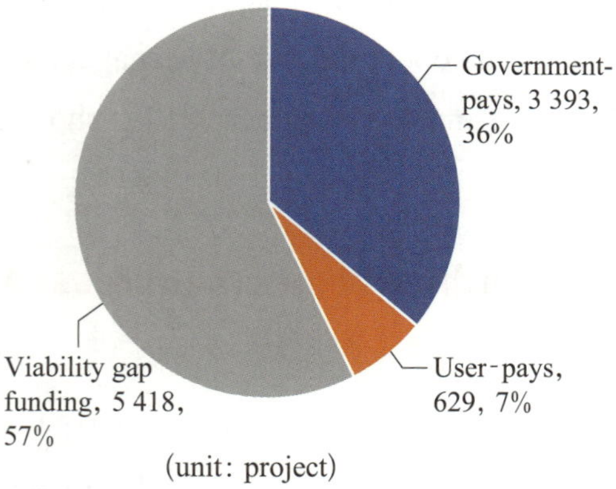

Figure 1–13 Number of Projects in Management Database by Payment Mechanism at the End of 2019

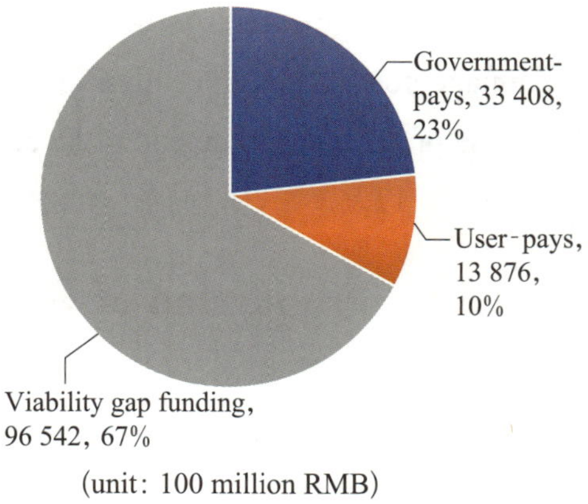

Figure 1–14 Investment Value of Projects in Management Database by Payment Mechanism at the End of 2019

2

Index System and Calculating Methodology

2.1 Construction of Index System

2.1.1 Basic Principles of Index System

The legitimacy of the Index System is directly related to the quality of the steps taken in index preparation and the validity of the interpretation of assessment results. To this end, the Index System that the Research Group established reflects all factors that affect the transparency of PPP information in an objective, reasonable and comprehensive manner, and also takes into account the availability and reliability of data. To establish a reliable PPP Market Transparency Assessment Index System, the Research Group defined key principles that should underpin the construction of an Index System. These key principles are hierarchy, commonality, continuity, as well as significance, impartiality and time-point.

(1) Principle of hierarchy within the Index System. Hierarchy refers to the multiplicity of levels within the Index System itself. Due to the multiple levels that PPP information covers based on PPP project life-cycles, the Index System must also be composed of a multi-level structure to reflect the features of each level in the PPP project life-cycle. At the same time, all the elements are linked to each other to form an organic whole, which is to reflect the full picture of PPP market transparency from the projects at different stages and levels. Specifically, with reference to the spirit of related administration measures, the index system for PPP market transparency can be divided into three levels, namely, the overall index, a secondary index based on the five phases of PPP projects, and underlying specific index for tasks within each phase of a PPP project. Therefore, the transparency index can be classified into a general index and then sub-indexes at identification, preparation, procurement, implementation, and transfer stages. Of course, given that different projects may be at different stages (i.e. phases in the project cycle), not every individual project's transparency index covers all the five stages.

(2) Principle of commonality and comparability of available information.

The Research Group assessed the transparency of each PPP project, for which there is information unique to specific PPP project. Therefore, the Research Group selected the indicators that can be applied across all the project samples for the sake of comparability. Those inapplicable to all projects, such as "design documents and approval documents", "government's authorization documents (if any) for the adjustment and updates at the project procurement stage", "increase or decrease of the capital", etc., were not included in the Index System for the time being. However, the Research Group has provided some policy suggestions at the end of the Report on the administration measures for improving the disclosure of such information.

(3) Principle of continuity for on-going measurement of transparency. Since this is the third time we assess the transparency of PPP market, the Index System is required to not only reflect the progress made by China in PPP project information disclosure in 2019, but also seamlessly link with the systems in 2017 and 2018, so that the index continuity will be maintained with consideration of potential future changes. In other words, the Index System shall have strong dynamic adaptability. The Research Group hopes that the information disclosure status of China's PPP market can be continuously assessed longitudinally through long-term tracking.

(4) Principle of significance in weighting scores. While the selection of indicators should be as comprehensive as possible, the selection should also be able to distinguish relative importance for transparency. For some particularly important indexes, as many fields as possible shall be selected. At the same time, the Research Group has set high scores for more important information and low scores for less important information through an expert survey. For example, the scores assigned to value-for-money evaluation and financial affordability assessment might be higher than those to basic project information.

(5) Principle of impartiality. As an assessment report on policy effectiveness, this China PPP Market Transparency Report is expected to have certain impacts on regions and projects upon release. Therefore, the Research Group considers that this Report must adhere to the principle of fairness and impartiality, treat all projects equally and elaborate on each and every achievement and problem. It is necessary to truthfully present the objective conditions of information disclosure in different regions and different types of PPP projects, and at the same time, make as clear as possible the objective and exogenous reasons that lead to discrepancies in the results in various regions and industries.

(6) Principle of common time-point. This Research Group assessed the disclosure of all project information in the Management Database on the PPP Integrated Information Platform of the Ministry of Finance as of December 31, 2019, which falls into the concept of inventory, that is, the object of assessment is the accumulated information disclosure status of all PPP projects existing before this time-point. Restricted by the availability of data, the assessment did not address the dynamic characteristics such as the specific time of disclosure. For example, some indicators involved disclosure in due time, so theoretically, in addition to whether or not information was disclosed, the Research Group also assessed the timeliness of such disclosure, which is an important assessment basis as well. However, as the Research Group could not obtain detailed information such as the specific time point of disclosure, such information has not been included in the Index System this time.

2.1.2 Design Basis for Index System

(1) Design basis. To assess information disclosure in PPP market, the primary basis is the relevant policies as promulgated by the Ministry for Finance and/or the China Public Private Partnerships Center (CPPPC). On January 23, 2017, the Ministry of Finance promulgated the *Interim Measures for Administration of Information Disclosure for Public-Private Partnership Integrated Information Platform* (namely, the No. 1 Document). This is the main operating guide for local competent authorities to disclose information on PPP projects. Therefore, the rules in the No. 1 Document are the essential basis for the design of PPP market transparency index system. The Index System that the Research Group designed aligns with the requirements of the No. 1 Document. In principle, the information not required by the No. 1 Document was not included into the index system, for the sake of fairness to all regions.

(2) Data sources. According to the requirements of the China Public Private Partnerships Center, all local PPP projects must be included and published on the PPP Integrated Information Platform set up on the homepage of the CPPPC website. Considering the need for consistency of data sources, the Research Group has chosen the PPP Integrated Information Platform as the main source. Therefore, in this Report, the main basis for index design is the No. 1 Document, and the data mainly comes from the PPP Integrated Information Platform. Because the No. 1 Document has come into force only recently, there are still some areas that need to be improved. For example, many fields are required to be disclosed by the No. 1 Document, but they are not displayed in the project data base component of the official CPPPC website. As a result, such fields were not included in the index system. After more information is disclosed on the website in the future, the Research Group will seek further improvements. Finally, due to the slight adjustment to several fields disclosed by the PPP Integrated Information Platform of the Ministry of Finance, the relevant indicators have also been updated in the evaluation this time.

(3) Assessment object. On November 10, 2017, the General Office of the Ministry of Finance issued the Circular on Regulating Project Database of the National PPP Integrated Information Platform, which requires the establishment of Project Reserve List and Project Management Database on the basis of the Project Database. The document defines that "the Project Reserve List corresponds to the identification stage, which incorporates the candidate projects that local government departments have the intention to adopt the PPP model, but have not completed the value-for-money evaluation and the financial affordability assessment; and the Project Management Database covers the stages of preparation, procurement, implementation, and transfer". In conjunction with the policy advices of competent departments, the Research Group has limited the assessment object to projects that have at least commenced the preparation stage, that is, projects that have been entered into the Project Management Database. In addition, the Research Group also excluded several projects that could not be found on the PPP Information Integration Platform and eventually 9 398 samples were accepted for the analysis, an increase compared with 2018.

(4) Method of acquisition. The Research Group mainly relied on the data available on the website of CPPPC①, and referred to the requirements in the No. 1 Document to select and acquire the source data and then make categorization. Upon the analysis by the Research Group, the index system incorporated a total of 80 index fields (reflecting each of the information disclosure obligations in the No. 1 Document), of which 5 were excluded in the transparency index system this year for various reasons (see in section 2.1.4). As a result, 75 index fields were identified as the basis to evaluate the PPP market transparency in China in 2019. The Research Group has extracted them one by one, by

① CPPPC has also provided some data directly to the Research Group, for which the Research Group would like to show gratitude.

direct reading and PDF files downloading from the CPPPC website.

It is worth noting that among the 75 fields, 33 fields needed to be acquired from PDF files. However, after reading them through, the Research Group found that there were a number of "forged" samples: for some projects, some PDF attachments were uploaded corresponding to certain fields, but they turned out to be blank or false files. This is because according to the system requirements, some items are mandatory. If the PDF files are not uploaded, the entire project cannot enter the database or perform the next steps for the project. As a result, some projects chose to upload false or blank PDF files. In order to identify and reduce such acts in the future and ensure robust accuracy and fairness, the Research Group conducted meticulous manual verification of all the PDF files of all projects and "punished" the "false uploads". Specifically, for the 33 fields related to PDF files, the scoring rules are as follows: if a true file is uploaded, it scores 1; if there is no upload, scores 0; if a fake file is uploaded, scores −1. In case of inadequate fields in an uploaded file, the Research Group marked it with 0.5.

2.1.3 Construction of Index System

The requirements of the No. 1 Document require that certain specified information in PPP projects should be immediately disclosed, and the remainder disclosed in "due time". Among the requirements, the requirements on immediate disclosure were easy to identify and process, but those on disclosure in "due time" were quite difficult, because the Research Group had to define "due time". However, as per the No.1 Document, "disclosure in due time" mostly refers to "disclosure within six months after entering into the implementation stage". Therefore, the Research Group decided to follow the approach applied in 2017 and 2018, that is, to select the projects that had entered the implementation stage by the end of June 2019 for assessment. For those projects, if they had not disclosed corresponding information as of December 31, 2019, the Research Group would conclude that they failed to disclose relevant information "in due time", and as a result, performed poorly in terms of "disclosure in due time".

However, adopting such an approach led to a gap between the research samples for immediate disclosure and those for disclosure in due time. Specifically, as of the end of December 2019, the total number of samples entering the Management Database was 9 398, all of which could be used as assessment samples for immediate disclosure; however, there were only 5 162 projects having entered the implementation stage by the end of June 2019 and could be used for the assessment on disclosure in due time. For individual projects, some projects contain information for both immediate disclosure and disclosure in due time, and some contain information for immediate disclosure only, so they cannot be assessed under the same framework. Therefore, for the transparency of individual projects, the PPP information transparency index produced by the Research Group includes two independent fields — one on immediate disclosure, the other on disclosure in due time. Considering that the Research Group had to assess the transparency of the PPP market at regional and industry levels eventually, the Research Group used the analytic hierarchy process to weigh the index on immediate disclosure and the index on disclosure in due time, thus calculating the general index.

Both the index on immediate disclosure and the index on disclosure in due time include two levels — staged index and specific index. PPP projects are generally divided into five stages: identification stage, preparation stage, procurement stage, implementation stage, and transfer stage. However, there are no PPP projects having entered transfer stage in China, so it was not covered by both indexes. In addition, due to the lack of appropriate index fields on disclosure in due time, the corresponding index didn't contain the information at implementation stage either. Therefore, in the end the index on immediate disclosure included four stages: identification, preparation, procurement, and implementation; the index on disclosure in due time included three stages: identification, preparation, and procurement.

The hierarchy diagram of our final index system is shown in Figure 2–1. The specific index systems for immediate disclosure and disclosure in due time are shown in Table 2–1 and Table 2–2 respectively.

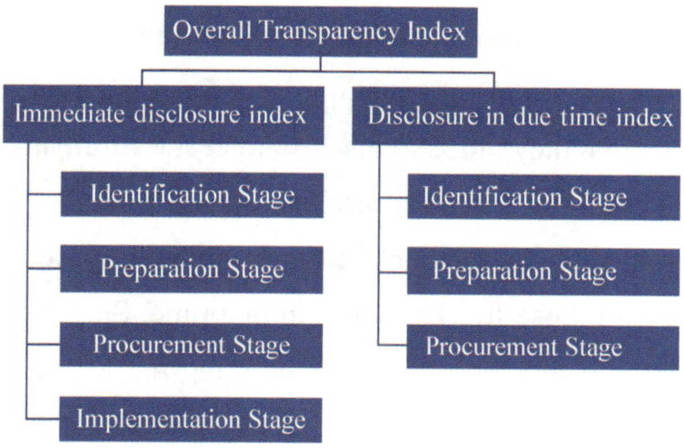

Figure 2–1 Hierarchy Diagram of PPP Transparency Index

Table 2-1 Index System for Immediate Disclosure

Primary Index	Specific field	Remarks
Identification Stage	Total investment	
	Partnership duration	
	Secondary industries	
	Operation mode	
	Return mechanism	
	Time of project initiation	
	Type of initiation	
	Name of initiator	
	Project profile	
	Name of the agency responsible for completing implementation program	
	Contact person of the agency responsible for completing implementation program	
	Contact number of the agency responsible for completing implementation program	
	Contact person of project	
	Contact number of project	
	Contact person of financial affairs	
	Contact number of financial affairs	
	Land use area of project	
	Proposed development year	
	Description of implementation program	
	Implementing organization	
	Contact person of implementing organization	
	Contact number of implementing organization	
	Selection of the mode of purchasing social capital	
	Cooperation scope (identification)	
	Value-for-money qualitative evaluation indicators and weights, scoring standards, scoring results	
	Conclusions on whether value-for-money evaluation passes or not (including opinions of the finance departments)	
	Financial expenditure liabilities of the project and those of the PPP projects implemented and to be implemented in the year and annual budget arrangements, and the ratio of expenditure for all the PPP projects out of the budget in each year in the expenditure of the general public budget	

(continued)

Primary Index	Specific field	Remarks
Identification Stage	Measurement basis, key factors and indicators of the financial affordability assessment	
	Conclusions on whether the financial affordability assessment passes or not	
Preparation Stage	Proposed investment value of social capital	
	Proposed government investment value	
	Name of government approving implementation program	
	Authorization documents of the government, including the authorization to the implementing agency, the contracting parties of the PPP project contract, the government's investment representatives, etc.	
	Approval time of implementation program by the government at the same level	
	Government's approval documents with respect to implementation program	
Procurement Stage	Prequalification announcements (including prequalification application documents)	
	Announcement of pre-bid winners and transaction results, the announcement of the bid-winning and transaction results and the letter of acceptance	
	Review opinions on proposed PPP contract by the competent industry authority at the same level	
	Review opinions on proposed PPP contract by the finance department at the same level	
	Review opinions on proposed PPP contract by the legal department at the same level	
	Whether people's government at the same level has approved the proposed PPP contract	
	Date of approval	
	Review opinions by the people's government at the same level on incorporating the government's financial expenditure liability which span two years into the mid-term financial plan	
	Date of review	
Implementation Stage	Name of project company	
	Establishment time of project company	
	Registered capital of project company	
	Economic nature of project company	
	Subscription by shareholders	
	Authorization by the people's government at the same level to government's investment representatives	

(continued)

Primary Index	Specific field	Remarks
Implementation Stage	Material breach and withdrawal of performance bond, handling of public complaints, etc.	—
	Decisions made by the government at the corresponding level or its functional departments that may have a significant impact on the project	—
	Major disputes, litigations or arbitrations with respect to the project or the parties directly related to the project	—
	Directory of the PPP projects at the same level, pilot library thereof and changes to the projects as well as the budget, implementation and settlement of government for the PPP projects as approved by the people's congress at the same level	—
	Authorization by the people's government at the same level to government's investment representatives	
Transfer stage	Composition of the transfer working group, transfer procedures, transfer standards, and other transfer programs	—
	List of the assets or facilities or equities to be transferred, assessment report on the assets or equities to be transferred, performance test program	—
	Release of various guarantees or equities on the assets or facilities to be transferred	—
	Test results on the satisfaction of the transfer standards for project facilities	—
	Post assessment report and the subsequent operation mode of the project	—

Note: "—" indicates that the item is temporarily not applicable, and was not included in the index system for 2019. However, as data system improves and data availability rises, it may be included in the index system in the future.

Table 2–2 Index System for Disclosure in Due Time

Primary index	Specific field	Remarks
Identification stage	Value-for-money evaluation report and approval documents	
	Financial affordability assessment report and approval documents	
	Proposals for new or renovated or expanded projects and approval documents	
	Feasibility study report	
	Design documents and approval documents	
	Assets appraisal report with respect to the stocked public assets or equities	
Preparation stage	Completion time of value-for-money evaluation	
	Completion time of financial affordability assessment	
	Project implementation program as examined and approved and amendments thereto	

(continued)

Primary index	Specific field	Remarks
Procurement stage	Prequalification: announcement time	
	Prequalification: prequalification time	
	Procurement: announcement time	
	Procurement results: time of review on response documents	
	Procurement results: time of negotiation about confirmation	
	Procurement results: time of government review	
	Procurement results: time of contract signing	
	Procurement results: time of contract announcement	
	Procurement results: media for contract announcement	
	Project investment amount specified in contract	
	Procurement documents	
	Concluding observations with respect to prequalification, and the list of prequalification experts	
	Concluding observations with respect to response documents, and the list of review experts	
	List of the working group of negotiation about confirmation	
	Appendixes to PPP project contracts	
	Responsibility confirmation documents for expenditure by the government at the same level	
Implementation stage	Financing limit, key terms and closing conditions	—
	Review of the project construction permits, construction progress, quality and cost and others made based on the PPP project contracts	—
	Annual operation of private capital partners or the project company and satisfaction of the operational performance	—
	Project company's performance monitoring report, interim assessment report, major changes or termination of the project, project pricing and previous adjustments	—
	Cost monitoring and review of the project company, alteration agreements on the PPP project contracts or supplementary agreements	—
	Related content of the financial report of the project company, including payment for the project, the government subsidy granted to the project, and the assets and liabilities of the project company and others	—

Note: "—" indicates that the item is temporarily not applicable, and was not included in the index system for 2019. However, as data system improves and data availability rises, it may be included in the index system in the future.

2.1.4 Explanatory Notes to Other Core Issues

(1) Notes to fields not included in index system. Some of the fields available on the PPP Center website were not included in the 2019 transparency index system (see Table 2–1 and Table 2–2 for details). The main reasons are as follows: 1) some fields are not applicable to all projects. For example, "government's authorization documents for the adjustment and updates during the project procurement process", "increase or decrease of the capital" are not applicable to all projects and are not subject to mandatory disclosure; 2) time points for judging on disclosure in due time are absent. The disclosure requirement of some fields is before April 30 of the year following the performance of certain operation. Since whether or not the operation was performed, and the time of performance is unknown, several fields in the implementation stage such as "cost monitoring and review of the project company", "alteration agreements on the PPP project contracts or supplementary agreements", etc. could not be included in the scope of assessment; 3) when there is no information, it cannot be judged whether incidents have occurred. For temporary major issues, such as "material breach and withdrawal of performance bond, handling of public complaints, etc.", which request the disclosure within 10 days, but when there is no information, it cannot be judged whether relevant incidents have occurred or they were not disclosed, so they were not included as well. For these issues, upon the improvement of the project information management system, they may enter the assessment scope in the future. Some thoughts and suggestions from the Research Group are also provided in the Report.

(2) This Report assesses whether information disclosure is in place, rather than the "quality" of the information disclosure. This Report has assessed the information disclosure of PPP projects, including completeness and importance, etc., but apart from obvious forging, the assessment does not touch upon the "quality" of specific content. Specifically, for a field (i.e. a defined information disclosure obligation contained in the No. 1 Document), if a project has disclosed corresponding information, it wins scores in the assessment, no matter the work is done well or poorly. For example, the PDF files of financial affordability report, as important information, were verified by the Research Group manually one by one, and at the same time, experts may assign a higher score to them. These are the factors considered in the assessment. As to whether a financial affordability report is normative, scientific, has sufficient argument and reliable conclusion, etc., is not the research subject of this Report. Because logically speaking, even if the financial sustainability report may not be standardized or poor in quality, as long as the responsible party chooses to disclose the report in a real and public manner, it wins scores under the assessment process used. Of course, the Research Group may go beyond "information transparency assessment" in the future and conduct special assessments on the standardization of PPP work in a certain region or field reflected by these important reports.

2.2 Calculating Methodology

2.2.1 Introduction to Calculating Methodology

For multi-index assessment, weights directly affect the results. There are many ways to determine weights. According to different sources of raw data, they can be roughly divided into two categories: subjective weighting and objective weighting. Subjective weighting is to obtain results by experts based on subjective judgments, such as Delphi method, AHP (Analytic Hierarchy Process), expert scoring method, etc., which invites authoritative experts to compare the importance among different fields, but the approach compromises objectivity. Objective weighting is to obtain results based on the numerical calculations of fields. It does not rely on subjective judgments, so it has strong objectivity, but cannot necessarily reflect the importance relations among different fields, nor can it necessarily satisfy the requirements of decision makers. Representatives of objective weighting are principal components analysis and coefficient of variation. Both subjective and objective weightings have their advantages and disadvantages. In calculating the weights of the fields of each rule hierarchy on the upper-hierarchy targets, the Research Group used subjective weighting — AHP; when calculating the weights of specific fields on the upper-rule hierarchy, the Research Group utilized expert scoring method.[①]

① The Research Group used the coefficient of variation method when calculating the weight of each specific indicator on the upper-rule hierarchy. It turned out that the results obtained by the coefficient of variation were in high consistency with those obtained by expert scoring. The decision to choose expert scoring method was made given that the method could better reflect the views on indicator importance of different sectors of the society, including industry authorities, university scholars, and social capital owners, rather than relying solely on the statistical characteristics of indicators. This makes it easier for each locality to locate problems in PPP information disclosure and make improvements in a targeted manner.

2.2.2 Analytic Hierarchy Process

Analytic Hierarchy Process (AHP) is a comprehensive assessment method for system analysis and decision making, which can quantify qualitative problems in a relatively rational manner. The main feature of AHP is that by building a hierarchical structure, it converts judgments into the importance comparison between two factors, thereby transforming qualitative decision into quantitative decision, which is easier to justify.

In an AHP model construct, a decision matrix is formed through investigation and judgment. When the decision matrix passes consistency check, it is accepted to calculate the weight of each index; if the consistency check fails, the element values of the decision matrix need adjustment until it passes the consistency check. Specifically, the steps of AHP are as follows:

Step 1: Establish hierarchical model. Upon the in-depth analysis on the factors that affect PPP information transparency, subdivide the factors into several hierarchies according to their subordination relationship. The top is target hierarchy, the middle is rule hierarchy, and the specific fields are at the lowest. The hierarchical model for this Report is shown in Figure 2–1.

Step 2: Build decision matrix. Construct decision matrix to compare the relative importance of two specific fields. As the schematic diagram of the PPP project transparency hierarchy in this Report shows, two classified indexes are involved. Therefore, three decision matrixes were built, namely the general index decision matrix (to judge the relative importance of immediate disclosure index and disclosure in due time index when compiling the general index of PPP market transparency), the immediate disclosure index decision matrix (to judge the relative importance of sub-indexes at identification, preparation, procurement, and implementation stages when compiling the immediate disclosure index), and the disclosure in due time decision matrix (to judge the relative importance of sub-indexes at identification, preparation, and procurement stages when compiling the disclosure in due time index).

In general, to compare the influence of n factors c_1, c_2, ..., c_n on the factors on upper hierarchy, the decision matrix requires that the relative importance of two factors on the factors on upper hierarchy be compared each time, and the relative importance is usually expressed in values of 1–9. Value is assigned to each factor that constitutes the decision matrix c_{ij} (the meaning of the values is shown in Table 2–3, which is usually assigned by experienced experts). All comparison results constitute “paired comparison matrix”, also called “positive reciprocal matrix”.

$$C=\begin{pmatrix} c_{11} & c_{12} & \cdots & c_{1n} \\ c_{21} & c_{22} & \cdots & c_{2n} \\ \vdots & \vdots & \vdots & \vdots \\ c_{n1} & c_{n2} & \cdots & c_{nn} \end{pmatrix}$$

$$C=(c_{ij})_{n\times n},\ c_{ij}>0,\ c_{ji}=\frac{1}{c_{ij}},\ c_{ii}=1.$$

If the positive reciprocal matrix C meets $c_{ij}\times c_{jk}=c_{ik}$, then C is called complete consistency matrix.

Table 2–3 Meaning of Decision Matrix Scale

Scale c_{ij}	Definition	Meaning
1	Equally important	The impact of c_i is the same as that of c_j
3	Slightly more important	The impact of c_i is slightly stronger than that of c_j
5	Relatively more important	The impact of c_i is stronger than that of c_j
7	More important	The impact of c_i is obviously stronger than that of c_j
9	Extremely more important	The impact of c_i is absolutely stronger than that of c_j
2, 4, 6, 8	Middle value of two adjacent scales	The impact ratio of c_i to c_j is between two adjacent scales
1/2, …, 1/9	Reciprocal	The impact ratio of c_i to c_j is the reciprocal of the α_{ij} above

Step 3: Calculate the maximum eigenvalue of decision matrix and its eigenvector. The process of determining the weight of each index with decision matrix is actually to obtain the eigenvector of the decision matrix. By solving the maximum eigenvalue of the reciprocal matrix, the corresponding eigenvector can be obtained and then normalized to be the weight vector.

$$CW=\lambda_{\max} W$$

Step 4: Consistency check. First, calculate the consistency index CI of the $n\times n$ decision matrix:

$$CI = \frac{\lambda_{max} - n}{n-1}$$

Secondly, calculate the average random consistency index *RI*. 1) Randomly select numbers from 1–9 and their reciprocals to form a $n \times n$ positive reciprocal matrix and calculate its maximum eigenvalue. 2) Repeat 1 000 times to obtain the maximum eigenvalues of 1 000 random positive reciprocal matrices, and calculate the mean value of the 1 000 max. eigenvalues *k*. 3) Obtain the average random consistency index *RI*.

$$RI = \frac{k - n}{n-1}$$

Finally, calculate the consistency ratio *CR* and check consistency.

$$CR = \frac{CI}{RI}$$

When $CR<0.1$, it is generally considered that the inconsistency degree of matrix *A* is within tolerance range, and its eigenvector can be used as a weight vector. Otherwise, the decision matrix needs to be modified (repeat Steps 2 and 3) until *CR* is less than 0.1.

Step 5: Calculate weight vector. By normalizing the eigenvector corresponding to the maximum eigenvalue of the decision matrix that has passed consistency check, the weight of the factor on the factors of upper hierarchy can be obtained.

Accordingly, the Research Group invited 11 representatives from universities and colleges (3), government (3), corporate partners (3) and intermediary consulting (2) to fill in the three decision matrices, then calculated the weights of each stage through the AHP described above, and finally obtained the mean values of the weights assigned by these experts. Appendix I shows the decision matrix survey forms for experts. Table 2–4 shows the table of weights calculated based on the decision matrixes provided by experts. For immediate disclosure, the weights of the sub-indexes at identification, preparation, procurement, and implementation stages were 0.19, 0.19, 0.4, and 0.22; regarding disclosure in due time, the weights of the sub-indexes at identification, preparation, procurement stages were 0.25, 0.30 and 0.45; and when being consolidated into the general index of PPP market transparency, the weights of the two disclosure modes were 0.61 and 0.39 respectively.

Table 2–4 Table of Weights Based on Decision Matrixes by Experts

Transparency index of immediate disclosure		Transparency index of disclosure in due time		General index	
Stage	Weight	Stage	Weight	Sub-index	Weight
Identification stage	0.19	Identification stage	0.25	Disclosure in due time	0.39
Preparation stage	0.19	Preparation stage	0.30	Immediate disclosure	0.61
Procurement stage	0.4	Procurement stage	0.45	—	—
Implementation stage	0.22	—	—	—	—

2.2.3 Weight Calculation Method

After the weighting of each middle hierarchy on upper hierarchy was finalized through AHP, it was also required to determine the weighting of the bottom hierarchy (that is, each specific field) on upper hierarchy. In this regard, the Research Group applied the experts scoring method.

Based on the information earlier in this Report, especially the "principle of significance", the Research Group scored the specific fields by means of expert scoring, giving them certain weights. The fields were divided into "common", "important" and "especially important", corresponding to 1 point, 2 points, and 3 points respectively. The higher the point is, the field is more significant. 11 experts from college, government, business, and consulting were invited for scoring. Table 2–5 and Table 2–6 show the results of expert scoring. It needs to be further noted that the scores of the above indicators were compared with each other within a certain stage, rather than directly compared among all. To clarify this, the Research Group also listed the specific weights corresponding to the scores in each stage in Table 2–5 and Table 2–6.

Table 2–5 Expert Scoring Results on Specific Fields of Immediate Disclosure

Stage	Specific field	Score	Weight
Identification stage	Total investment	2.455	4.4
	Partnership duration	2.273	4.1
	Secondary industries	1.091	1.9

(continued)

Stage	Specific field	Score	Weight
Identification stage	Operation mode	2.182	3.9
	Return mechanism	2.909	5.2
	Time of project initiation	1.636	2.9
	Type of initiation	1.455	2.6
	Name of initiator	1.182	2.1
	Project profile	2.000	3.6
	Name of the agency responsible for completing implementation program	1.909	3.4
	Contact person of the agency responsible for completing implementation program	1.364	2.4
	Contact number of the agency responsible for completing implementation program	1.364	2.4
	Contact person of project	1.455	2.6
	Contact number of project	1.455	2.6
	Contact person of financial affairs	1.455	2.6
	Contact number of financial affairs	1.455	2.6
	Land use area of project	2.000	3.6
	Proposed development year	2.000	3.6
	Selection of the mode of purchasing social capital	2.455	4.4
	Description of implementation program	2.364	4.2
	Implementing organization	1.455	2.6
	Contact person of implementing organization	1.455	2.6
	Contact number of implementing organization	1.364	2.4
	Cooperation scope (identification)	2.182	3.9
	Value-for-money qualitative evaluation indicators and weights, scoring standards, scoring results	2.545	4.5
	Conclusions on whether value-for-money evaluation passes or not (including opinions of the finance departments)	2.636	4.7
	Financial expenditure liabilities of the project and those of the PPP projects implemented and to be implemented in the year and annual budget arrangements, and the ratio of expenditure for all the PPP projects out of the budget in each year in the expenditure of the general public budget	2.818	5.0
	Measurement basis, key factors and indicators of the financial affordability assessment	2.636	4.7

(continued)

Stage	Specific field	Score	Weight
Identification stage	Conclusions on whether the financial affordability assessment passes or not	2.455	4.4
Preparation stage	Proposed investment value of social capital	2.182	18.2
	Proposed government investment value	2.273	18.9
	Name of government approving implementation program	1.727	14.4
	Authorization documents of the government, including the authorization to the implementing agency, the contracting parties of the PPP project contract, the government's investment representatives, etc.	2.000	16.7
	Approval time of implementation program by the government at the same level	1.727	14.4
	Government's approval documents with respect to implementation program	2.091	17.4
Procurement stage	Prequalification announcements (including prequalification application documents)	2.364	11.2
	Announcement of pre-bid winners and transaction results, the announcement of the bid-winning and transaction results and the letter of acceptance	2.545	12.1
	Review opinions on proposed PPP contract by the competent industry authority at the same level	1.909	9.1
	Review opinions on proposed PPP contract by the finance department at the same level	2.000	9.5
	Review opinions on proposed PPP contract by the legal department at the same level	1.909	9.1
	Whether people's government at the same level has approved the proposed PPP contract	2.455	11.6
	Date of approval	2.455	11.6
	Review opinions by the people's government at the same level on incorporating the government's financial expenditure liability which span two years into the mid-term financial plan	2.727	12.9
	Date of review	2.727	12.9
Implementation stage	Name of project company	1.636	15.6
	Establishment time of project company	1.545	14.8
	Registered capital of project company	1.818	17.4
	Economic nature of project company	1.455	13.9
	Subscription by shareholders	2.000	19.1
	Authorization by the people's government at the same level to government's investment representatives	2.000	19.1

Table 2–6 Expert Scoring Results on Specific Fields of Disclosure in Due Time

Stage	Specific field	Score	Weight
Identification stage	Value-for-money evaluation report and approval documents	3.000	18.0
	Financial affordability assessment report and approval documents	3.000	18.0
	Proposals for new or renovated or expanded projects and approval documents	2.333	14.0
	Feasibility study report	2.667	16.0
	Design documents and approval documents	2.677	16.1
	Assets appraisal report with respect to the stocked public assets or equities	3.000	18.0
Preparation stage	Completion time of value-for-money evaluation	1.556	33.3
	Completion time of financial affordability assessment	1.556	33.3
	Project implementation program as examined and approved and amendments thereto	1.556	33.3
Procurement stage	Prequalification: announcement time	1.778	5.5
	Prequalification: prequalification time	1.667	5.2
	Procurement: announcement time	1.889	5.9
	Procurement results: time of review on response documents	1.556	4.8
	Procurement results: time of negotiation about confirmation	1.889	5.9
	Procurement results: time of government review	1.778	5.5
	Procurement results: time of contract signing	1.778	5.5
	Procurement results: time of contract announcement	1.889	5.9
	Procurement results: media for contract announcement	1.444	4.5
	Project investment amount specified in contract	2.556	8.0
	Procurement documents	2.889	9.0
	Concluding observations with respect to prequalification, and the list of prequalification experts	2.111	6.6
	Concluding observations with respect to response documents, and the list of review experts	2.111	6.6
	List of the working group of negotiation about confirmation	1.222	3.8
	Appendixes to PPP project contracts	2.556	8.0
	Responsibility confirmation documents for expenditure by the government at the same level	3.000	9.3

2.2.4 Indicator Synthesis

In multi-index assessment, synthesis refers to the integration of assessment values of different fields on different aspects of a subject through a certain formula to produce a holistic assessment. There are many mathematical methods that can be used for synthesis. Common synthesis models are weighted arithmetic mean, weighted geometric mean, or their combination. All three have their features and applicable occasions, without absolute difference in advantages or disadvantages. After comprehensively comparing the three methods, the Research Group chose weighted arithmetic mean, the formula of which is as follows:

$$d = \sum_{i=1}^{n} w_i d_i$$

Wherein, d is the general index, w_i is the normalized weight of each assessment index, d_i is the assessment score of single index, and n is the number of assessment indexes. Synthesis is based on a bottom-to-top layer-by-layer sequence. First, calculate the indexes on each hierarchy, and then weigh and consolidate the indexes to obtain the general index (see Chapter 4 for detailed calculation process).

Specifically, the disclosure status of each field from the website was firstly acquired and then given a score (a total of four scores, namely, 1 represents disclosure and no obvious forging; 0 represents no disclosure; 0.5 represents partial disclosure; −1 stands for “forged” disclosure). Subsequently, the scores of these fields were consolidated by the expert scoring method or coefficient of variation to calculate the scoring average (percentage system) at a certain stage (for example, disclosure in due time at identification stage). Subsequently, weights were generated by Analytic Hierarchy Process, sub-indexes at different stages were synthesized into immediate disclosure index or disclosure in due time index. Finally, the immediate disclosure index or disclosure in due time index was weighted to obtain the PPP market transparency index.

It should be noted that based on the Index System and calculation methods, theoretically, a project’s general transparency index (or staged index) may reach 100 points, indicating that the project has correctly and completely disclosed the information required by the Research Group; the lowest score can be negative, indicating that the project has disclosed much false information. 0 indicates that the project has not disclosed any information required by the Research Group, or it has disclosed some information, which was yet offset by certain forged disclosure. Of course, such circumstances were rare, especially upon the synthesis of a number of fields.

It needs to be emphasized that when calculating the general index, some projects did not cover all five stages, in order to ensure index stability, weighting normalization was used to ensure the consistency of relative weights. For example, for immediate disclosure index, the weights of identification, preparation, procurement, and implementation stages were 0.19, 0.19, 0.4, and 0.22, respectively. But for a project with only the first three stages, the weights would be:

Recognition Stage=0.19/(0.19+0.19+0.4)=0.244

Preparation Stage=0.19/(0.19+0.19+0.4)=0.244

Procurement Stage=0.4/(0.19+0.19+0.4)=0.512

3

Primary Results and Overall Analysis

3.1 Introduction to Sample Data

3.1.1 Sample Overview

As previously outlined, the Index System was classified into two groupings: the immediate disclosure index and the disclosure in due time index. Among them, the immediate disclosure index covered 9 398 projects, an increase of 762 compared with the 8 636 projects in 2018; the disclosure in due time index involved 5 162 projects, representing an increase of 1 612 compared with the previous year. Furthermore, among the 9 398 total samples in 2019, 1 398, 1 678 and 6 322 projects were at the stages of preparation, procurement, and implementation, respectively. As can be seen from Figure 3–1, compared with 2018, the proportion of samples entering the implementation stage to the overall sample size in 2019 increased significantly from 54% to 67%, while both the proportions of samples still in preparation and procurement stages saw decline.

Upon regulation in 2018, PPP projects have come to a phase of standardized and orderly advancement. As a result, the total number of projects in 2019 did not change much from the previous year, with a lower percentage of removal. In the following paragraphs we will find the total transparency index in 2019 changed little from 2018.

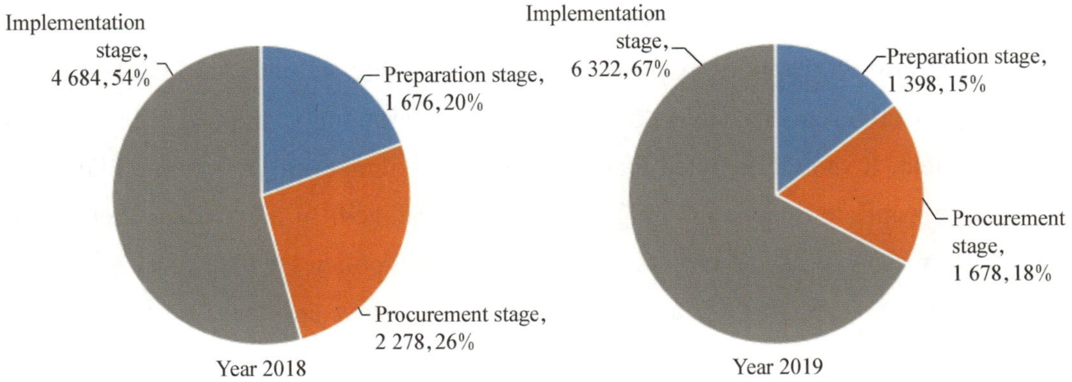

Figure 3–1 Distribution of Sample Projects by Stage in 2018 and 2019

Nevertheless, the section 4 of this Chapter still provides a discussion on the causes for the gap in PPP transparency scores between 2019 and 2018.

3.1.2 Index Methodology

Chapter 2 highlights the index system which consists of a total of 75 index fields, based on the CPPPC website, of which 33 index fields were manually read from the website to verify authenticity. Among the remaining 42 fields obtained directly from the website or CPPPC, they were assigned "1" if the field recorded disclosed information or "0" if there was no information disclosed in the field. While as for the manually read fields, a more detailed scoring system was applied: "1" point was allocated for complete disclosure, "0.5" points for partial disclosure, "0" points for no disclosure, and "–1" points for false or erroneous disclosure (e.g. if there is a blank PDF file).

Standard definitions were developed to define Partial and False Disclosure, to support consistency in the points allocation. Partial disclosure was defined as a field which contained multiple items of information, but only part of which had been disclosed. For example, if the field "value-for-money qualitative evaluation indicators and weights, scoring standards, scoring results" included only the scoring standards or results, then 0.5 point would be assigned. Similarly, the value-for-money evaluation report and financial affordability assessment report requires the disclosure of the "value-for-money evaluation report and approval documents by the competent industry authority and the finance industry at the same level" as well as the "financial affordability report and approval documents by the finance department at the same level". Some projects only disclosed the value-for-money evaluation report and the financial affordability assessment report, but no approval documents, or vice versa. In these instances, a score of 0.5 was also assigned. False disclosure with a penalty of "–1" which primarily applies to those circumstances where an uploaded PDF file was a blank document, or an erroneous document, or the information contained did not match with the field. It should be noted that in a very small number of cases some PDF files without appropriate documents lodged were not penalized. In these cases there were justifiable reasons (e.g. the project commenced before policies took effect) and under such circumstance, it was not assessed as false disclosure, and there no penalty was awarded, to avoid any unfair assessment.

Here we take the "value-for-money evaluation report and approval documents by the competent industry authority and the finance industry at the same level" in disclosure in due time as an example to introduce our manual data collection. As shown in Figure 3–2, among the 5 162 samples subject to disclosure in due time, 4 164 have completely disclosed the "value-for-money evaluation report and approval documents by the competent industry authority and the finance industry at the same level", 390 made partial disclosure, 580 no disclosure, and 28 had disclosed false or wrong documents. From 2018 to 2019, the complete disclosure rate under this index dropped from 88% to 81%, the false disclosure rate from 1% to 0.54%, and the non-disclosure rate rose sharply from 2% to 11%.

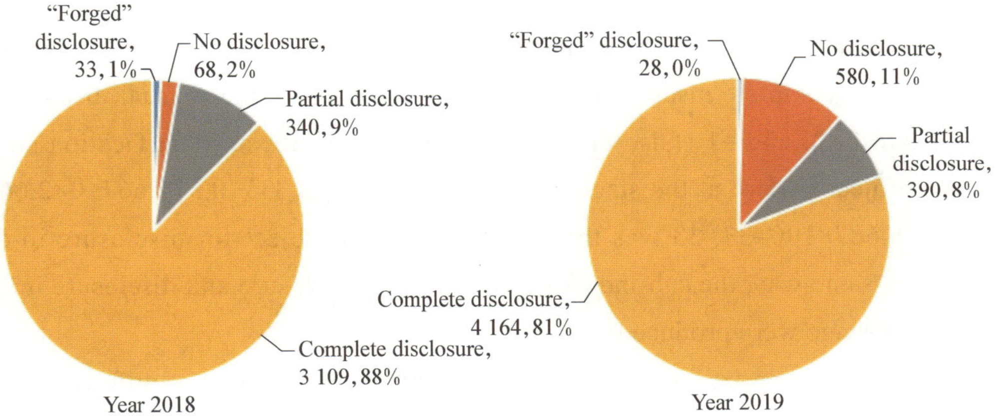

Figure 3–2 Disclosure of Value-for-money Evaluation Report and Attachment

Once the scores were assigned, the final score of each field was determined by multiplying the score by the weighting (relative importance) determined through expert scoring (as outlined in Chapter 2).

3.2 Calculation of National General Index

3.2.1 Index Synthesis

With the score of each index, the Research Group would calculate the score of a PPP project at a certain stage (standardized to be a percentage out of 100), which is the sub-index at the stage. Take the disclosure in due time index at identification stage as an example: the stage contains six information items: "value-for-money evaluation report and approval documents by the competent industry authority and the finance industry at the same level", "financial affordability assessment report and approval documents by the finance department at the same level", "proposals for new or renovated or expanded projects and approval documents" and "feasibility study report or fund application report or report for project approval, and approval documents by competent authority; assets appraisal report with respect to the stocked public assets", "design documents and approval documents", and "asset evaluation report with respect to the stocked public assets or equity, and various programs and others (if applicable) that may be involved in the transfer of stocked assets or equity". The six fields scored 3 points, 3 points, 2.333 points, 2.667 points, 2.667 points and 3 points respectively in expert scoring. Then, the total score of disclosure in due time at the identification stage was 16.667 points. Suppose a project was given 1 (complete disclosure), 1 (complete disclosure), 0.5 (partial disclosure), 0.5 (partial disclosure), 0 (no disclosure), and −1 (false disclosure) in the six fields at identification stage, then the project's score at the stage was $[1\times3+1\times3+0.5\times2.333+0.5\times2.667+0\times2.667+(-1)\times3]/16.667\times100=33$. 33 was the sub-index of the project for disclosure in due time. In the same way, the sub-indexes of immediate disclosure and disclosure in due time at each stage were produced.

Table 3–1 summarizes the sub-indexes of immediate disclosure at different stages. Of the 9 398 immediate disclosure samples, the average scores were 89.71 at the identification stage, 84.48 at the preparation stage, 73.61 at the procurement stage, and 71.17 at the implementation stage. The results demonstrate that immediate information disclosure at the identification and preparation stages was generally satisfactory, yet poorer at the procurement and implementation stages. From the perspective of management mechanism, most of the information required to be disclosed at the identification and preparation stages must be submitted before PPP projects are included into the database. Due to the rigorous review by competent authorities for database entry, the scores were generally higher. While after coming to the procurement and implementation stages, project progress wouldn't be hindered by the failure to upload information to the PPP Integrated Platform in time as required. As the information disclosure at these stages was not under proper regulation, lower scores were seen. Compared with 2018, the scores at the procurement and implementation stages in 2019 showed large increase, while slight decrease was seen at the identification and preparation stages.

Table 3–1 Immediate Disclosure Indexes at Different Stages

Stage	Year 2019			Year 2018		
	Sample size	Mean value	Standard deviation	Sample size	Mean value	Standard deviation
Identification stage	9 398	89.71	4.38	8 636	94.36	6.63
Preparation stage	9 398	84.48	25.39	8 636	91.45	18.78
Procurement stage	8 000	73.61	21.19	6 962	61.88	43.02
Implementation stage	6 322	71.17	28.86	4 684	60.59	30.75

Table 3–2 shows the distribution of immediate disclosure indexes at different stages, implying that negative scores are possible where false or erroneous documents were published; and conversely projects with strong information disclosure have the potential to score 100 points. Conversely projects with strong information disclosure has the potential to score 100 points. The Research Group paid attention to these "abnormal" projects and dealt with them specifically, in a bid to urge responsible departments to make up for shortcomings as soon as possible, and promote standardized management of PPP projects. However, we are more concerned with the information disclosure performance of most projects, since it represents the information transparency across the entire PPP market. Therefore, Figure 3–2 also highlights scores at the 75 and 25 percentiles. By comparing the distribution of the transparency indexes at all stages of immediate disclosure in 2019 and 2018, we can see that the immediate disclosure at the identification stage in 2019 was slightly worse than that in 2018, as proven by the fact that both the upper quartile and the lower quartile in 2019 were lower than those in 2018; and the minimum value and 25 percentile at the preparation stage of immediate disclosure in 2019 were –34.09 points and 66.67 points, respectively, both far lower than the –19.7 points and 91.67 points in 2018. This indicates that for those projects with low scores, their information disclosure at the preparation phase of immediate disclosure in 2019 was far poorer than that in 2018; while regarding those with higher scores, few differences were seen in the preparation stage of immediate disclosure between 2018 and 2019, as the 75 percentiles and maximum values in the two years were exactly the same. As for the procurement stage, lower-scored projects did much better in immediate disclosure in 2019 than in 2018, since the 25 quantile in 2019 was as high as 74.14 points, contrasted by 9.93 points in 2018. Finally, at the implementation stage, the 25 quantiles in the two years

were basically the same; but the minimum value in 2019, 0 points, was much higher than the –38.26 points in 2018. In general, the conclusions made based on careful examination of the index distribution are consistent with the information provided by Table 3–1. In terms of immediate disclosure, the projects performed worse in the identification and preparation phases in 2019 than in 2018, yet significantly better at the procurement and implementation stages than in 2018.

Table 3–2 Immediate Disclosure Indexes at Different Stages

Stage	Year 2019			
	Minimum value	25 percentile	75 percentile	Maximum value
Identification stage	58.44	88.64	92.21	97.56
Preparation stage	–34.09	66.67	100	100
Procurement stage	0	74.14	87.07	100
Implementation stage	0	61.74	100	100
Stage	**Year 2018**			
	Minimum value	**25 percentile**	**75 percentile**	**Maximum value**
Identification stage	53.25	91.72	100	100
Preparation stage	–19.7	91.67	100	100
Procurement stage	–32.06	9.93	100	100
Implementation stage	–38.26	61.73	83.48	100

Table 3–3 shows the disclosure in due time sub-indexes at different stages. Out of the 5, 162 assessment objects, the average score was 44.63 at the identification stage, 95.81 at the preparation stage, and 70.37 at the procurement stage. Disclosure was poorer at the identification stage relative to the preparation stage. One explanation for this could be that the information required at the identification stage includes value-for-money evaluation report, financial affordability assessment report and some other core documents, and a number of projects failed to properly disclose these documents. Comparison of performance in disclosure in due time between 2018 and 2019 shows that the average scores at the preparation stage in the two years didn't vary much, the average score of the procurement stage in 2019 was slightly higher than that in 2018, and that of the identification stage in 2019 was 11 points less than that in 2018.

Table 3–3 Disclosure in Due Time Indexes at Different Stages

Stage	Year 2019			Year 2018		
	Sample size	Mean value	Standard deviation	Sample size	Mean value	Standard deviation
Identification stage	5 162	44.63	20.03	3 550	55.04	18.34
Preparation stage	5 162	95.81	11.66	3 550	94.81	13.46
Procurement stage	5 162	70.37	16.18	3 550	65.21	20.60

Table 3–4 reports the distribution of the transparency indexes at each stage of disclosure in due time, including minimum and maximum values, upper quartile and lower quartile. From the table, we can conclude that in terms of disclosure in due time, most projects disclosed the required information in the preparation and procurement stages, with 100% disclosure at the 75 percentile for the preparation stage; while 25% of the projects received a score that was less than 43.97 at the identification stage. Therefore, if action is to taken to improve the overall transparency of PPP projects concerning disclosure in due time, the focus should be on the complete disclosure of several core reports such as value-for-money evaluation report and financial affordability assessment report. Only after these shortcomings are addressed will the transparency of disclosure in due time increase greatly. Comparing with the same in 2018, in 2019 the score of the identification stage was slightly lower, while that of the procurement stage was higher. This is quite similar to the cross-phase comparison result of immediate disclosure.

Table 3–4 Disclosure In Due Time Indexes at Different Stages

Stage	Year 2019			
	Minimum value	25 percentile	75 percentile	Maximum value
Identification stage	–63.96	43.97	52.97	100
Preparation stage	0	100	100	100
Procurement stage	–9.68	62.29	85.12	90.66
Stage	**Year 2018**			
	Minimum value	**25 percentile**	**75 percentile**	**Maximum value**
Identification stage	–52	52	66	100
Preparation stage	0	100	100	100
Procurement stage	–43.25	51.21	80.62	100

3.2.2 General Index

With transparency index at each stage, the Research Group synthesized the immediate disclosure index and disclosure in due time index based on the weights of the sub-index at each stage obtained by AHP as explained in the Chapter 2. Table 3–5 shows the general indexes of immediate disclosure and disclosure in due time. It shows that the mean values of immediate disclosure index and disclosure in due time index were 79.14 and 71.57 respectively. Compared with 2018, the two indicators in 2019 basically remained stable, with slight increase.

Table 3–5 Immediate Disclosure and Disclosure in Due Time Indexes

Index	Year 2019			Year 2018		
	Sample size	Mean value	Standard deviation	Sample size	Mean value	Standard deviation
Immediate disclosure	9 398	79.14	13.95	8 636	77.61	21.46
Disclosure in due time	5 162	71.57	13.90	3 550	71.55	13.03

Also the immediate disclosure index and the disclosure in due time index, were synthesized for the national PPP market transparency index based on the weights of immediate disclosure index and disclosure in due time index calculated by AHP. The conclusion is, by the end of December 2019, the national PPP market transparency index was 76.19 ($79.14\times0.61+71.57\times0.39$), slightly higher than 2018 at 75.25. Figure 3–3 shows the national PPP market transparency index, immediate disclosure index, disclosure in due time index, and the average transparency sub-index by stage. Consistent with the results shown from Table 3–1 to Table 3–4 above, Figure 3–3 indicates that the major changes from 2018 to 2019 include higher scores in the procurement and execution phases, and lower scores in the identification and preparation phases.

3.3 Heterogeneity Analysis of National General Index

Based on the analysis above, the national PPP market transparency index was calculated based on the average transparency index of around 9 400 PPP projects

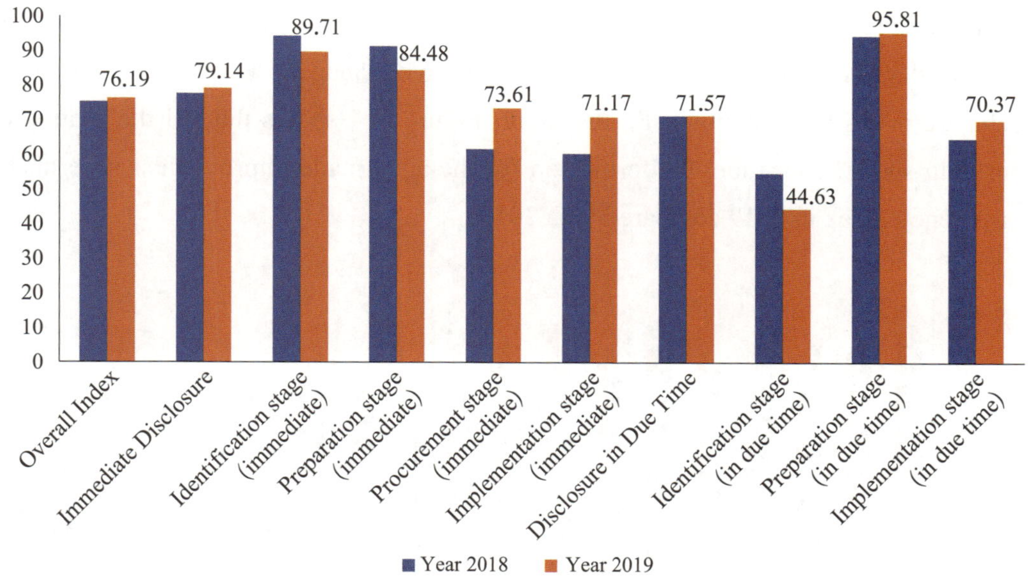

Figure 3–3 National PPP Market Transparency Index and Sub-index by Stage

across China. As discussed previously, the average transparency may have masked the heterogeneity between individual projects. Therefore, in order to offer a more in-depth and intuitive display of the transparency of the national PPP market, in this section, the analysis needs to focus on different perspectives, such as industry sector, type, etc., A more detailed discussion at the provincial and municipal levels will also be provided in the following two chapters.

3.3.1 PPP Transparency Index by Sector

Figure 3–5 examines the PPP market transparency by sector. Figure 3–4 examines the PPP market transparency by sector. Although some differences were noted, they were not substantial. For example, the highest transparency index was 78.47 for the social security sector, and the lowest was 72.05 for the forestry sector, showing a gap of merely 6 points. From 2017 to 2018, smaller gap between industries was already observed, and it was further narrowed in 2019. Upon analysis on the immediate disclosure index and the disclosure in due time index by industry, as well as the sub-indexes at different stages, findings are similar. Therefore, generally PPP projects in different sectors showed no significant heterogeneity in information disclosure requirements and practices. It also means the existing rules and regulations for the disclosure of PPP project information are generally applicable to all sectors. Since PPP projects in different sectors are often managed and supervised by authorities with expertise in the respective industry sector, the above results also indicated that these authorities have managed PPP project information disclosure in a similar manner. Furthermore, Figure 3–4 shows that all the industries other than sports, education, and provision for the aged made improvement in terms of transparency index in 2019 compared with 2018.

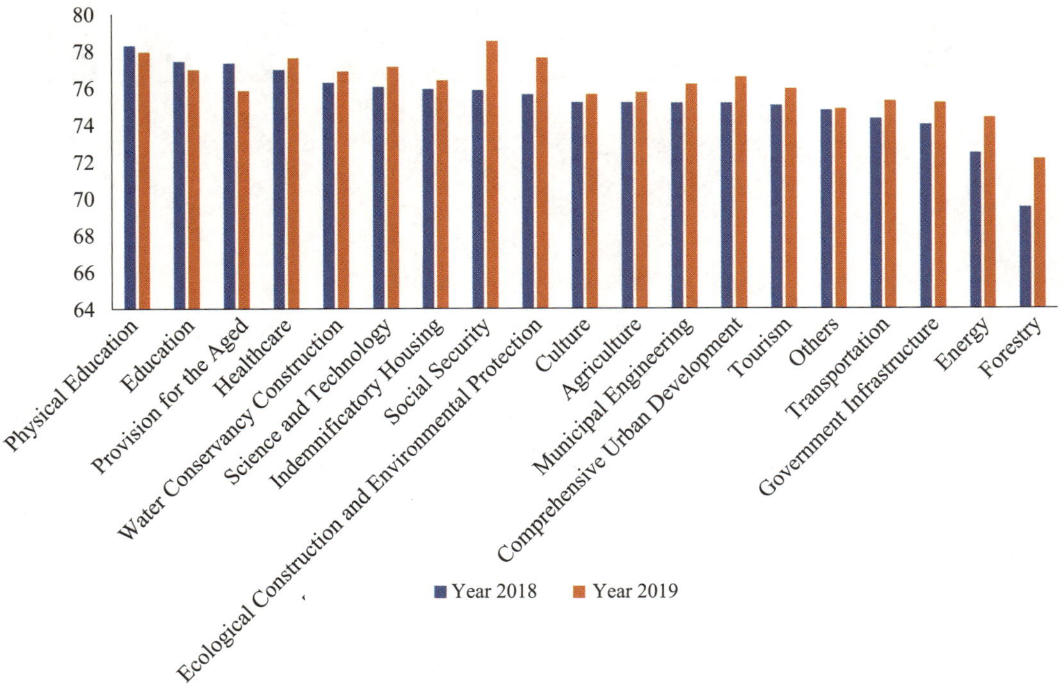

Figure 3–4 PPP Market Transparency Index by Sector

3.3.2 Transparency Indexes of Demonstration Projects and Non-demonstration Projects

As for demonstration and non-demonstration projects, as shown by Figure 3–5, the score gap between demonstration projects and non-demonstration ones in 2019 was not significant, with the general index of the former slightly higher than that of the latter. According to the evaluation results in the past three years, the overall index of demonstration projects increased from 72.3 in 2017 to 74.9 in 2018, and then to 77.19 in 2019 — indicating a moderate growth rate; while the overall index of non-demonstration projects surged from 62.0 in 2017 to 75.3 in 2018, and then 76.01 in 2019 — a significant slowdown in growth. This indicates that the variable "whether it is a demonstration

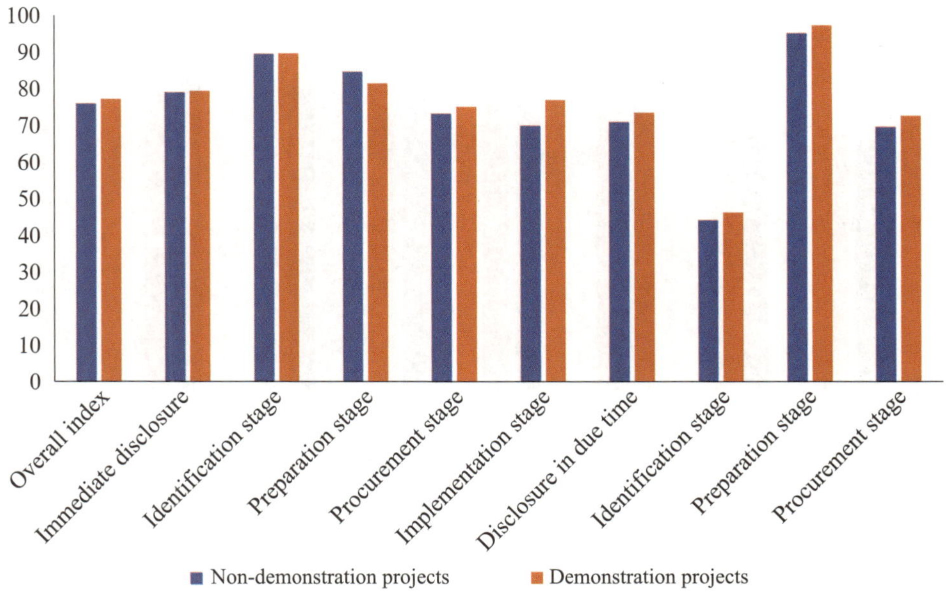

Figure 3–5 Transparency Indexes of Demonstration Projects and Non-demonstration Projects in 2019

project", as time goes by, is increasingly ungrounded to justify the difference in transparency scores between projects.

3.3.3 Time of Project Initiation and Transparency Indexes

In this section, we further examine the relationship between the time when a PPP project is initiated and its transparency score, in order to identify the reasons for the large gaps in the transparency scores between PPP projects. Figure 3–6 summarizes the average scores of projects launched in different years in the two assessments at the end of 2018 and at the end of 2019. It shows that the later a PPP project is launched, the better performance it delivers in information disclosure, resulting in a higher PPP transparency index. Specifically, in the assessment conducted at the end of 2019, the transparency index scored by projects launched before 2012 was around 63.1 points, while the projects launched in 2019 had an average score of 81.2 points. This result is reasonable, since more and more information needs to be published with higher and higher requirements as a project progresses. Comparison between the assessment results at the end of 2018 and the end of 2019 indicates that the projects initiated at the same time presented similar average scores at the end of 2018 and the end of 2017.

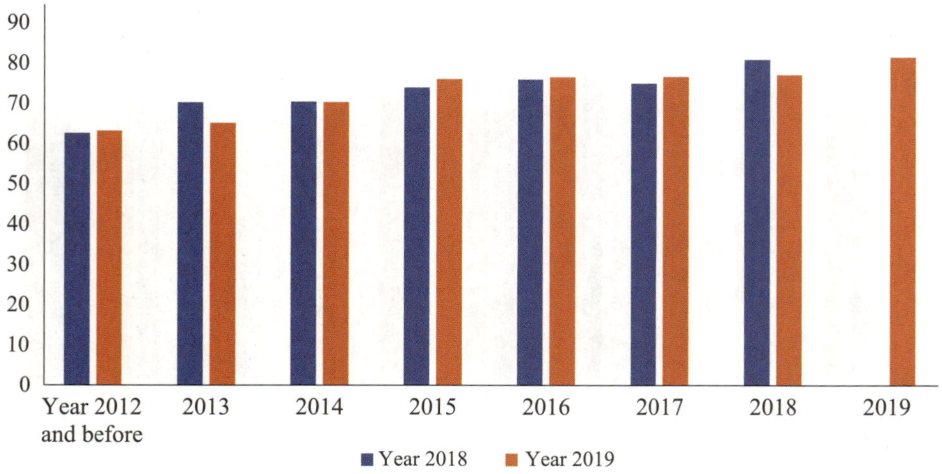

Figure 3–6 Transparency Indexes of PPP Projects by Initiation Time

3.4 Further Discussion: Analysis of Cross-phase Differences in Transparency Index

As shown from the foregoing, the gap in the PPP transparency indexes between the end of 2018 and the end of 2019, including the immediate disclosure indexes, disclosure in due time indexes and general indexes, is not significant. Further analysis on the heterogeneity between industries, demonstration and non-demonstration projects, and different time of initiation also shows insignificant cross-phase differences in the PPP transparency indexes. Nonetheless, we will keep analyzing the possible reasons for the cross-phase differences in the transparency indexes, which is crucial and politically significant, as this will help us timely discover the strengths and weaknesses of our management over PPP project information, and better improve the quality and efficiency of PPP projects. In other words, it is beneficial to understand what improvements have been made in PPP information disclosure in 2019 compared to 2018, what deficiencies still stand out, and what the corresponding causes are. For example, in the second section above, we revealed that the increase in the transparency score in the procurement phase and the decrease in the identification phase may be one of the important factors driving the cross-phase changes in the PPP transparency indexes. The two variances in opposite directions seem to be offset by each other after being added up to the immediate disclosure index and disclosure in due time index. However, with such results, we can still propose to PPP information regulators highly targeted suggestions such as "to maintain the good performance of information disclosure in the procurement phase, and improve the same at the identification stage in the next year".

In this section, we focus on the cross-phase changes in the PPP market transparency scores caused by the changes in the assessment objects themselves. The Research Group has examined and grouped the projects assessed in 2019 and 2018. In specific, the samples were divided into three categories: 1) withdrawn project, which was included in the evaluation at the end of 2018, but was later removed from the database, thus was not included in the assessment in 2019, with a total number of 861; 2) inventory project, which was engaged in the assessments in both 2018 and 2019, totaling 7 779; and 3) new project, which was added to the database after 2018 and before the end of 2019, with a total number of 1 619. The withdrawn projects only had transparency scores for 2018; the new projects were scored in 2019 only; and inventory projects had recorded scores in both 2018 and 2019. Comparing the sample sizes of the three categories, it is easy to find: the evaluation samples in 2019 were more stable than those in 2018. About 90% of the 8 640 projects in 2018 were still in the database at the end of 2019. In 2019, the proportions of withdrawn and new projects were not high, which explains to a large extent why the general index in 2019 was not changed much from that in 2018.

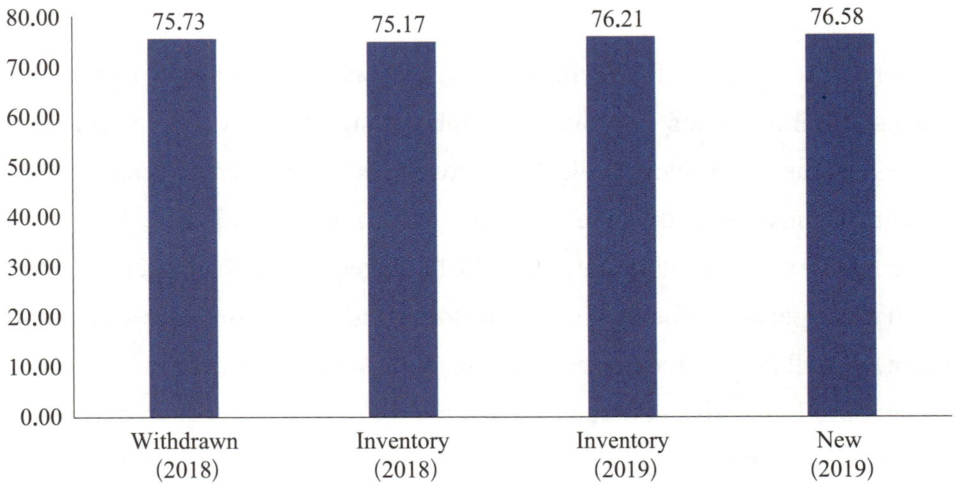

Figure 3–7 Transparency Scores by Project Type

Figure 3–7 further proves the explanation above, as overall, few differences were cbserved in the transparency scores between these types of projects. First of all, those projects that were in the database in both 2018 and 2019 had a transparency score of 75.17

in 2018, but those that were removed from the database in 2019 delivered a transparency score of 75.73 in 2018 — even slightly higher than that of inventory projects. Figure 3–8 is a more detailed display of the score gap between the projects removed in 2018 and those remained, which shows that the inventory projects had delivered similar performance in information disclosure with the withdrawn projects at all stages.

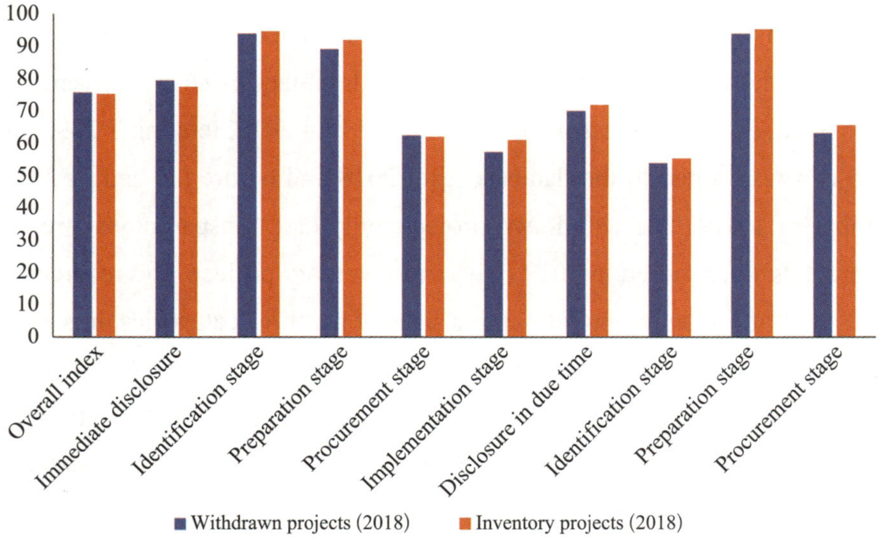

Figure 3–8 2018 Scores of Projects Withdrawn in 2019 and Inventory Projects

Second, the projects that remained in the database had also improved their performance in information disclosure, though not significantly. As can be seen from Figure 3–9, as far as inventory projects are concerned, their average score in 2018 was 75.17, significantly lower than the 76.21 in 2019. In addition, Figure 3–9 shows that the major reason why inventory projects in 2019 scored higher than in 2018 is that they improved their performance at the procurement and execution stages of immediate disclosure, as well as the procurement stage of disclosure in due time in 2019. However, their scores in the identification and preparation phases of immediate disclosure, and in the identification phase of disclosure in due time dropped in 2019 from 2018. These findings are basically consistent with our conclusions in section 2 concerning why the national PPP market transparency index in 2019 was different from that in 2018.

Finally, the score of new projects was slightly higher than that of inventory projects in 2019. Figure 3–7 shows that the transparency score of new projects in 2019 was 76.58, representing a minor gap between that of inventory projects, which was 76.21. Figure

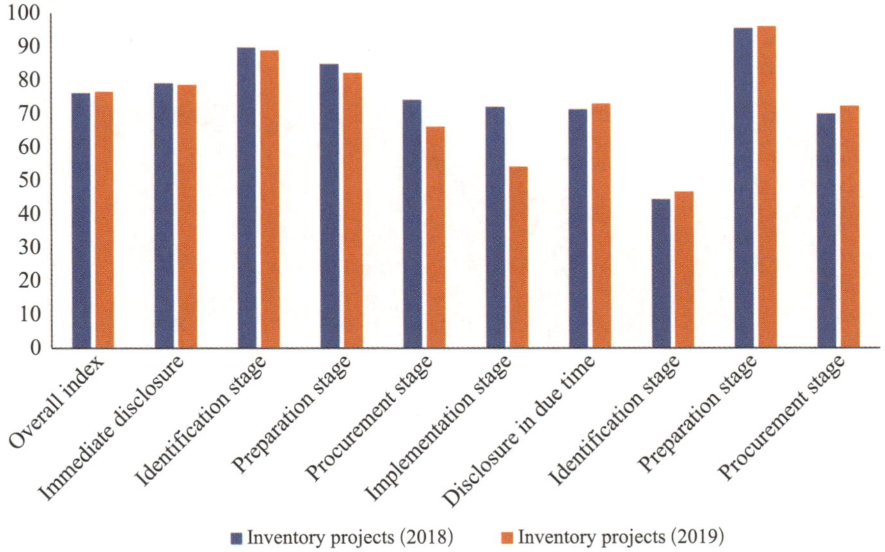

Figure 3–9 Scores of Projects Remaining in Database in Both 2018 and 2019

3–10, a further comparison by phase, shows that new projects performed better in 2019 than 2018 at all stages of disclosure in due time, but worse at all stages of immediate disclosure, especially the procurement and execution stages. This requires newly-increased PPP projects in the database to put extra efforts on immediate disclosure, so as to further improve information transparency.

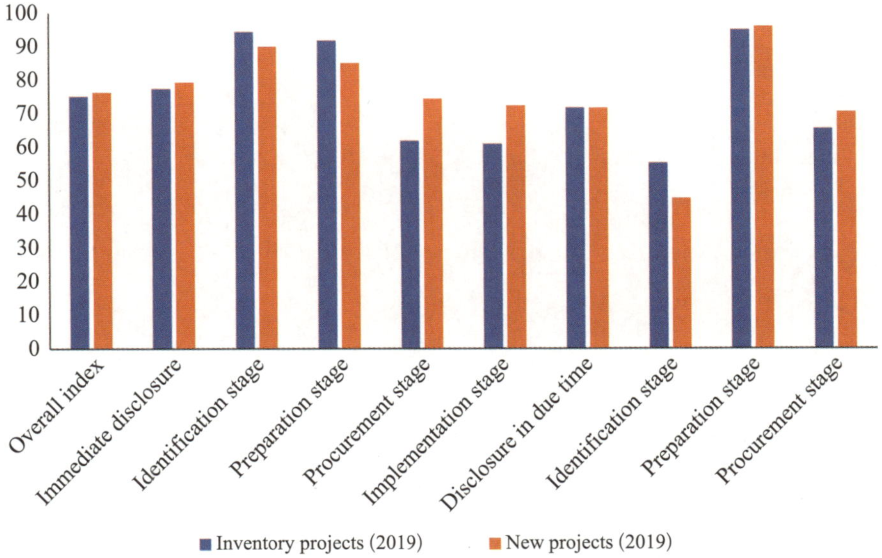

Figure 3–10 Scores of Inventory Projects and Newly-included Projects in 2019

4

Provincial Rankings and Analysis

4.1 Analysis on General Provincial Index

4.1.1 Provincial Ranking

The previous chapter provides the 2019 national PPP market transparency index, while this Chapter will focus on provincial results. The calculation of the transparency index for each province was based on arithmetic average of the immediate disclosure index and the disclosure in time index for each province and multiplied by the weightings outlined in Chapter 2. (Based on the findings outlined in Chapter 2, the weight of immediate disclosure was 0.61, and the weight of disclosure in due time was 0.39). Table 4–1 shows the number of PPP projects and the transparency indexes of the 32 provincial-level units (provinces, municipalities, autonomous regions, and Xinjiang Production and Construction Corps, the same below) in 2019. From it the Research Group have come up with the following conclusions:

First, overall, the provincial average PPP market transparency index in 2019 was 73.68, a slight drop from last year (75.26). A possible reason is that more projects came to the stage of execution. In 2018, there were only 3 550 projects covered by disclosure in due time, while in 2019, the projects of the same category reached 5 162. The decline in the transparency index in terms of disclosure in due time led to changes in the overall market transparency index. Nevertheless, 73.68 is still higher than the mean value of all scores provided in the fiscal transparency reports by the Shanghai University of Finance and Economics research groups in the past 10 years (the provincial average fiscal transparency score in 2017 was only 48.3 points). It implies that as regulated by relevant departments, the PPP market is making faster progress in information disclosure than other financial segments.

Second, the PPP market information transparency index at the provincial level maintained at a satisfactory level, as the transparency scores of most provinces were concentrated between 70 and 85. However, compared with 2018, the provincial scores were more scattered. Specifically, in 2018 all of them were within the scope of 70–80, while in 2019, several provinces delivered a PPP transparency index below 70. It indicates as the PPP projects continue to advance, the transparency scores of the provinces began to gradually differentiate. In specific, the top five in transparency ranking were Guangxi (81.97), Hebei (81.29), Jilin (80.52), Shandong (80.20) and Yunnan (80.17). Xizang, Shanghai, Hainan, Beijing, and Tianjin performed relatively poorly, occupying the last five places in the ranking. By comparing with last year's ranking, we found that the provinces that made the greatest progress in PPP project information disclosure were Jiangsu (77.69) and Guangdong (77.20). Both of them rose by 17 places from the previous year to No.9 and No.12, respectively. Among all provinces, Qinghai recorded the largest decline in the list, as its information transparency index dropped from 78.16 in 2018 to 70.81 in 2019. Despite a decline of less than 8 points, since the score gap between provinces was small, Qinghai ranked No.26 in 2019, plummeting by 24 places from the previous year. Provinces such as Xinjiang, Shandong, Hebei, Shaanxi and Heilongjiang rose significantly in the list compared with 2018, while the ranks of Xinjiang Production and Construction Corps, Tianjin, Guangxi and Liaoning saw great decline.

Table 4–1 Provincial PPP Market Transparency Index and Ranking in 2019

Province	Year 2019 project quantity	Year 2019 transparency index	Ranking in 2019	Variance from last year	Year 2018 project quantity	Year 2018 transparency index
Gansu	124	81.97	1	+3	96	77.63
Hebei	390	81.29	2	+10	343	76.48
Jilin	170	80.52	3	+2	160	77.57
Shandong	765	80.20	4	+11	755	76.30
Yunnan	481	80.17	5	–2	446	77.91
Inner Mongolia	283	78.07	6	+5	276	76.63
Shaanxi	280	77.94	7	+9	262	76.16
Anhui	474	77.84	8	+5	448	76.40
Jiangsu	398	77.69	9	+17	366	73.33
Hunan	418	77.64	10	–4	418	77.21
Xinjiang	381	77.48	11	+14	364	73.39

(continued)

Province	Year 2019 project quantity	Year 2019 transparency index	Ranking in 2019	Variance from last year	Year 2018 project quantity	Year 2018 transparency index
Guangdong	519	77.20	12	+17	439	72.94
Guangxi	204	77.03	13	−12	170	78.47
Henan	752	76.17	14	+6	640	73.90
Liaoning	184	75.80	15	−8	134	76.92
Shanxi	396	74.15	16	−7	353	76.90
Zhejiang	513	73.86	17	−3	492	76.33
Fujian	351	73.80	18	+3	332	73.82
Guizhou	512	73.76	19	0	512	73.94
Sichuan	557	73.05	20	+4	512	73.47
Hubei	417	72.96	21	+1	392	73.79
Chongqing	43	72.23	22	+1	31	73.64
Heilongjiang	107	72.09	23	+9	92	71.72
Ningxia	47	71.57	24	−7	46	75.51
Jiangxi	355	71.52	25	−7	306	74.98
Qinghai	38	70.81	26	−24	32	78.16
Corps	18	69.28	27	−19	19	76.92
Tianjin	49	68.28	28	−18	32	76.81
Beijing	70	67.49	29	−2	60	73.29
Hainan	96	62.89	30	+1	99	72.08
Shanghai	5	60.77	31	−3	3	72.98
Xizang	1	52.22	32	−2	2	72.61

Notes: ① The projects contained in this table refer to the 9 398 PPP projects subject to immediate disclosure. The 5 162 PPP projects subject to disclosure in due time are a subset of it. ② "+" indicates an increase in the ranking, "–" indicates a fall in the ranking, the same below.

4.1.2 Provincial Rankings of Immediate Disclosure and Disclosure in Due Time

Figure 4–1 and Figure 4–2 show the provincial distribution of immediate disclosure indexes and disclosure in due time indexes of all provinces in 2018 and 2019. The results show that disclosure in due time index of each province was generally higher than the immediate disclosure index. This finding is consistent with that in Chapter 3, which implies again that all provinces have done a poorer job in immediate disclosure than in disclosure in due time on PPP projects.

While the provincial rankings of general transparency index, disclosure in due time index, and immediate disclosure index were generally consistent, it is important to qualify

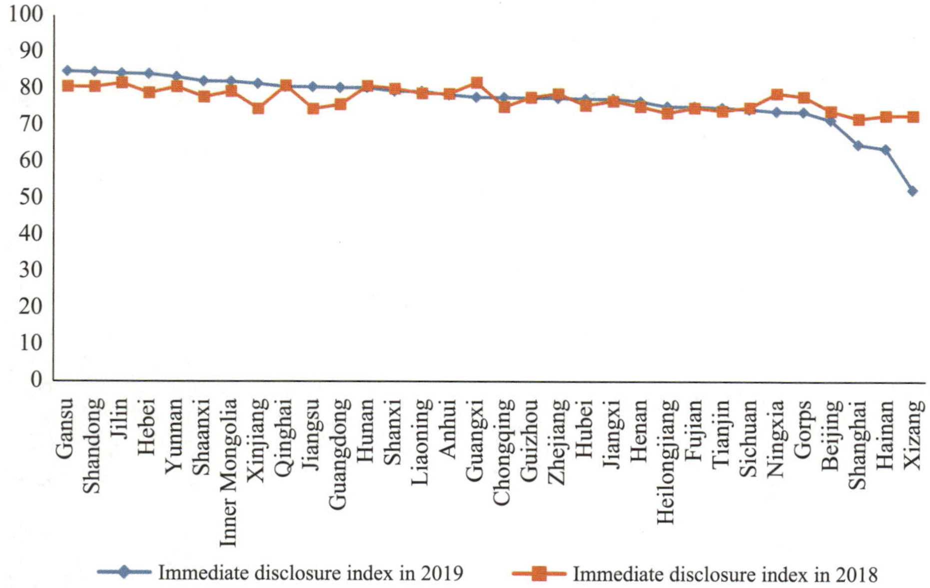

Figure 4–1 PPP Immediate Disclosure Index in 2018 and 2019 by Province

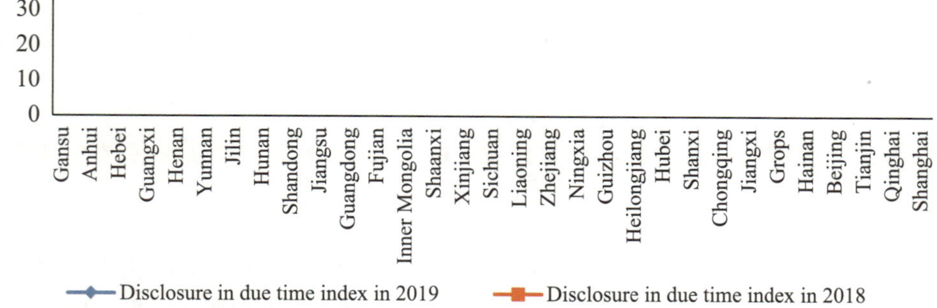

Note: Among them, as there were no projects subject to disclosure in due time in Xizang, Xizang did not participate in the corresponding ranking.

Figure 4–2 PPP Disclosure in Due Time Index in 2018 and 2019 by Province the impact of weightings on the results. As the weight allocated for immediate disclosure is higher than that for disclosure in due time (0.61 versus 0.39), it is more likely for the provinces that perform better in immediate disclosure to rank higher in the list of general index. For example, the top five provinces with the highest immediate disclosure index were also the top five in the ranking of general index. However, there still existed some differences in the provincial rankings of disclosure in due time index and immediate disclosure index. The No.2 in the ranking of immediate disclosure index Shandong ranked ninth in terms of disclosure in due time, indicating that the province did do well in immediate disclosure, but less desirable in disclosure in due time. Another example is Shanghai, which ranked last in terms of disclosure in due time, and the third from bottom in immediate disclosure, indicating that the city needs to put more efforts on both categories of disclosure. The gap between the two lists further indicates that each region has its own advantages and disadvantages in disclosing the information of PPP projects, and it is necessary for them to learn from each other, so that the overall transparency of PPP projects will come to a higher stage.

Comparison between the data in 2019 and 2018 shows no obvious trends in the cross-phase changes of both immediate disclosure and disclosure in due time indexes. That is, all provinces delivered a mixed performance in terms of PPP project information disclosure. As for immediate disclosure, there are 18 provinces and cities showing increase in index and 14 decline. Concerning the immediate disclosure index, the largest improvement came from Xinjiang, the score of which climbed from 74.63 in 2018 to 81.29 in 2019, followed by Jiangsu, Hebei, Guangdong and other provinces; while the largest drop was delivered by Xizang, from 72.61 in 2018 to 52.22 in 2019. As for disclosure in due time, there are 12 provinces and cities showing increase and 19 decrease. The largest increase in the disclosure in due time index was in Gansu, rising from 72.94 in 2018 to 77.66 in 2019. Xinjiang recorded the smallest increase in the same category, from 71.46 in 2018 to 71.52 in 2019, representing a growth of 0.07 points only. Tianjing dropped the most significantly in the disclosure in due time index, from 81.31 in 2018 to 58.24 in 2019. Generally speaking, as more projects enter the implementation stage, most provinces saw a downward trend in the disclosure in due time index, which necessitates more efforts from most provinces and cities concerning the information management of PPP projects in disclosure in due time.

4.1.3 Relationship between Transparency Index and Project Quantity

During index compilation, some experts and representatives from local finance departments suggested quantitative factors should also be taken into consideration. The rationale is that some provinces manage larger numbers of PPP projects, which may increase the difficulty in supervision and information disclosure, which in turn may result in a lower PPP transparency index. Therefore, in order to examine the relationship between the quantity of PPP projects managed in each region and its PPP market transparency, Figure 4–3 maps provincial PPP transparency indexes and project quantities. It indicates that the quantity of PPP projects does not have a significant negative relationship with the provincial PPP market transparency index, but instead shows certain positive correlation In the statistical sense, the speculation that "a region is managing too many PPP projects, so it scores low in the information transparency" does not seem to hold true.

Another doubt is that for the provinces with few PPP projects, which is deemed statistically insignificant, whether it is necessary to include them in the national ranking. In our report, no provincial-level units with too few projects were deleted. Instead, all were included in the rankings in order to thoroughly and objectively reflect the PPP information disclosure work done by each province. This is because it is hard to define a scope for sample size, for which different readers might have different standards. Instead,

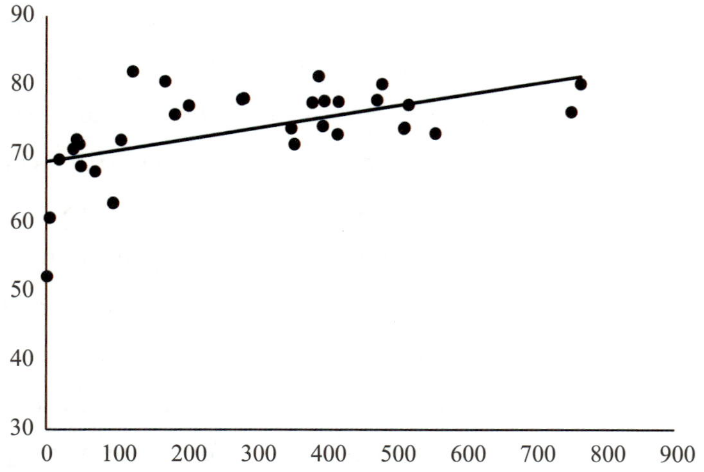

Figure 4–3 Scatter Diagram of Provincial Project Quantity and Transparency Index

they're free to intentionally omit the provinces they believe are operating few projects, and such omission doesn't affect the relative rankings of other provinces. Apart from that, it is also worthy of probing why the number of projects in a region is positively correlated with the region's PPP transparency index. One possible reason is that in regions with a large number of PPP projects, their competent authorities tend to arrange more management personnel or dedicated persons in charge.

4.2 Analysis on Provincial Index by Stage

4.2.1 Immediate Disclosure

The following is the analysis over the results of information disclosure by provinces in each stage of immediate disclosure and disclosure in due time. Table 4–2 shows the provincial rankings of 2019 PPP project immediate disclosure index and disclosure in due time index, as well as the variance from the previous year. As for immediate disclosure, Gansu, Shandong, Jilin, Hebei and Yunnan ranked as top five, while Xinjiang Production and Construction Corps, Beijing, Shanghai, Hainan and Xizang were in the last five places. Xinjiang presented largest rise in rank, from No.25 in 2018 to No.8 in 2019. The province with the most decline was Guangxi, which fell by 15 places from No.1 in 2018 to No.16 in 2019. In terms of disclosure in due time, Gansu, Anhui, Hebei, Guangxi and Henan occupied the top five places, while Hainan, Beijing, Tianjin, Qinghai and Shanghai ranked last. Shandong presented the highest surge in the ranking of disclosure in due time index, leaping from No.28 in 2018 to No.9 in 2019. The provinces recording the most decline were Tianjin and Shanghai, dropping by 28 places from the previous year to No.29 and No.31 respectively.

Table 4–2 Provincial Rankings of Immediate Disclosure Index and Disclosure in Due Time Index

Ranking	Year 2019 immediate disclosure index	Variance from 2018	Year 2019 disclosure in due time index	Variance from 2018
1	Gansu	+4	Gansu	+8
2	Shandong	+4	Anhui	+8
3	Jilin	−1	Hebei	+9

(continued)

Ranking	Year 2019 immediate disclosure index	Variance from 2018	Year 2019 disclosure in due time index	Variance from 2018
4	Hebei	+6	Guangxi	+4
5	Yunnan	+2	Henan	+12
6	Shaanxi	+10	Yunnan	0
7	Inner Mongolia	+2	Jilin	+17
8	Xinjiang	+17	Hunan	+11
9	Qinghai	−6	Shandong	+19
10	Jiangsu	+16	Jiangsu	+12
11	Guangdong	+8	Guangdong	+19
12	Hunan	−8	Fujian	+4
13	Shanxi	−5	Inner Mongolia	0
14	Liaoning	−3	Shaanxi	−7
15	Anhui	−3	Xinjiang	+6
16	Guangxi	−15	Sichuan	+7
17	Chongqing	+5	Liaoning	−13
18	Guizhou	−1	Zhejiang	−7
19	Zhejiang	−5	Ningxia	+8
20	Hubei	0	Guizhou	+11
21	Jiangxi	−3	Heilongjiang	+8
22	Henan	−1	Hubei	+3
23	Heilongjiang	+6	Shanxi	−5
24	Fujian	0	Chongqing	−4
25	Tianjin	+2	Jiangxi	−10
26	Sichuan	−3	Corps	−24
27	Ningxia	−14	Hainan	−1
28	Corps	−13	Beijing	−14
29	Beijing	−1	Tianjin	−28
30	Shanghai	+2	Qinghai	−25
31	Hainan	0	Shanghai	−28
32	Xizang	−2		

Table 4–3 shows the provincial rankings of 2019 PPP project immediate disclosure index, and the sub-indexes of all stages in immediate disclosure.

Gansu, Shandong, Jilin and Hebei performed well and consistently across all stages. Yunnan delivered desirable results in the identification, preparation and implementation stages, but ranked No.20 in the procurement stage, resulting in its fifth place in the overall ranking. Better disclosure at the implementation stage is expected to improve Yunnan's overall ranking. Inner Mongolia Autonomous Region ranked high in the procurement and implementation stages, but its poorer performance in the identification and preparation stages lowered its general immediate disclosure index score.

Xinjiang Production and Construction Corps, Beijing, Shanghai , Hainan and Xizang occupied the last five places in the ranking of immediate disclosure index. In particular, Beijing ranked No.5 in the identification stage, but its poor performance during other stages lowered its overall ranking. Xizang ranked first in the identification stage, but performed poorly at the procurement and implementation stages (ranked last for both), which led to its ranking toward the end of the list. Xinjiang Production and Construction Corps, Shanghai and Hainan performed poorly at all stages of information disclosure.

Table 4–3 Provincial Rankings of Immediate Disclosure Index and Sub-index at Each Stage in 2019

Ranking	Immediate disclosure index	Identification stage	Preparation stage	Procurement stage	Implementation stage
1	Gansu	Xizang	Xinjiang	Xinjiang	Yunnan
2	Shandong	Yunnan	Yunnan	Qinghai	Hebei
3	Jilin	Gansu	Shandong	Fujian	Jilin
4	Hebei	Jiangsu	Jilin	Shaanxi	Inner Mongolia
5	Yunnan	Beijing	Gansu	Shandong	Hunan
6	Shaanxi	Shandong	Hebei	Jiangxi	Shandong
7	Inner Mongolia	Xinjiang	Shanxi	Hebei	Gansu
8	Xinjiang	Jilin	Hubei	Inner Mongolia	Jiangsu
9	Qinghai	Hebei	Jiangxi	Guangdong	Henan
10	Jiangsu	Corps	Guangxi	Jiangsu	Beijing
11	Guangdong	Henan	Inner Mongolia	Jilin	Sichuan
12	Hunan	Shaanxi	Hunan	Anhui	Guangdong

(continued)

Ranking	Immediate disclosure index	Identification stage	Preparation stage	Procurement stage	Implementation stage
13	Shanxi	Qinghai	Qinghai	Gansu	Guangxi
14	Liaoning	Guangdong	Shaanxi	Tianjin	Shaanxi
15	Anhui	Chongqing	Jiangsu	Zhejiang	Zhejiang
16	Guangxi	Inner Mongolia	Guangdong	Hubei	Ningxia
17	Chongqing	Zhejiang	Guizhou	Henan	Anhui
18	Guizhou	Anhui	Henan	Ningxia	Liaoning
19	Zhejiang	Fujian	Corps	Hunan	Chongqing
20	Hubei	Liaoning	Liaoning	Yunnan	Fujian
21	Jiangxi	Heilongjiang	Chongqing	Shanghai	Guizhou
22	Henan	Shanxi	Heilongjiang	Sichuan	Corps
23	Heilongjiang	Guangxi	Tianjin	Guangxi	Shanghai
24	Fujian	Hunan	Zhejiang	Chongqing	Shanxi
25	Tianjin	Hubei	Anhui	Shanxi	Xinjiang
26	Sichuan	Jiangxi	Sichuan	Guizhou	Hubei
27	Ningxia	Sichuan	Fujian	Hainan	Qinghai
28	Corps	Tianjin	Ningxia	Heilongjiang	Tianjin
29	Beijing	Ningxia	Beijing	Beijing	Heilongjiang
30	Shanghai	Guizhou	Shanghai	Liaoning	Hainan
31	Hainan	Hainan	Xizang	Corps	Jiangxi
32	Xizang	Shanghai	Hainan	Xizang	Xizang

Qinghai did not deliver outstanding performance at any of the stages, but took up the first place in the ranking of immediate disclosure index. Xinjiang, No.1 at the preparation and procurement stages, and Yunan, No.1 at the implementation stage, ranked higher than Qinghai at almost all stages, but lower in the final ranking of immediate disclosure index as a whole. It demonstrates that the distribution of PPP projects by stage has certain impacts on the final results. Where a province has a higher percentage of PPP projects in preparation stage and the disclosure work done at this stage is excellent, then the province can easily achieve a high score. This is partly due to the calculation methods in Chapter 3, whereby the procurement and implementation stage weighting were "consolidated" into the preparation and identification stages. If a province does not have many PPP projects at preparation stage, its slight inadequacies at procurement and implementation stages may adversely affect the final general transparency index. For better clarification, Table 4–4 shows the distribution of PPP projects by stage in each province. It is easy to find out that Gansu was significantly higher than Xinjiang and Yunnan with regard to the proportion of projects at the preparation stage. It should also be noted that the purpose of highlighting the distribution difference in stages is to explain the results and possible reasons. It does not imply project companies should deliberately slow down the progress of PPP projects to raise the index.

Table 4–4 Quantity of PPP Projects by Stage in Each Province

Province	Total quantity	Preparation stage	Procurement stage	Implementation stage
Anhui	474	48	38	388
Beijing	70	5	3	62
Fujian	351	45	21	285
Gansu	124	36	32	56
Guangdong	519	49	68	402
Guangxi	204	40	60	104
Guizhou	512	119	94	299
Hainan	96	5	8	83
Hebei	390	54	59	277
Henan	752	151	164	437
Heilongjiang	107	23	15	69
Hubei	417	52	92	273
Hunan	418	79	77	262
Jilin	170	24	29	117
Jiangsu	398	44	68	286
Jiangxi	355	51	40	264
Liaoning	184	59	46	79
Inner Mongolia	283	27	52	204
Ningxia	47	2	5	40
Qinghai	38	8	8	22
Shandong	765	115	116	534

(continued)

Province	Total quantity	Preparation stage	Procurement stage	Implementation stage
Shanxi	396	92	132	172
Shaanxi	280	53	41	186
Shanghai	5	1	1	3
Sichuan	557	35	162	360
Tianjin	49	12	9	28
Xizang	1	0	1	0
Xinjiang	381	24	44	313
Corps	18	3	5	10
Yunnan	481	86	125	270
Zhejiang	513	45	58	410
Chongqing	43	11	5	27

4.2.2 Disclosure in Due Time

Table 4–5 shows the list of the top 10 provinces for the 2019 PPP project disclosure in due time index and sub-indexes at each stage. Gansu and Anhui performed well at all stages. In particular, Gansu ranked first and second at identification and procurement stages. Thanks to its outstanding performance in the identification stage, Guangxi ranked No.4 in the disclosure in due time index ranking. Since the information disclosure in procurement stage was of the highest importance (according to the calculation results of the expert decision matrix, the weight of procurement stage was 0.45), Hebei and Henan occupied the third and fifth places in terms of disclosure in due time with a high score in procurement stage.

Table 4–5 Provincial Rankings of Disclosure in Due Time Index and Sub-index at Each Stage in 2019

Ranking	Disclosure in due time index	Identification stage	Preparation stage	Procurement stage
1	Gansu	Gansu	Anhui	Henan
2	Anhui	Guangxi	Gansu	Hebei
3	Hebei	Anhui	Shandong	Jilin
4	Guangxi	Hebei	Hunan	Yunnan

(continued)

Ranking	Disclosure in due time index	Identification stage	Preparation stage	Procurement stage
5	Henan	Yunnan	Yunnan	Gansu
6	Yunnan	Jilin	Hebei	Shandong
7	Jilin	Xinjiang	Jiangsu	Anhui
8	Hunan	Fujian	Shaanxi	Jiangsu
9	Shandong	Henan	Ningxia	Hunan
10	Jiangsu	Hunan	Guangxi	Guangdong
11	Guangdong	Guangdong	Henan	Guangxi
12	Fujian	Shaanxi	Inner Mongolia	Xinjiang
13	Inner Mongolia	Sichuan	Chongqing	Inner Mongolia
14	Shaanxi	Inner Mongolia	Jilin	Fujian
15	Xinjiang	Corps	Liaoning	Heilongjiang
16	Sichuan	Jiangsu	Sichuan	Sichuan
17	Liaoning	Zhejiang	Guangdong	Shaanxi
18	Zhejiang	Liaoning	Zhejiang	Liaoning
19	Ningxia	Guizhou	Fujian	Guizhou
20	Guizhou	Shandong	Shanxi	Hubei
21	Heilongjiang	Ningxia	Guizhou	Shanxi
22	Hubei	Chongqing	Xinjiang	Ningxia
23	Shanxi	Hubei	Hubei	Zhejiang
24	Chongqing	Beijing	Heilongjiang	Hainan
25	Jiangxi	Shanxi	Jiangxi	Jiangxi
26	Corps	Jiangxi	Hainan	Beijing
27	Hainan	Heilongjiang	Beijing	Corps
28	Beijing	Hainan	Shanghai	Chongqing
29	Tianjin	Tianjin	Tianjin	Tianjin
30	Qinghai	Shanghai	Corps	Qinghai
31	Shanghai	Qinghai	Qinghai	Shanghai

The last five on the list were occupied by Hainan, Beijing, Tianjin, Qinghai and Shanghai. According to Table 4–3, Beijing, Shanghai and Hainan also performed poorly in immediate disclosure (see the previous analysis), ranking among the last on the list. It indicates that their PPP information disclosure approaches are in need of improvement.

Figure 4–4 consolidates the indexes of provincial units at each stage of immediate disclosure and disclosure in real time. The comparison highlights that the disclosure of information at identification and preparation stages was more complete, while the indexes at procurement and implementation stages were generally lower. Such results are basically in line with expectations as the more detailed information at the identification and preparation stages is likely to determine if a PPP project progresses, and is often more valued by the regulatory authorities and social participants, hence resulting in the higher corresponding indexes.

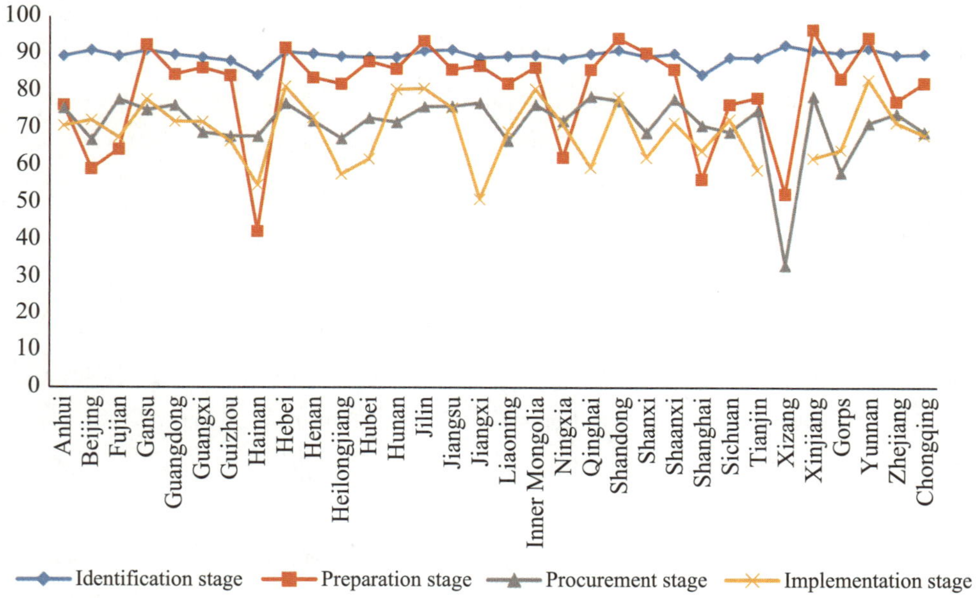

Figure 4–4 Provincial Distribution of Immediate Disclosure Transparency Indexes by Stage in 2019

Figure 4–5 shows the indexes of provincial units at various stages of disclosure in due time. Unlike the case in immediate disclosure, the information disclosure performance at identification stage does not appear to be as comprehensive as in the preparation and procurement stages. This may be attributed to the identification stage requiring two important PDF files, namely the "Two Assessments" (value-for-money evaluation and financial affordability assessment). The Research Group conducted a very strict review of the two files, and there were many projects with no disclosure or false disclosure, consequently contributing to a generally low index of each province at this stage.

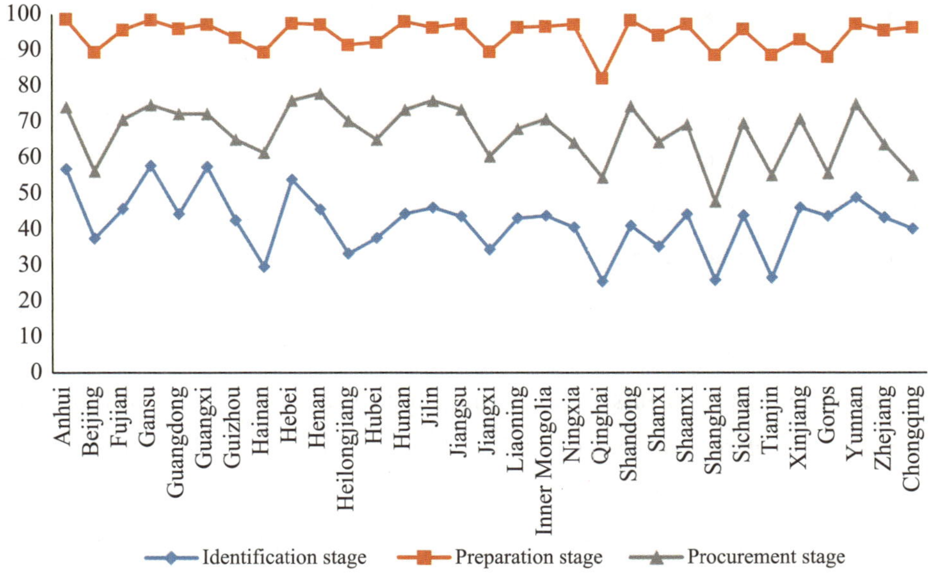

Figure 4–5 Provincial Distribution of Disclosure in Due Time Indexes by Stage in 2019

4.3 Analysis on Provincial Transparency Indexes of "Two Assessments and One Program"

The "Two Assessments and One Program" refer to the "value-for-money evaluation report and approval documents by the competent industry authority and the finance industry at the same level", the "financial affordability assessment report and approval documents by the finance department at the same level" and "attachments to implementation program". The "Two Assessments and One Program" takes a very important position at the identification stage and preparation stage of a PPP project, and is also an indispensable step in the normal operation of PPP projects in China, enough to determine whether a PPP project can be implemented smoothly or not. Accordingly, this section briefly summarizes the disclosure of these key reports in all provinces.

The "Two Assessments and One Program" documents contain extensive amounts of complex information, prepared in PDF files and published on the website. It is not unusual for the PDF files to extend to tens or even hundreds of pages for the public to review. Three PDF files were the focus of the Research Group for manual reading and checking — "value for money", "financial affordability", "implementation program". Table 4–6 shows the provincial rankings of the scores of the three PDF files. It can be seen that the rankings are highly consistent with that of disclosure in due time index. For example, Gansu took the first place in "financial affordability assessment report and approval documents by the finance department at the same level" and the second in "value-for-money evaluation report and approval documents by the competent industry authority and the finance industry at the same level". It is due to the province's excellent performance concerning the two indicators that it managed to rank first in the disclosure in due time index. Shanghai ranked the last in the same ranking, mainly attributable to its low score in the disclosure of the three documents, which showed that the city needs to dedicate more efforts to this aspect. Anhui took the second place in the ranking of "attachments to implementation program", but due to its low scores in "value-for-money evaluation report and approval documents by the competent industry authority and the finance industry at the same level" and "financial affordability assessment report and approval documents by the finance department at the same level", its general index of disclosure in due time ranked No.2. Hebei performed well in "Two Assessments and One Program", ranking among three in all three documents, so it retained its third place in the overall ranking of disclosure in due time index. Guangxi, Henan and Yunnan delivered a mixed performance in "Two Assessments and One Program", so they ranked 4th to 6th in the general ranking.

Table 4–6 Provincial Transparency Rankings of "Two Assessments and One Program"

Ranking	Disclosure in due time index	Value-for-money	Financial affordability	Implementation program
1	Gansu	Yunnan	Gansu	Guangxi
2	Anhui	Gansu	Hebei	Anhui
3	Hebei	Hebei	Hunan	Hebei
4	Guangxi	Henan	Yunnan	Jiangsu
5	Henan	Shaanxi	Henan	Beijing
6	Yunnan	Guangxi	Shaanxi	Liaoning
7	Jilin	Inner Mongolia	Inner Mongolia	Xinjiang
8	Hunan	Hunan	Guangxi	Ningxia
9	Shandong	Anhui	Shandong	Jilin
10	Jiangsu	Shandong	Anhui	Hubei
11	Guangdong	Fujian	Fujian	Zhejiang

(continued)

Ranking	Disclosure in due time index	Value-for-money	Financial affordability	Implementation program
12	Fujian	Jiangsu	Jiangsu	Hainan
13	Inner Mongolia	Jilin	Guangdong	Henan
14	Shaanxi	Sichuan	Jilin	Gansu
15	Xinjiang	Guangdong	Sichuan	Shanghai
16	Sichuan	Zhejiang	Corps	Fujian
17	Liaoning	Ningxia	Ningxia	Jiangxi
18	Zhejiang	Xinjiang	Zhejiang	Guizhou
19	Ningxia	Corps	Chongqing	Guangdong
20	Guizhou	Shanxi	Xinjiang	Shaanxi
21	Heilongjiang	Liaoning	Liaoning	Inner Mongolia
22	Hubei	Chongqing	Shanxi	Tianjin
23	Shanxi	Guizhou	Guizhou	Hunan
24	Chongqing	Hubei	Hubei	Heilongjiang
25	Jiangxi	Heilongjiang	Heilongjiang	Sichuan
26	Corps	Jiangxi	Jiangxi	Chongqing
27	Hainan	Shanghai	Shanghai	Qinghai
28	Beijing	Tianjin	Tianjin	Yunnan
29	Tianjin	Qinghai	Beijing	Shanxi
30	Qinghai	Beijing	Qinghai	Shandong
31	Shanghai	Hainan	Hainan	Corps

In the future, the Research Group will consider carrying out a number of special assessments to check not only whether these key fields or core PDF files are disclosed, but also the content quality of these reports, with an aim to further promote the standardization and transparency of PPP projects.

5

Municipal Rankings and Analysis

5.1 Municipal Distribution of PPP Projects

Drawing on the same methodology for comparative analysis of the PPP market transparency indexes at national level and at provincial level in Chapter 3 and Chapter 4, this Chapter presents some analysis on the transparency of the PPP market in some cities with a large number of PPP projects. In the 338 prefecture-level cities (autonomous prefecture, prefecture, league, etc., are all defined as “city” hereinafter), 326 cities have introduced the PPP model. The PPP model is far-reaching, especially in 22 provinces and autonomous regions, that is, Guangdong, Shandong, Henan, Xinjiang, Anhui, Yunnan, Liaoning, Hunan, Guangxi, Jiangsu, Hubei, Inner Mongolia, Hebei, Shanxi, Zhejiang, Jiangxi, Shaanxi, Jilin, Sichuan, Fujian, Guizhou and Ningxia, where PPP projects have covered all prefecture-level cities.

Some cities have mature PPP markets, while others are relatively new to PPP projects. For the purposes of this Report, the Research Group selected the cities that have introduced a large number of PPP projects for analysis. Specifically, 46 cities were selected as samples for analysis of municipal PPP market transparency. They were cities above the prefecture level with more than 50 projects registered in the PPP Integrated Information Platform as of December 31, 2019. For the results of the PPP Market Transparency Index in cities above the prefecture level with more than 20 projects, please see Appendix Ⅳ. The 46 cities that met the criteria were: Aksu of Xinjiang, Dongguan of Guangdong, Rizhao of Shandong, Weifang of Shandong, Jining of Shandong, Tangshan of Hebei, Changchun of Jilin, Chengde of Hebei, Yuxi of Yunnan, Heze of Shandong, Bijie of Guizhou, Linyi of Shandong, Nanjing of Jiangsu, Pingdingshan of Henan, Kunming of Yunnan, Xi’an of Shaanxi, Guiyang of Guizhou, Xuzhou of Jiangsu, Zhengzhou of Henan, Fuyang of Anhui, Hangzhou of Zhejiang, Zunyi of Guizhou, Xiangxi of Hunan, Ningde of Fujian, Liupanshui of Guizhou, Luoyang of Henan, Lishui of Zhejiang, Jinzhong of Shanxi, Chifeng of Inner Mongolia, Urumqi of Xinjiang,

Chengdu of Sichuan, Wenzhou of Zhejiang, Zhumadian of Henan, Qingdao of Shandong, Linfen of Shanxi, Nanyang of Henan, Quanzhou of Fujian, Yibin of Sichuan, Xinyang of Henan, Zhangzhou of Fujian, Taizhou of Zhejiang, Wuhan of Hubei, Ganzhou of Jiangxi, Beijing, Qiannan of Guizhou, and Haikou of Hainan.

Table 5–1 Number of Cities in Each Province Having Introduced PPP Model

Province	Number of cities with PPP	Total number of cities	Province	Number of cities with PPP	Total number of cities
Yunnan	16	16	Jiangxi	11	11
Inner Mongolia	12	12	Hebei	11	11
Jilin	9	9	Henan	17	17
Sichuan	21	21	Zhejiang	11	11
Ningxia	5	5	Hainan	2	3
Anhui	16	16	Hubei	13	13
Shandong	17	17	Hunan	14	14
Shanxi	11	11	Gansu	13	14
Guangdong	21	21	Fujian	9	9
Guangxi	14	14	Guizhou	9	9
Xinjiang	14	14	Liaoning	14	14
Shaanxi	10	10	Qinghai	6	8
Jiangsu	13	13	Heilongjiang	12	13
Xizang	1	7			

5.2 Municipal PPP Market Transparency Index

5.2.1 Municipal Ranking

Of the 46 cities selected, all of which could be described as relatively mature PPP markets, the overall ranking of PPP market transparency index in 2019 is shown in Table 5–2. Aksu, Xinjiang, ranked first, with an index of 82.81 points, 6.73 points higher than the national average; followed by Dongguan, Guangdong and Rizhao, Shandong, scoring 82.48 and 82.06 points, respectively. In addition, cities with a total score of 80 points or above include Weifang of Shandong, Jining of Shandong, Tangshan of Hebei, Changchun of Jilin, Chengde of Hebei, Yuxi of Yunnan, Heze of Shandong and Bijie of Guizhou. The index outcomes suggest that these cities have performed well in terms of PPP information disclosure.

Table 5–2 Overall Transparency Indexes of Selected Cities in 2019

Ranking	City	Number of projects in 2019	Overall index in 2019	Variance from general index in 2018	Overall index in 2018	Overall index in 2017
1	Aksu, Xinjiang	66	82.81	15.39	67.43	55.89
2	Dongguan, Guangdong	108	82.48	13.62	68.86	79.76
3	Rizhao, Shandong	56	82.06	3.88	78.18	81.07
4	Weifang, Shandong	93	81.79	4.72	77.08	60.76
5	Jining, Shandong	82	81.62	6.93	74.69	78.48
6	Tangshan, Hebei	52	81.58	5.03	76.55	78.84
7	Changchun, Jilin	50	81.46	5.11	76.35	71.10
8	Chengde, Hebei	56	81.41	3.45	77.96	79.88
9	Yuxi, Yunnan	57	81.41	3.82	77.59	76.43
10	Heze, Shandong	74	80.85	3.66	77.19	66.56
11	Bijie, Guizhou	65	80.09	4.85	75.24	64.12
12	Linyi, Shandong	76	79.88	4.84	75.04	70.63
13	Nanjing, Jiangsu	90	79.43	8.25	71.19	64.99
14	Pingdingshan, Henan	59	78.39	2.96	75.43	66.57
15	Kunming, Yunnan	54	78.06	0.33	77.73	75.03
16	Xi’an, Shaanxi	83	78.06	1.68	76.38	66.28
17	Guiyang, Guizhou	51	77.61	–0.53	78.14	59.17
18	Xuzhou, Jiangsu	58	77.36	2.77	74.59	54.67
19	Zhengzhou, Henan	56	77.09	5.51	71.58	60.58
20	Fuyang, Anhui	62	77.09	–2.33	79.41	70.39
21	Hangzhou, Zhejiang	66	76.61	0.31	76.29	57.97
22	Zunyi, Guizhou	114	76.43	–0.74	77.17	65.79
23	Xiangxi, Hunan	50	75.98	0.05	75.92	67.31
24	Ningde, Fujian	63	75.97	6.06	69.91	65.20

(continued)

Ranking	City	Number of projects in 2019	Overall index in 2019	Variance from general index in 2018	Overall index in 2018	Overall index in 2017
25	Liupanshui, Guizhou	50	75.93	3.85	72.08	44.07
26	Luoyang, Henan	57	75.86	5.34	70.52	53.95
27	Lishui, Zhejiang	62	75.85	−3.07	78.92	72.40
28	Jinzhong, Shanxi	50	75.81	0.54	75.26	76.76
29	Chifeng, Inner Mongolia	56	75.29	−1.97	77.26	56.48
30	Urumqi, Xinjiang	64	75.18	1.64	73.54	54.59
31	Chengdu, Sichuan	55	74.99	0.10	74.90	84.67
32	Wenzhou, Zhejiang	83	74.90	−0.26	75.16	54.95
33	Zhumadian, Henan	69	74.70	−4.05	78.75	62.52
34	Qingdao, Shandong	74	74.27	−1.67	75.94	72.47
35	Linfen, Shanxi	58	73.67	−7.08	80.75	72.37
36	Nanyang, Henan	71	73.58	5.10	68.48	51.76
37	Quanzhou, Fujian	66	73.54	−2.08	75.62	76.05
38	Yibin, Sichuan	62	72.90	−1.87	74.77	67.20
39	Xinyang, Henan	52	72.43	−4.79	77.22	58.46
40	Zhangzhou, Fujian	60	72.08	−3.29	75.37	70.12
41	Taizhou, Zhejiang	67	70.93	−6.84	77.77	62.08
42	Wuhan, Hubei	67	70.41	−0.99	71.40	73.19
43	Ganzhou, Jiangxi	95	70.34	−2.19	72.53	65.61
44	Beijing	70	67.49	−7.43	74.92	52.25
45	Qiannan, Guizhou	53	66.16	−12.00	78.16	54.51
46	Haikou, Hainan	52	57.86	−13.10	70.96	42.96

By comparison with the indexes in 2018, it can be found that some prefecture-level cities scored significantly higher in 2019 than in 2018. Among them, the largest increase was delivered by Aksu of Xinjiang, the 2019 overall score of which increased by 15.39 points compared to 2018, and followed by Dongguan of Shandong, with an increase of 13.62 points from 2018. However, it can also be found that the indexes of many cities above the prefecture level decreased in 2019 from 2018, especially Qiannan of Guizhou and Haikou of Hainan. They recorded the largest decline from 2018 by 13.10 and 12 points, respectively.

5.2.2 Comparison with National Average

The distribution of the general transparency indexes of 46 cities shows that as the PPP model gains popularity, no significant differences were seen in PPP market information transparency between most cities. Exceptions include Beijing, Qiannan of Guizhou and Haikou of Hainan. The information transparency indexes of all the three cities were below 70 points, especially Haikou, which delivered an index less than 60 points. By variation in the market transparency index, the 46 cities can be roughly classified into two groups, as shown in Figure 5–1. The first group includes 22 cities with leading PPP market transparency performance across the nation, i.e. those ranking between Aksu of Xinjiang and Zunyi of Guizhou; the second group includes 24 cities that lagged behind the national average, i.e. those ranking between Xiangxi of Hunan and Haikou of Hainan. As most of the cities analyzed manage large numbers of PPP projects, business unfamiliarity should not be a factor for poor PPP market transparency indexes delivered by the cities in the second group. Instead, it means that some cities do need to strengthen their efforts related to PPP information disclosure to avoid the negligence in standardized management.

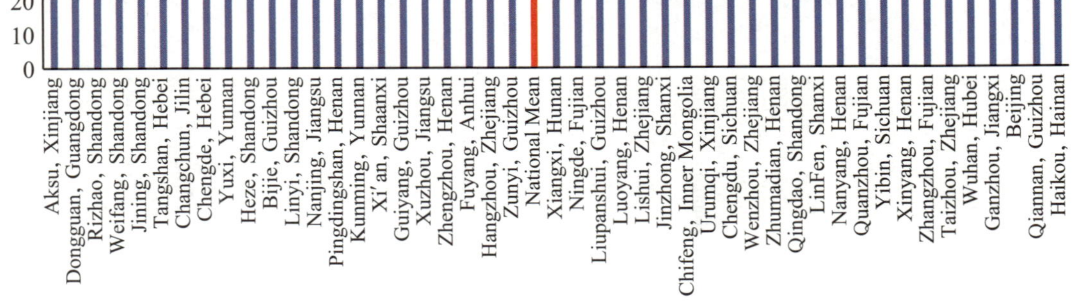

Figure 5–1 Distribution of Transparency Indexes of Selected Cities in 2019

5.2.3 Analysis on Municipal Index by Immediate Disclosure/Disclosure in Due Time

Figure 5–2 and Figure 5–3 show the distribution of the immediate disclosure indexes and the disclosure in due time indexes of 46 cities. As shown in Figure 5–2, the average immediate disclosure index in 2019, 78.6 points, was much higher than that in 2017 — 58.67 points, and similar to that in 2018 — 77.95 points. At the same time, it can be observed from Figure 5–3 that many cities scored almost the same in terms of disclosure in due time in 2019 and 2018. Also, most cities from Aksu of Xinjiang to Zunyi of Guizhou scored higher in both immediate disclosure and disclosure in due time indexes in 2019 than 2018; while most cities from Xiangxi of Hunan to Haikou of Hainan did the opposite. It indicates that the good performance of cities in PPP project information transparency was attributable to their high scores in both immediate disclosure and disclosure in due time. On the other hand, there were a number of cites delivering worse performance in both dimensions.

As far as immediate disclosure is concerned, the top three cities that made the largest improvement in 2019 compared with 2018 are: Aksu of Xinjiang (from 67.11 to 85.02 points), Dongguan of Guangdong (from 70.25 to 84.61 points) and Nanjing of Jiangsu (from 73.37 to 83.41 points). And Taizhou of Zhejiang, Qiannan of Guizhou, and

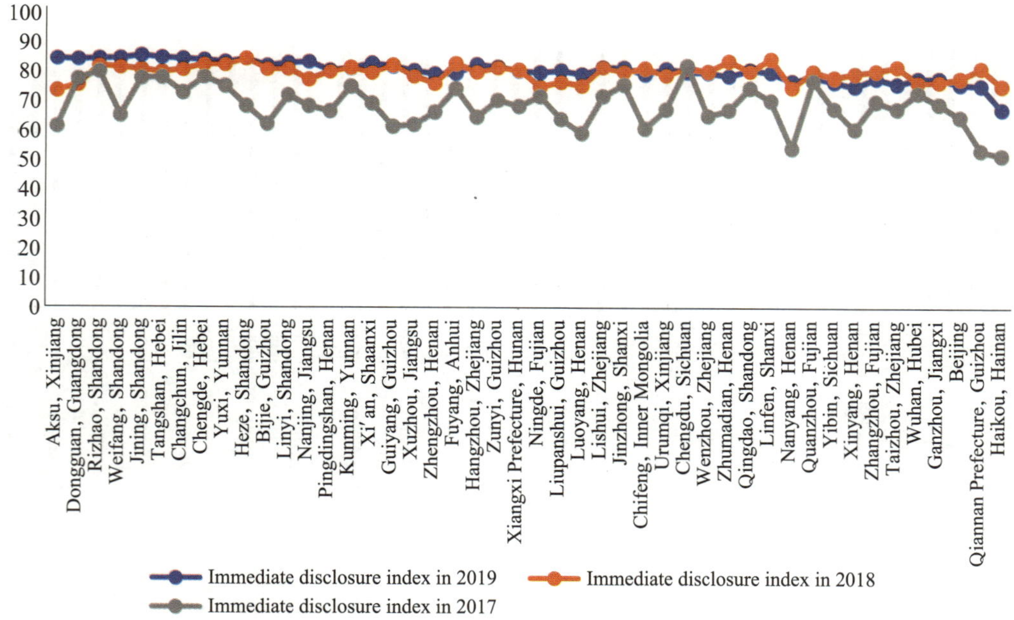

Figure 5–2 Distribution of Immediate Disclosure Indexes of Selected Cities in 2017–2019

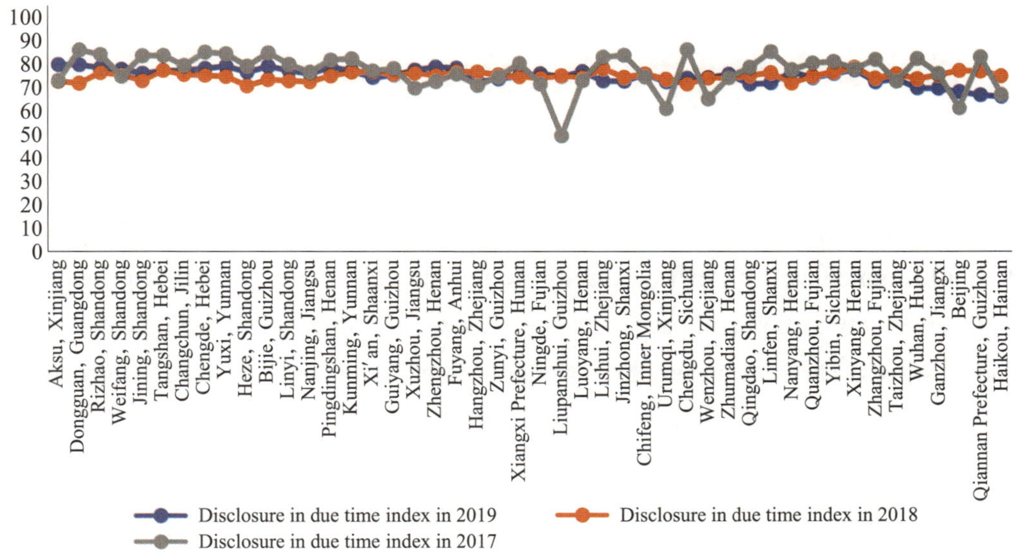

Figure 5–3 Distribution of Disclosure in Due Time Indexes of Selected Cities in 2017–2019

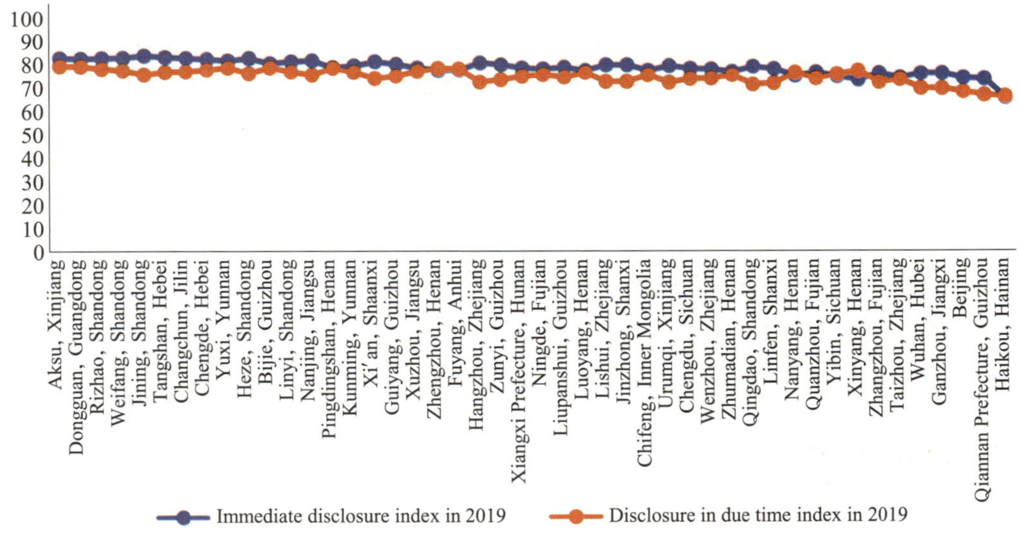

Figure 5–4 Distribution of Immediate Disclosure Indexes and Disclosure in Due Time Indexes of Selected Cities in 2019

Haikou of Hainan are the most representative cities delivering worse performance than the previous year. In terms of disclosure in due time, the top three cities that delivered the largest increase in score in 2019 are: Aksu of Xinjiang, Dongguan of Guangdong, and Heze of Shandong; on the contrary, the largest decrease was seen in Beijing, Qiannan of Guizhou and Haikou of Hainan. Figure 5–4 indicates that the overall immediate disclosure index is higher than the index of disclosure in due time in 2019, calling for more efforts in the information disclosure in due time by cities.

5.2.4 Analysis on Municipal Index by Stage

The municipal sub-indexes at different stages are shown in Figure 5–5 and Figure 5–6. Figure 5–5 shows the immediate disclosure index of each city at the stages of identification, preparation, procurement and implementation. The results indicate that in relation to immediate information disclosure requirements, cities have performed better during the identification and preparation phases, with scores generally higher than those at other stages. The reason may be that the high completeness of basic information in identification and preparation stages helps attract social capital and directly improves the tendering results of PPP projects. As a result, it is likely most project management departments will pay more attention to immediately disclosing information required at the two stages, resulting in average indexes of 89.59 and 83.07 respectively. The average information transparency indexes at procurement and implementation stages were 74.01 and 70.79 respectively, lower than the other two, along with high fluctuation. Meanwhile, it should also be noted that the immediate disclosure indexes of some cities in the preparation stage were lower than those in procurement and implementation stages. In particular, Haikou of Hainan scored only 23.53 points in the preparation stage of immediate disclosure, which calls for more efforts from the city in this respect.

Conversely, for disclosure in due time, the index at identification stage was significantly lower than preparation and procurement phases. The identification stage average index was

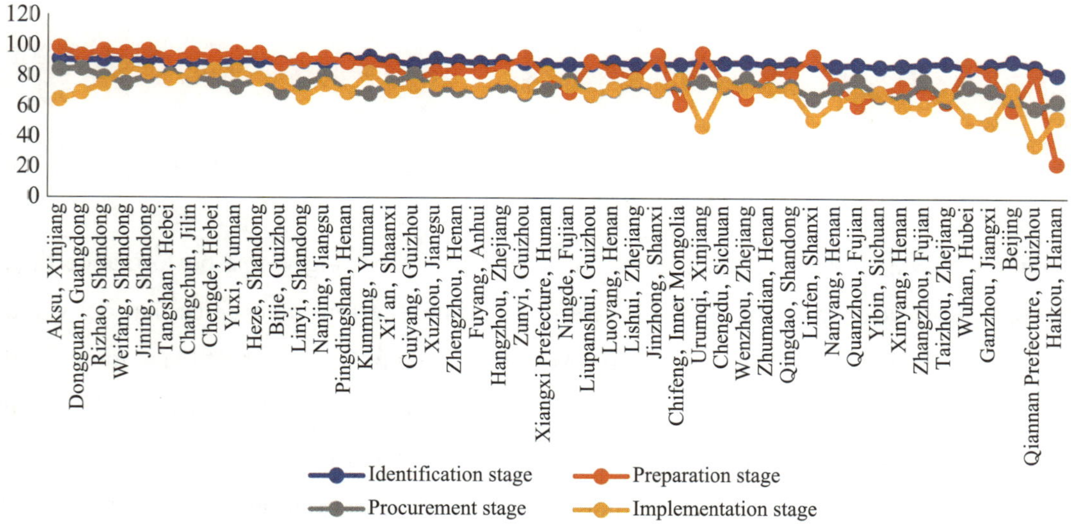

Figure 5–5 Staged Distribution of Immediate Disclosure Indexes of Selected Cities in 2019

44.72, while the index at the preparation stage averaged up to 96.29. The likely reason for such difference relates to the requirement raised by disclosure in due time at the identification stage as to disclose value-for-money evaluation report, financial affordability assessment report and other essential attachments. All of these were rigorously reviewed by the Research Group. Many reports were found problematic and/or “forged”. Therefore, the non-standard reporting of value-for-money and financial affordability led to the poorest performance of disclosure in due time at identification stage among all stages. No outstanding fluctuation is found in the disclosure in due time index of the three stages among 46 cities.

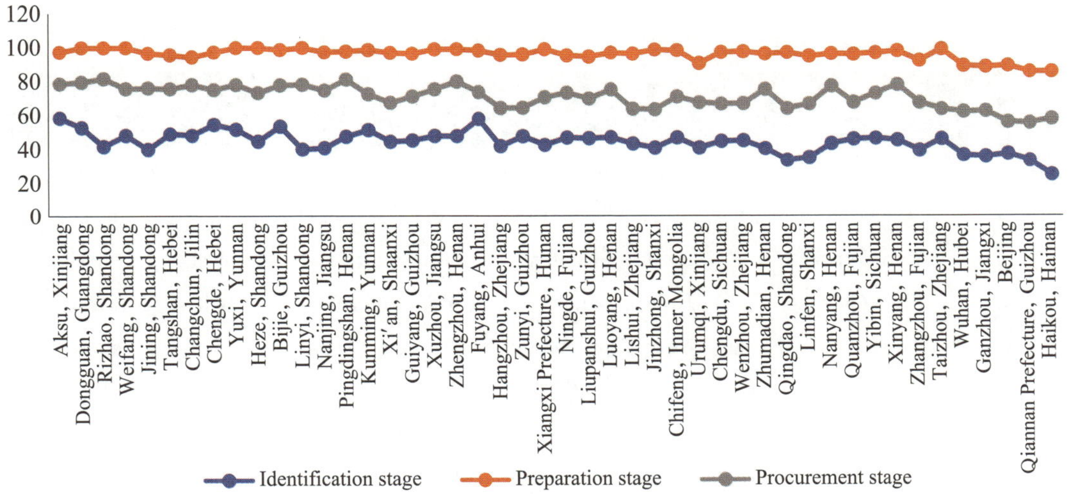

Figure 5–6 Distribution of Disclosure in Due Time Indexes of Selected Cities in 2019 by Stage

The results are a signal to local authorities that due attention should be made to the information disclosure effort for the “Two Assessments”, and the quality level, as well as a reminder to the national competent authorities to keep tightening the regulatory requirements for “Two Assessments”. Due to the pervasiveness of the problem, it is necessary to propose a more detailed and operable policy guide for these key tasks.

5.3 Analysis on Municipal Transparency Indexes of “Two Assessments and One Program”

This section is a continuation of the provincial analysis, examining the transparency of the “Two Assessments and One Program” in key cities. Table 5–3 shows the performance of Dongguan of Guangdong, Bijie of Guizhou, Yuxi of Yunnan and Pingdingshan of Henan in disclosing the "Two Assessments and One Program" is worthy of recognition. Dongguan and Pingdingshan ranked first in the disclosure of information relating to value-for-money and financial affordability, with a perfect score. According to the definition above, there was neither incomplete disclosure nor "false" disclosure of information found in these cities. However, the overall index of Pingdingshan did not rank high, because other indicators that need to be disclosed were not reported to the system in time - implementation program in particular.

Table 5–3 Municipal Transparency Rankings of "Two Assessments and One Program

Ranking	Disclosure in due time index	Value-for-money	Financial affordability	Implementation program
1	Aksu, Xinjiang	Dongguan, Guangdong	Dongguan, Guangdong	Aksu, Xinjiang
2	Dongguan, Guangdong	Pingdingshan, Henan	Pingdingshan, Henan	Fuyang, Anhui
3	Yuxi, Yunnan	Rizhao, Shandong	Bijie, Guizhou	Nanjing, Jiangsu
4	Bijie, Guizhou	Bijie, Guizhou	Yuxi, Yunnan	Chengde, Hebei
5	Pingdingshan, Henan	Yuxi, Yunnan	Weifang, Shandong	Xuzhou, Jiangsu
6	Zhengzhou, Henan	Heze, Shandong	Heze, Shandong	Changchun, Jilin
7	Rizhao, Shandong	Chifeng, Inner Mongolia	Chifeng, Inner Mongolia	Beijing
8	Fuyang, Anhui	Linyi, Shandong	Linyi, Shandong	Lishui, Zhejiang
9	Chengde, Hebei	Weifang, Shandong	Zhengzhou, Henan	Tangshan, Hebei
10	Weifang, Shandong	Kunming, Yunnan	Kunming, Yunnan	Quanzhou, Fujian
11	Xinyang, Henan	Zhengzhou, Henan	Xiangxi, Hunan	Urumqi, Xinjiang
12	Xuzhou, Jiangsu	Aksu, Xinjiang	Aksu, Xinjiang	Haikou, Hainan
13	Changchun, Jilin	Xinyang, Henan	Rizhao, Shandong	Zhumadian, Henan
14	Linyi, Shandong	Jinzhong, Shanxi	Xinyang, Henan	Nanyang, Henan
15	Kunming, Yunnan	Xiangxi, Hunan	Jinzhong, Shanxi	Luoyang, Henan
16	Tangshan, Hebei	Xuzhou, Jiangsu	Yibin, Sichuan	Wuhan, Hubei
17	Luoyang, Henan	Xi'an, Shaanxi	Ningde, Fujian	Hangzhou, Zhejiang
18	Nanyang, Henan	Chengde, Hebei	Chengde, Hebei	Liupanshui, Guizhou
19	Heze, Shandong	Ningde, Fujian	Xi'an, Shaanxi	Taizhou, Zhejiang
20	Yibin, Sichuan	Jining, Shandong	Luoyang, Henan	Wenzhou, Zhejiang
21	Ningde, Fujian	Luoyang, Henan	Fuyang, Anhui	Guiyang, Guizhou

(continued)

Ranking	Disclosure in due time index	Value-for-money	Financial affordability	Implementation program
22	Jining, Shandong	Fuyang, Anhui	Jining, Shandong	Yibin, Sichuan
23	Chifeng, Inner Mongolia	Nanjing, Jiangsu	Nanyang, Henan	Zhengzhou, Henan
24	Nanjing, Jiangsu	Yibin, Sichuan	Nanjing, Jiangsu	Chengdu, Sichuan
25	Zhumadian, Henan	Wenzhou, Zhejiang	Wenzhou, Zhejiang	Xinyang, Henan
26	Guiyang, Guizhou	Taizhou, Zhejiang	Taizhou, Zhejiang	Zunyi, Guizhou
27	Xiangxi, Hunan	Quanzhou, Fujian	Quanzhou, Fujian	Ganzhou, Jiangxi
28	Liupanshui, Guizhou	Zunyi, Guizhou	Zunyi, Guizhou	Qingdao, Shandong
29	Quanzhou, Fujian	Nanyang, Henan	Chengdu, Sichuan	Qiannan, Guizhou
30	Wenzhou, Zhejiang	Tangshan, Hebei	Tangshan, Hebei	Xi’an, Shaanxi
31	Xi’an, Shaanxi	Guiyang, Guizhou	Guiyang, Guizhou	Bijie, Guizhou
32	Chengdu, Sichuan	Liupanshui, Guizhou	Hangzhou, Zhejiang	Pingdingshan, Henan
33	Taizhou, Zhejiang	Lishui, Zhejiang	Liupanshui, Guizhou	Chifeng, Inner Mongolia
34	Zunyi, Guizhou	Chengdu, Sichuan	Lishui, Zhejiang	Zhangzhou, Fujian
35	Lishui, Zhejiang	Zhumadian, Henan	Xuzhou, Jiangsu	Ningde, Fujian
36	Jinzhong, Shanxi	Changchun, Jilin	Zhumadian, Henan	Dongguan, Guangdong
37	Hangzhou, Zhejiang	Linfen, Shanxi	Changchun, Jilin	Heze, Shandong
38	Zhangzhou, Fujian	Zhangzhou, Fujian	Linfen, Shanxi	Kunming, Yunnan
39	Urumqi, Xinjiang	Hangzhou, Zhejiang	Zhangzhou, Fujian	Yuxi, Yunnan
40	Linfen, Shanxi	Urumqi, Xinjiang	Urumqi, Xinjiang	Xiangxi, Hunan
41	Qingdao, Shandong	Wuhan, Hubei	Wuhan, Hubei	Linfen, Shanxi
42	Wuhan, Hubei	Ganzhou, Jiangxi	Qingdao, Shandong	Jinzhong, Shanxi
43	Ganzhou, Jiangxi	Qingdao, Shandong	Ganzhou, Jiangxi	Jining, Shandong
44	Beijing	Qiannan, Guizhou	Qiannan, Guizhou	Weifang, Shandong
45	Qiannan, Guizhou	Beijing	Beijing	Linyi, Shandong
46	Haikou, Hainan	Haikou, Hainan	Haikou, Hainan	Rizhao, Shandong

Chifeng of Inner Mongolia, despite its desirable performance in disclosing value-for-money evaluation and financial affordability assessment reports, ranked among the last in the index of disclosure in due time, mainly attributable to its poor work regarding implementation program. Haikou of Hainan and Beijing ranked among the last in disclosing information on value-for-money and financial affordability, with average performance in terms of implementation program.

5.4 Analysis on Cross-phase Variance in Overall Index

As per the Circular on Regulating Project Database of the National PPP Integrated Information Platform (Cai Ban Jin [2017] No. 92) issued by the Ministry of Finance, the PPP projects that fail to conduct the "Two Assessments" in accordance with the regulations should be removed from the database. Specifically, the projects that have entered the procurement stage but have not carried out the value-for-money evaluation or financial affordability assessment (except for those that entered the procurement stage before April 7, 2015 but have not carried out the financial affordability assessment and those that entered the procurement stage before December 18, 2015 but have not carried out value-for-money evaluation); and the projects that have conducted the value-for-money evaluation and financial affordability assessment, but the assessment methods and procedures were not in line with the regulations. Furthermore, as a large number of PPP projects come to the stage of implementation, they are required to disclose the information on social capital partners, project construction progress, project quality compliance inspection, as well as the annual operation and business performance compliance of private capital partners or project companies, and interim assessment reports — all of which fall into the scope of immediate disclosure; and for disclosure in due time, they must make public their financing limit, key terms and closing conditions, which is often deemed hard to complete. In conclusion, the increased difficulty in information disclosure at the implementation stage is likely to suppress the overall index in 2019. As analyzed in Chapter 3, the PPP market transparency index in 2019 did not change much compared with 2018. This may be due to two factors: 1) The substantial increase in the proportion of projects in the implementation stage led to the decrease in the general index in 2019; 2) The removal of some projects raised the index on the other hand.

In this section, the data at the city level is used for further analysis. Figure 5–7 shows the relationship between the proportion of projects at implementation stage and the change to the general index from 2018 to 2019, which is in negative correlation. In other words, the higher the proportion of projects at implementation stage, the lower the general index. This may be because at the implementation stage, disclosure in due time was more difficult to complete than immediate disclosure, which in turn lowered the information transparency indexes of some projects in 2019.

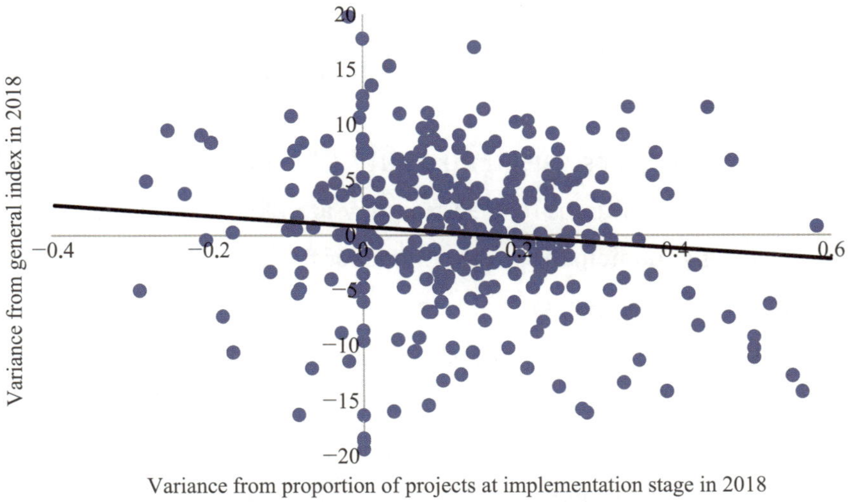

Figure 5–7 Relevance between Variance from Proportion of Projects at Implementation Stage in 2018 and Variance from General Index in 2018

Figure 5–8 shows the relationship between the proportion of projects withdrawn in 2019 and the change to the general index from 2018 to 2019, which is in positive correlation. It indicates that in 2019, the financial departments at all levels made further progress in the centralized review and clean-up of projects in the Management Database. The higher the proportion of removed projects, the greater the improvement in the PPP market transparency.

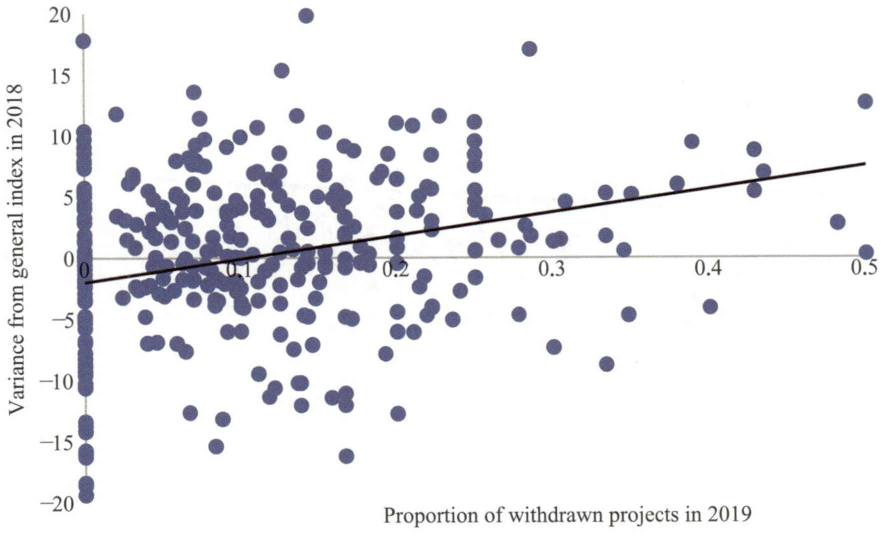

Figure 5–8 Relevance between Proportion of Withdrawn Projects in 2019 and Variance from General Index in 2018

5.5 Relevance of Economy & Finance to General Index

In this section, the cities listed in the 2017 China City Statistical Yearbook are selected as an object of research. In specific, they are 289 cities at the prefecture level and above, including 4 municipalities directly under the Central Government, 15 deputy provincial capital cities, 17 provincial capital cities and 253 prefecture-level cities. Based on the data of these cities and the 2019 PPP Information Disclosure Index, in combination with the quantitative analysis method, a scatter diagram concerning the 2019 PPP Market Transparency Index (vertical axis) and the gap between fiscal revenue and expenditure in 2017 (horizontal axis) is obtained. The selection of data on these 289 cities in 2017 is out of the following considerations: First, the cities cover 90% of the Chinese population and can basically represent the situation nationwide. Second, the data on GDP per capita, fiscal revenue, and fiscal expenditure in 2017 is chosen to avoid endogenous problems; while the source - China City Statistical Yearbook can also ensure the authority of the data.

Figure 5–9 shows a positive correlation between the 2019 PPP Market Transparency Index and the gap between fiscal revenue and expenditure in 2017. That is, the larger the gap, the higher the 2019 PPP Market Transparency Index is. This may be because a region

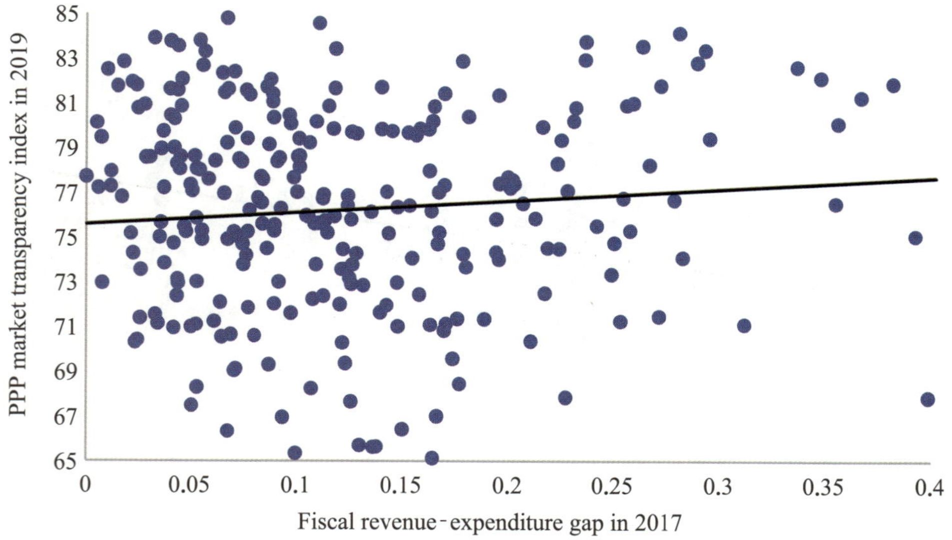

Figure 5–9 Relevance between Fiscal Revenue-Expenditure Gap in 2017 and PPP Market Transparency Index in 2019

with larger fiscal gap is more motivated to seek financing through PPP. To attract social capital, it is more obligated to standardize its work on PPP projects, so the transparency index of the region will be higher. Figure 5–10 shows that GDP per capita is negatively correlated with the PPP transparency index in 2019, that is, the more slowly a region grows economically, the higher its PPP transparency index.

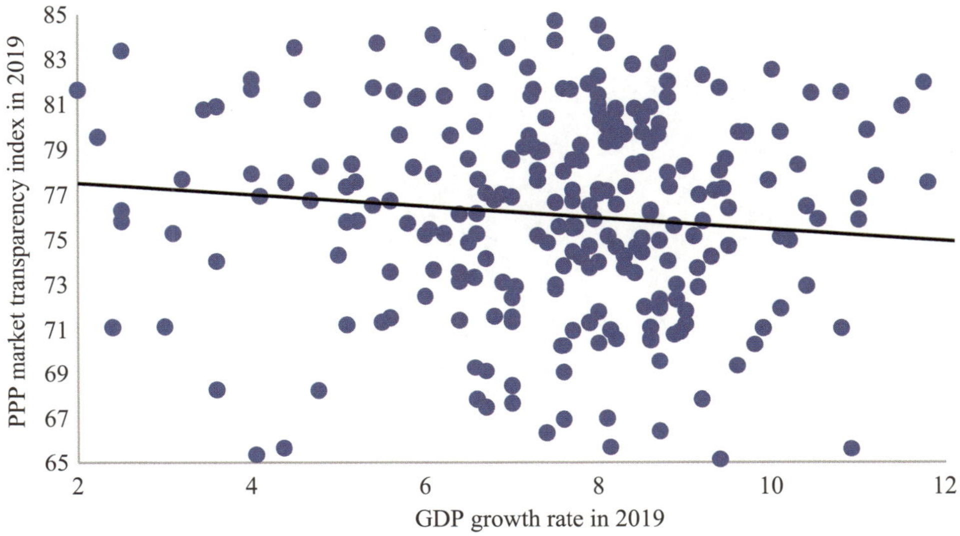

Figure 5–10 Relevance between GDP Growth Rate in 2019 and PPP Market Transparency Index in 2019

6

Evaluation of Information Disclosure by PPP Intermediaries

6.1 Significance of Evaluating Intermediaries' Transparency

PPP projects reflect the long-term partnerships between public and private capital, and are subject to long-term quality test. Therefore, interested parties have more and higher requirements for professional consulting services in PPP projects than in traditional projects, and it is a common practice by foreign countries to resort to professional consulting agencies in PPP projects. In order to improve the quality and efficiency of project development and implementation, the Ministry of Finance issued an array of files, indicating that for the purpose of optimizing project design and scheme, professional intermediary technologies and services shall be introduced into PPP projects. For instance, in 2014, the *Operational Guidelines for Public-Private Partnership Model (Trial)* (Cai Jin [2014] No.113) noted to actively employ professional third parties into prominent performance. In 2015, the Ministry of Finance issued the *Circular on Further Effectively Implementing the Demonstration of Public-Private Partnership Projects* (Cai Jin [2015] No.57), further putting forward that professional intermediaries of high competence shall be employed for providing technical support to demonstration projects.

In practical terms, PPP projects involve multi-parties and intricacies. During the process of identification, preparation, procurement, implementation, and transferring, PPP projects require various expertise in audit, law and finance. It is unlikely for government officers to equip with all required techniques and easily have the entire process under control. With core competitiveness and practical experiences in respective fields, intermediaries can help government to design value-for-money evaluation reports and feasibility study reports, thus increasing the leverage held by government during its negotiation with social capital.

However, many companies transformed into PPP intermediaries as relevant consulting services demands upsurge along with PPP projects' boom in China. Consequently, there is an unevenness of capacity among Chinese PPP intermediaries.

Some might even not be qualified for providing necessary professional techniques. Therefore, relevant regulatory departments set a high priority on supervising PPP intermediaries, and hence formulated the *Interim Measures for the Administration of PPP Consulting Agency Database* (Cai Jin [2017] No.8) and the like. Those files stipulated that the information submitted by PPP intermediaries shall be subject to verification and disclosure, and the information inquiry function in the PPP Consulting Agency Database shall be made available to the whole society. By actively accepting the supervision by service receivers and all sectors of society, PPP intermediaries shall improve the quality of PPP consulting services, and build up a standardized and orderly PPP consulting services market.

To examine and promote the information transparency of PPP intermediaries in China and hence to well maintain a favorable market environment for the sustainable development of PPP market, referring to the aforesaid compilation of PPP project information transparency index, the Research Group has compiled transparency indexes for PPP intermediaries, thereby evaluating the information transparency of PPP intermediaries.① However, given the wide disparity between PPP intermediary information transparency and PPP project information transparency in terms of index system and assessment object, the Research Group provided separate index compilation and analysis rather than compiling these two into one single index system.

6.2 Construction of Index System and Calculating Methodology

Prior to the results of PPP intermediary information transparency index, a brief introduction of the index system and calculating methodology of PPP intermediary information transparency evaluation is provided in this section.

6.2.1 Design Principle and Basis for Index System

(1) Design principle for index system. Due to the multiple layers of meaning contained by intermediary information, index system should correspondingly be

① It needs to be stated again that this evaluation is restricted to the disclosure of information by PPP intermediaries, rather than the evaluation of information quality or PPP intermediaries' overall operation compliance, scale and market share.

composed with multiplicity to reflect the nature of each layer. Therefore, referring to the compilation of PPP project information transparency index, the Research Group also divided the compilation of PPP intermediary information transparency index and evaluation into several categories. Specifically, with reference to the spirit of related administration measures and the status of the PPP Consulting Agency Database in the PPP Integrated Information Platform, the index system for PPP intermediary information transparency was divided into three levels, namely, the overall index, a secondary index (including institutions' basic information, the information on the PPP projects undertaken by the institutions, as well as their website information), and underlying specific index.

(2) Data sources and design basis for index system. According to the requirements of the China Public Private Partnerships Center, all information concerning PPP intermediaries must be published on the PPP Consulting Agency Database Information Disclosure System of the PPP Integrated Information Platform set up on the homepage of the CPPPC website. Considering the need for consistency of data sources, the Research Group chose the specific index fields in the Database as the evaluation basis and main source. The fields are divided into two parts — institutions' basic information and the information on the PPP projects undertaken by the institutions. In addition, for further enrichment of the index system, the Research Group logged in to the official websites of the institutions one by one to check the disclosure of information related to PPP, thereby constituting the secondary index — website information.

(3) Assessment object. In conjunction with the policy advices of competent departments and in consideration of practical operability, the Research Group limited the assessment objects to intermediaries that had been included into the PPP Consulting Agency Database Information Disclosure System of the PPP Integrated Information Platform and meanwhile published on the Platform, amounting to 357 institutions.

(4) Data acquisition. The Research Group mainly relied on the data available on the website of CPPPC[①], and logged in to the official website of each intermediary to acquire the source data and then make categorization. Upon the analysis by the Research Group, the index system incorporated a total of 29 index fields. The Research Group has extracted them one by one, by direct reading, copying and pasting from the CPPPC website.

---

① The data in this Chapter were all manually collected by the Research Group.

6.2.2 Index System for Evaluation of PPP Intermediary Information Disclosure

Subject to the aforesaid principles and methods, the hierarchy diagram of PPP intermediary information transparency index system is shown in Figure 6–1. The index system for the evaluation of PPP intermediary information transparency consisted of the overall index, three secondary sub-indexes (basic information, project information, and website information of intermediaries), and the lowest hierarchy — specific indexes.

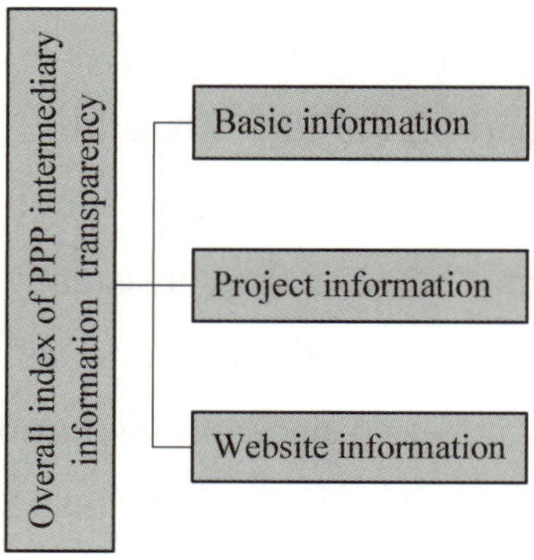

Figure 6–1 Hierarchy Diagram of PPP Intermediary Information Transparency Index

The specific index system for the evaluation of PPP intermediary information disclosure is shown in Table 6–1. The scoring system for these specific indexes was simplified. Most indexes were assigned "1" if the field recorded disclosed information or "0" if there was no information disclosed in the field. While for exceptional indexes containing multiple items of information, an intermediate score of "0.5"was specially designed. Take the index field of "website information" as an example, "1" was given to an institution with its website published on the official website of CPPPC; "0.5" for an institution with a website available for access through search engines like Baidu, but unpublished at CPPPC; otherwise, "0" points. Regarding the news published on the intermediary websites, the following scoring system was applied: "0" points for non-coverage, "0.5" points for coverage but the latest three pieces of news were released more than 30 days from the date of data acquisition, and "1" point for coverage and the latest three pieces of news were released no more than 30 days from the date of data acquisition. Clearer distinction could be achieved by such design.

Table 6–1 PPP Intermediary Information Transparency Assessment Index System

Secondary index	Specific field
Basic information	Name of company
	Organization introduction
	Business scope
	Date of incorporation
	Year established
	Corresponding address
	Postal code
	Official website
	Performance statistics
	Evaluation by principal
	Key executives
	Honors
	Qualifications
	Record of withdrawals
Project information	Name of project
	Project phase
	Region
	Industry
	Investment volume
	Demonstration level
	Performance category of consulting service industry
	Project manager (PM)
	Business experience of PM in PPPs
	Name of principal
	Signature page of consulting service contract
Website information	Executives
	Qualifications
	Business projects
	Latest news

6.2.3 Calculating Methodology for Indicator Synthesis

For multi-index assessment, weights directly affect the results. Considering the comparability with last year's evaluation results, we applied the same index synthesis approach as last year. Specifically, in the process of synthesizing specific indicators into secondary indexes, the coefficient of variation was applied. The basic idea of the method is to weight each field based on its degree of variation in observed values. Specifically, if the coefficient of variation of a field is large, it means that the field has greater explanatory power in measuring the overall difference in assessment object, and such field should be given a bigger weight.

For the specific process of determining index weight by the coefficient of variation method: first, calculate the coefficient of variation of each field, which indicates the absolute degree of variation of each field:

$$CV_i = \frac{S_i}{\bar{x}_i}, i=1, 2, 3, \cdots, n$$

Wherein, S_i is the standard deviation of each field, $\bar{x}_i$ is the mean value of each field. Then, normalize the coefficient of variation of each field to obtain the weight of each field:

$$q_i = \frac{CV_i}{\sum_{i=1}^{n} CV_i}, i=1, 2, 3, \cdots, n$$

Finally, the secondary indexes were synthesized into the general index. At this point, the secondary indexes — intermediary information, project information and website information were given a weight of 1/3 each.

6.3 Analysis on Intermediary Transparency Index

6.3.1 Basic Features

Table 6–2 is the basic descriptive statistics of the PPP intermediary information transparency index, which shows that the average transparency index of 357 intermediaries recorded 75.2, close to the national average score in PPP project transparency (See details in Chapter 3). Specific to the three secondary sub-indexes, Table 6–2 also indicates that the intermediaries did the best job in disclosing the information on the projects they were engaged in, with a score of 90.89 points, followed by the disclosure of their basic information on the PPP Integrated Information Platform, with an average of 76.09 points. Under the index system designed by the Research Group, the information collected from the official websites of the intermediaries scored the lowest in terms of transparency, which was 58.63 points only. By year, the overall transparency index of PPP intermediaries in 2019 was basically the same as in 2018, with little change; by sub-index, in 2019 they did a better job in disclosing basic information, yet less satisfactory in terms of project information and website information. From the prospective of policies, there is not much room for improvement in disclosing project information, but more efforts are required for the information disclosure surrounding intermediary websites.

Table 6–2 Description Statistics of Index

Variable	Year 2018			Year 2019		
	Observed value	Mean value	Standard deviation	Observed value	Mean value	Standard deviation
Overall index	352	75.76	20.56	357	75.20	17.25
Basic information	352	70.42	28.49	357	76.09	22.41
Project information	352	94.57	14.67	357	90.89	20.06
Website information	352	62.30	41.02	357	58.63	39.00

Figure 6–2 shows the histograms of the overall transparency index of PPP intermediaries, as well as their scores in the three secondary indexes. Most PPP intermediaries delivered good performance in disclosing project information and their own basic information; while the disclosure of website information presented polarization, which means that some institutions did well, and some poorly. This result leads to the large standard deviation of website information disclosure as shown in Table 6–2.

Table 6–3 provides the lists of intermediaries ranking among top 10 and last 10 in terms of the PPP Intermediary Transparency Index. Huachun Construction Engineering Project Management Co., Ltd., Anhui Tendering Group Inc. and Tianjin Fangyou Engineering Consulting Co., Ltd. did an excellent job in information disclosure. As

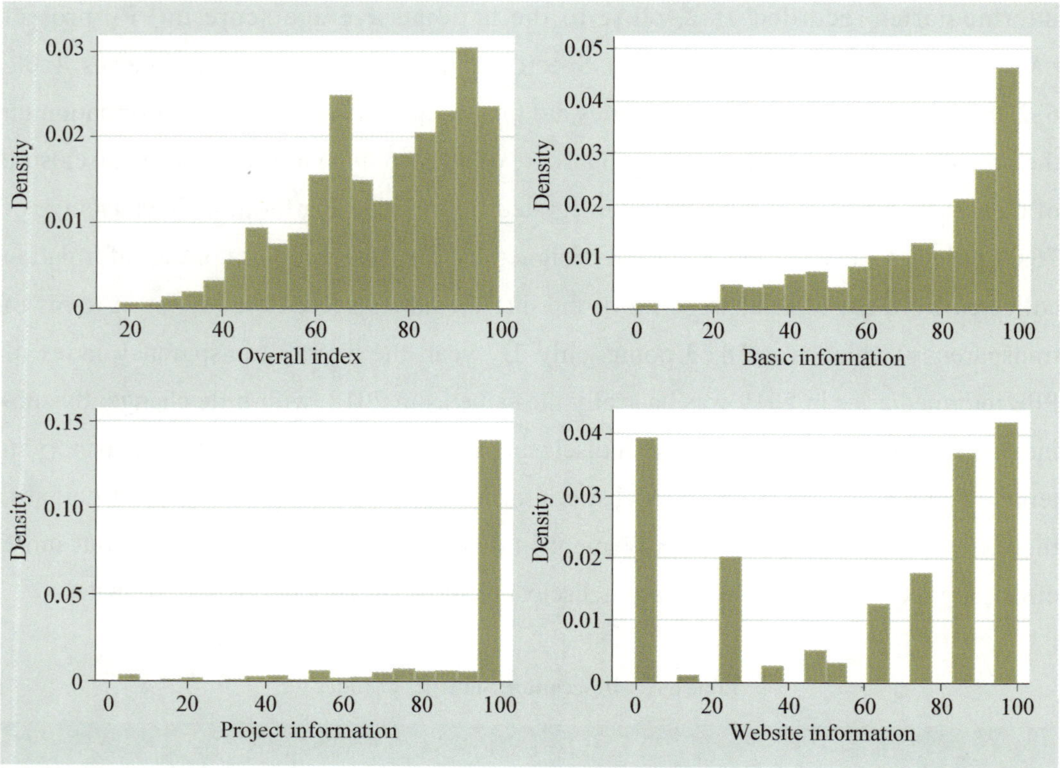

Figure 6–2 Histograms of Overall Index and Sub-Indexes of PPP Intermediary Information Transparency

assessed by the 29 indicators for intermediaries' information disclosure, the three obtained a score close to 100 points. However, the results in Table 6–3 also show that there are some intermediaries that failed to disclose information properly, with an average score of only 18–40 points. Thus it is necessary for regulatory authorities to urge them to put more efforts in information disclosure, especially in terms of website information. Compared with the previous year, the top ten list was not changed much. In other words, most of the top ten intermediaries in the previous year maintained their positions this year. In particular, thanks to its improvement made in website information disclosure, China Far East International Tendering Co., Ltd. emerged as a newcomer to the top 10 list, ranking at No.5; so did Shanghai Jumbo Consulting Co., Ltd., which climbed by 13 places. Bigger changes were seen on the last ten list, yet most of the subsidiaries were still those given low ranks last year. Shandong Delin Enterprise Management Consulting Co., Ltd. and CHC Think Tank (Beijing) Consulting Co., Ltd. were not included as evaluation samples last year, so the variance in ranking does not apply to the two.

Table 6–3 Top 10 and Last 10 PPP Intermediaries in the Ranking of Information Transparency Index

Ranking	Name of intermediary	Overall index	Variance from last year
1	Huachun Construction Engineering Project Management Co., Ltd.	99.48	+2
2	Anhui Tendering Group Inc.	99.48	0
3	Tianjin Fangyou Engineering Consulting Co., Ltd.	99.48	+1
4	Jonten Certified Public Accountants (Limited Liability Partnership)	99.35	+6
5	China Far East International Tendering Co., Ltd.	99.35	+51
6	China CNTC International Tendering Corporation	99.03	−1
7	CAMCE WHU Design & Research Co., Ltd.	98.90	−1
8	Beijing Zhongjiao Construction Engineering Consulting Co., Ltd.	98.77	−1
9	Shanghai Jumbo Consulting Co., Ltd.	98.06	+13
10	China Virtue (Beijing) International Engineering Technology Co., Ltd.	97.93	+3
……			
348	Xinjiang Lianxin Fanglue Enterprise Management Consulting Co., Ltd.	39.72	−16
349	Shandong Delin Enterprise Management Consulting Co., Ltd.	37.90	0
350	Wuhan Kaiyuan Real Estate Information Development Co., Ltd.	36.72	−11
351	Tianjin Yitian Engineering Cost Consulting Co., Ltd.	34.84	−40
352	Beijing Caike Zhihe Management Consulting Co., Ltd.	33.12	−13
353	Guizhou Zhongjian Zhengyan Investment Management Co., Ltd.	32.12	−7
354	Heze Jiangtian Assets Evaluation Firm	31.62	−6
355	Beijing Guanghuan Shidai International Consulting Co., Ltd.	29.96	−15
356	CHC Think Tank (Beijing) Consulting Co., Ltd.	24.32	0
357	Xinjiang Chengtai Construction Engineering Management Consulting Co., Ltd.	18.13	−40

6.3.2 Relevance between PPP Intermediary Information Disclosure and Project Volume

Figure 6–3 shows the relationship between the PPP Intermediary Transparency Index and the number of PPP projects engaged. The conclusion is highly aligned with that last year: the more PPP projects an intermediary is involved in, the higher its score is. In terms of both theory and practice, the number of PPP projects and the information disclosure by intermediaries are in a relationship of mutual promotion. The larger number of projects an institution is engaged in means the institution is larger in scale and more standardized in management, leading to higher attention to information disclosure, and then higher score in information transparency; in turn, the better an intermediary does in information disclosure, the more attractive it is to customers, so that it is able to participate in more PPP projects. As a result, a significant positive correlation is developed between the PPP intermediary transparency score and the number of PPP projects participated by intermediaries.

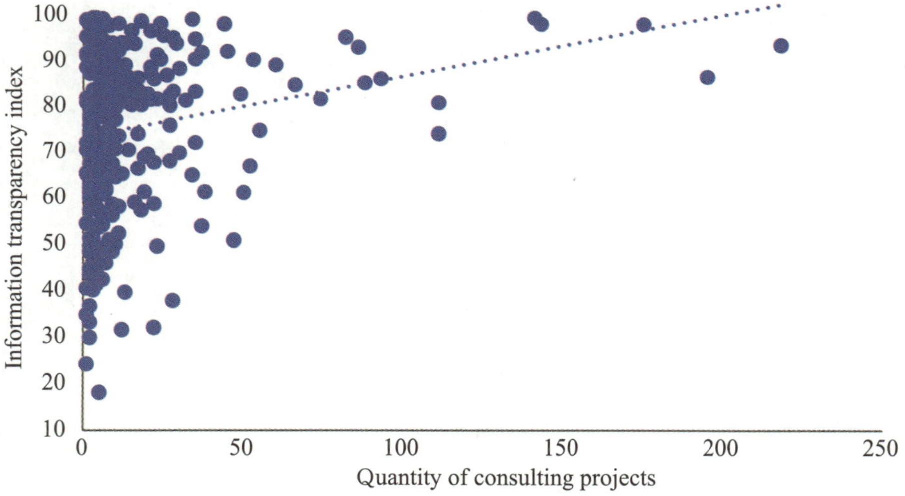

Figure 6–3 Diagram of Relationship between PPP Intermediary Information Transparency Index and Quantity of Consulting Projects

6.3.3 Relevance between PPP Intermediary Information Disclosure and Company Qualifications

The relevance between the information transparency index and qualifications of intermediaries is studied in this section. According to Figure 6–4, the longer an intermediary operates, the better it does in information disclosure. That is, there is a prominent positive correlation between the "age" of intermediaries and the information transparency index. This is also quite similar to what was discovered in the previous year. But it is a general statistical finding only, which does not mean that all newly established PPP intermediaries delivered unsatisfactory performance in information disclosure. Instead, as shown by Figure 6–4, some new intermediaries obtained a transparency score of up to 80 or even more than 90.

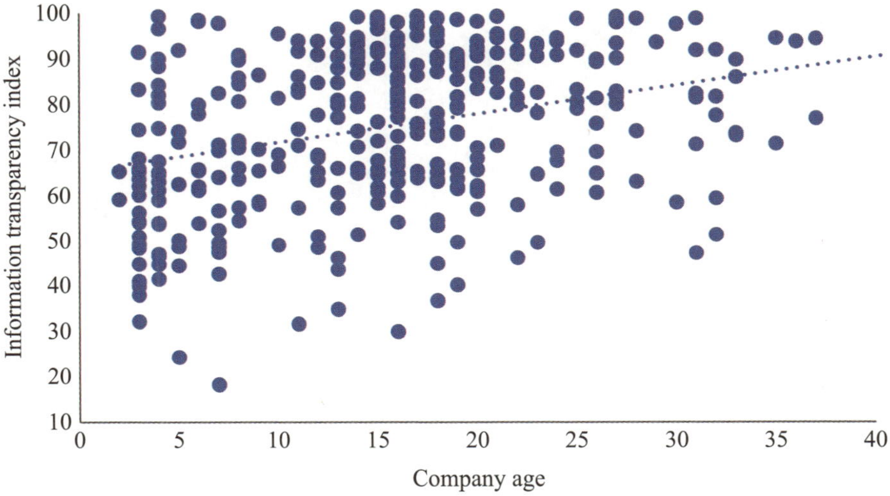

Figure 6–4 Scatter Diagram of Relationship between PPP Intermediary Information Transparency Index and Company Age

7

Report Summary and Outlook

7.1 Report Summary

PPPs is the acronym for Public-Private Partnerships. At present, China's PPP model is not only a means of market-oriented investment and financing by government, but also has become a comprehensive and systematic market and social reform for the provision of public infrastructure and services. Therefore, all stakeholders (both internal and external) have high expectations for the further development and implementation of PPP, hoping it could play a key role in leading the reform of public finance system and assisting the public sector in deepening reform. In this context, standardized arrangements for the management of PPP projects are particularly important. In particular, the timely and complete information disclosure of PPP projects is the basis for standardized management of PPP projects. From 2017, a number of documents issued by the Ministry of Finance have made provisions concerning the information disclosure of PPP projects. In particular, the *Interim Measures for Administration of Information Disclosure for Public-Private Partnership Integrated Information Platform* (Cai Jin [2017] No. 1) released in early 2017 specified all the requirements for information disclosure of PPP projects. When it came to 2018, the removal of PPP projects from management database became a key mission in PPP management. In specific, more than 2 000 PPP projects that failed to meet the management specifications were cleaned and removed from management database, while many new projects were added to the database as well. From the beginning of 2019, as more PPP projects come to the implementation stage, how to effectively promote the disclosure in due time of PPP projects becomes increasingly important. Meanwhile, the public has higher and higher requirements for the quality of PPP project information disclosed. On March 31, 2020, the Ministry of Finance released the Guideline for PPP Project Performance Management, proposing a complete appraisal system for PPP performance. While clarifying who to take accountability, the document has also incorporated truthfulness, openness, transparency and quality into specific assessment rules.

In this context, the Research Group of PPP Research Center at Shanghai University of Finance and Economics, following the evaluation of the information disclosure of PPP projects in the past two years, carried out a detailed assessment on the latest status as of December 31, 2019. The Research Group assessed in detail the information disclosure work of 9 398 projects included into the management database as of the end of 2019, and compiled a set of "2019 China PPP Market Transparency Index", which incorporates 75 index fields and is divided into transparency index of immediate disclosure, transparency index of disclosure in due time, and transparency sub-indexes at each stage, i.e. identification, preparation, procurement, and implementation. Regarding the synthesis of indexes, the Research Group adopted an approach combining analytic hierarchy process (AHP) and expert scoring: for specific indexes under sub-indexes, different scores were set according to the importance determined by selected experts; and for the synthesis of sub-indexes, the Research Group adopted AHP, a method commonly used in the compilation of similar indexes, thus guaranteeing the reliability of the index preparation method. In the end, through the statistical analysis of final results, the Research Group obtained the following findings:

First, the overall national PPP market transparency index 2019 was 76.19, a slight improvement from 2018. As of December 31, 2019, the overall national PPP market transparency index recorded 76.19 (out of 100, the same below), an increase of about 1 point from 75.25 in 2018. In specific, the transparency index of immediate disclosure was 79.14, an increase of 1.5 points from last year (77.61), while the transparency index of disclosure in due time was 71.57, almost the same as last year (71.55). Further analysis on heterogeneity shows no obvious difference in the transparency scores between industries or between demonstration and non-demonstration projects; while time of project initiation had significant impacts on the score, as the later a project is initiated, the more transparent it is regarded.

Second, change in the evaluation object was an important cause for the cross-phase differences in the PPP market transparency indexes in 2019 from 2018. First, the substantial increase in the proportion of projects entering the implementation phase led to a decrease in the transparency in 2019. Second, by decomposing the effects generated by withdrawal, inventory and new increase, we found that projects with low transparency scores that were withdrawn or remained in the database improved their information disclosure work. On the other hand, newly increased projects scored slightly higher than inventory projects. These factors jointly contributed to a higher PPP market transparency score in 2019.

Third, larger differences between provinces were presented in the PPP market transparency index. The transparency indexes of most provinces were between 70–80 — they formed up the second group. The top five provinces, all scoring more than 80 points, constituted the first group. The last six provincial-level regions all recorded a PPP market transparency score of less than 70 points, belonging to the third group. In specific, the top five in transparency ranking were Gansu (81.97), Hebei (81.29), Jilin (80.52), Shandong (80.2) and Yunnan (80.17). By comparing with last year's ranking, we found that the provinces that made the greatest progress in PPP project information disclosure were Jiangsu (77.69) and Guangdong (77.20). Both of them rose by 17 places from the previous year to No.9 and No.12, respectively.

Fourth, more than half of the cities scored higher than 2018, and the rest showed decline. The Research Group selected 46 cities that managed a relatively large number of PPP projects (>50 projects in the management database) for more detailed analysis. Comparison with the indexes in 2018 shows that some cities above the prefecture level scored significantly higher in 2019 than in 2018. Among them, the largest increase was delivered by Aksu of Xinjiang, the 2019 overall score of which increased by 15.39 points compared to 2018; and followed by Dongguan of Guangdong, with increase of 13.62 points from 2018. However, it can also be found that the indexes of many cities above the prefecture level decreased in 2019 from 2018, especially Qiannan of Guizhou and Haikou of Hainan. They recorded the largest decline from 2018 by 13.10 and 12 points, respectively. The five cities of the highest PPP market transparency index in 2019 were: Aksu of Xinjiang (82.81), Dongguan of Guangdong (82.48), Rizhao of Shandong (82.06), Weifang of Shandong (81.79), and Jining of Shandong (81.62).

Fifth, PPP intermediaries showed minor cross-phase differences in information disclosure, with their transparency indexes positively related to qualifications and business volumes. We made an analysis on the status quo of information disclosure by PPP intermediaries. The main findings are as follows: the average transparency index of intermediaries was 75.20. In secondary indexes, projects engaged by intermediaries scored relatively high in terms of information disclosure, but some of them delivered less satisfactory performance in active information disclosure, with a further decrease in willingness from last year. Further analysis also found that intermediaries' transparency indexes showed a clear positive correlation with the number of PPP projects they were engaged in and how long they had been operating.

7.2 Policy Suggestions

To conclude the above analysis, in 2019 China has made steady progress regarding the information disclosure in PPP market compared with the previous year. The results observed in this Report suggest the progress in PPP information disclosure is leading reform in infrastructure and services. Notwithstanding these achievements, the Research Group also identified issues related to the disclosure of PPP market information. Therefore, the following are offered as policy improvement opportunities and enhancements, with a view to further improving the PPP information disclosure work, further raising the information disclosure transparency in the PPP market, and promoting the standardized management of PPP projects in China.

First, to increase the assessment on disclosure timeliness. According to the operation and management rules of PPP projects, the Ministry of Finance has classified the information disclosure work of PPP projects into "immediate disclosure" and "disclosure in due time". In the analysis of PPP projects in this Report, and the calculation of the PPP market transparency index, projects were divided into these two categories of immediate disclosure and disclosure in due time. The results of the review by the Research Group indicate some areas would benefit from improvement. Specifically, in relation to disclosure in due time, in addition to assessing whether or not the information has been disclosed, it is also advisable to record and evaluate the specific time of disclosure. For example, some information is required to be disclosed within 6 months after entering the implementation stage. Since there was no time of information disclosure recorded, all projects were examined that entered the implementation stage by the end of June 2019 and reviewed as to whether corresponding information was disclosed by the end of 2019. It was not possible to determine if the timeliness was compliant. For a further example, some projects entered the implementation stage in early 2019, but they did not disclose information until the end of 2019, failing to meet the requirement of "disclose within six months after entering the implementation stage". However, since it was impossible to identify specific time points, the researchers were unable to make precise make assessments regarding timeliness. For another example, some information is required to be disclosed before April 30 of the year following the end of corresponding activities, which involves the time when corresponding activities ended and the time when the information was disclosed. In practice, it may be feasible to add the data that records information disclosure time to the backstage of the PPP Integrated Information Platform. On the webpage, a graphic of a light may be designed as a prompt for the failure to timely disclose relevant information. For example, for a field with information disclosure overdue for over 30 days, a yellow light is displayed; for a field with information disclosure overdue for over 60 days, a red light shows.

Second, to improve the operational norms for the disclosure of "inapplicable" information and temporary major events. PPP projects cover a wide range of sectors and fields, which have varied cooperation methods, return mechanisms, etc. It is difficult to ascertain in analyzing results if information is required to be disclosed but not lodged, or if it is not applicable. Accordingly, this limits the extent of research scope when analyzing PPP information disclosure performance. A possible remedy may be to require the project to insert a notation to the effect of "the information item does not apply to this project". From this, it is possible to discern whether the information item is inapplicable, or if the project has failed to disclose the information. In addition, there should be similar requirements for the management of disclosure on major temporary events. For instance, for the disclosure of information on temporary major events such as "material breach and withdrawal of performance bond, handling of public complaints, etc.", projects should be requested to state that "as of now, the project has no material breach and withdrawal of performance bond, handling of public complaints and other issues to be disclosed" or similar expressions, if there are no corresponding events. This practice is common in the information disclosure management standards of listed companies, commercial banks and other institutions.

Third, to improve the classification of management of information subject to immediate disclosure and disclosure in due time. As mentioned above, classification is an important measure. However, through investigation by the Research Group and discussion with experts, it was determined the classification criteria require further improvement. For example, some information subject to disclosure in due time may be transferred to immediate disclosure; and some immediate disclosure work which is time-consuming, may be transferred to disclosure in due time category. Input through the professional opinions of the representatives from project companies, consulting agencies and the academic community will support improvement in the classification of management information.

Fourth, to enhance the supervision over the information disclosure by PPP projects at implementation stage and above. The above analysis demonstrates that the PPP projects at the stage of implementation tended to perform less desirably in information disclosure than those at identification and preparation stages. The reason is that the projects in the implementation stage lack the pressure to make disclosure, since they've already been included into the database. Therefore, in order to motivate these projects, more effective regulatory approaches are required. A possible approach is to incorporate the information disclosure by PPP projects in the implementation stage into performance management, and link it with the financial subsidies, tax incentives, etc. of the following stage, so as to urge relevant departments and project executors to pay more attention.

Fifth, to strengthen the supervision and inspection of the disclosure of key information in PPP projects. Based on the above analysis, the Research Group identified there were substantial differences in the implementation of information disclosure at different stages. For example, for disclosure in due time, the assessment results of value-for-money evaluation report and financial affordability assessment report at identification stage was less desirable compared with others. Accordingly, it is a recommendation of the Research Group that the supervision and inspection over disclosure outcomes should be strengthened. Random inspection may be utilized to supervise the disclosure of these project reports. In addition, concerning the information to be disclosed at implementation stage, it may be necessary to improve the system and regulations, urging responsible parties to disclose relevant information in a proactive and timely manner. For example, it is feasible to link the information disclosure work of the project company at the implementation stage with government payment by means of contractual covenants, etc. Finally, automatically screening the documents by keyword identification may be helpful in the prevention of false uploads. The screening could require attachments without certain keywords were not approved for upload, thereby improving the quality of information disclosure.

Sixth, to further clarify the disclosure accountability and division of labor.

Since the *Interim Measures for Administration of Information Disclos*ure for Public-Private Partnership Integrated Information Platform took effect on March 1, 2017, there has been significant progress in PPP information disclosure, as also verified by the assessment results we obtained over the past three years. However, there are still some challenges to be resolved in the disclosure of PPP information. Any lack of accountability is likely to bring a series of systemic problems to PPP information disclosure. According to the Article 4 of Cai Jin [2017] No. 1, "Local finance departments at all levels will, in conjunction with the related departments of the government at the same level, promote, guide, coordinate and supervise the PPP project information disclosure work within their respective administrative region and carry out the following work in combination with local conditions". In the actual implementation, finance departments need to coordinate water conservancy bureaus, transportation bureaus, sports bureaus, social capital and third-party consulting agencies to collect and consolidate information. As the information disclosure work has limited binding power to the related departments of the government at the same level other than the finance department, it is difficult for local financial systems to update the data in a timely manner. Such circumstance may be mitigated in regions without abundant financial resources, for if the progress of information disclosure does not match with that of project construction, the government can choose to delay payment to punish relevant departments. However, the restraint can hardly be realized in regions with poor financial resources, which make the conditions worse in those places where it is already difficult to attract high-quality social capital based on their local conditions. Therefore, it is necessary to further clarify the accountability and to build supporting incentive mechanisms.

Seventh, to promote the information disclosure by PPP intermediaries. PPP projects reflect long-term partnerships, and are subject to long-term quality test. There are higher requirements for solutions and agreements in PPP projects than in traditional projects, and it is a common practice by foreign countries to resort to professional consulting agencies in PPP projects. Therefore, PPP intermediaries play an important role in the compliant operation and management of PPP projects. The discussion in Chapter 6 shows that there is still much room for the improvement of the information disclosure by PPP intermediaries. Roughly, there are two aspects. On the one hand, it is necessary for PPP intermediaries to disclose their own information. More fields may be added to the PPP Consulting Agency Database for them to fill in, such as the number of employees, personnel structure, leading teams, etc. On the other hand, during the operation of PPP projects, it is necessary to strengthen the disclosure of such information as intermediaries' participation, dedication, types of projects they were involved before, and the classification of intermediaries. The following information may be disclosed as well: the proportion of projects that have been engaged by an intermediary and removed from the Management Database; whether it is serving a local government and a social capital owner that has cooperation with the government at the same time (to avoid conflicts related to business ethics). Such requirements pose pressure on PPP intermediaries, so that they can be more cautious in their participation in PPP projects.

7.3 Outlook

That's all for the 2019 China PPP Market Transparency Report. Based on the index compilation and analysis in 2017 and 2018, and by means of index preparation, substantial data and analysis on the information disclosure of PPP projects in China as of the end of 2019 are provided. The Report has not only maintained the continuity of the index system and index compilation methods, but also produced some new findings. While there have been several continuous refinements to assess the information transparency of the China PPP market, there are still many deficiencies in terms of index system setting, index preparation methods, and specific analysis. The Research Group recommends that future changes should consider:

First, the index system can be improved. As stated in the Report, due to the absence of information and many other reasons, the PPP market transparency index was intentionally divided into immediate disclosure index and disclosure in due time index. As the PPP integrated information platform grows mature, and especially when the time of disclosure can be accurately incorporated into the database, it is expected to combine the two in the future. Moreover, in addition to assessing whether related information is disclosed, it is also possible to further assess disclosure timeliness. With the advancing of the PPP, more and more projects will enter implementation and transfer stages, and the information disclosure work at these stages will be of higher significance, then the index system may also appropriately focus on those stages.

Second, information quality may be included in the assessment. As we have mentioned in the preceding part, this Report only assesses the information disclosure work of PPP projects, but not the quality of the information disclosed. For example, the Research Group has assessed whether the value-for-money evaluation report and financial affordability assessment report were disclosed but without assessment of their quality. Therefore, the content of these key project reports should direct special assessment and analysis in the future, examining the standardized management of PPP projects in all regions and of all stakeholders.

Appendix Ⅰ Determination Matrix Survey for Experts

Engaged by the Asian Development Bank, the PPP Research Center of Shanghai University of Finance and Economics is undertaking the *2019 China PPP Market Transparency Assessment Report*, which involves preparing an index to holistically reflect the achievements and deficiencies in the information disclosure efforts within China's PPP market. In the process of index preparation, the amount of information contained in each specific indicator and its degree of importance vary greatly. Therefore, the Research Group intends to determine the relative weight among the influencing factors of information transparency of PPP projects through an expert survey (the hierarchy chart is shown in Figure 3–1).

To this end, the Research Group has designed the survey below based on the Analytic Hierarchy Process (AHP), which makes paired comparison on the importance of influencing factors at the same hierarchy. The measurement scale is divided into 9 levels, of which the values of 9, 7, 5, 3 and 1 correspond to absolutely more important, more important, relatively more important, slightly more important, and equally important, while 8, 6, 4 and 2 indicate that the importance is between two adjacent levels.

In the tables below, the left cells indicate that the factors on the left are more important than those on the right, and the right cells indicate that factors on the right are more important than those on the left. Please tick "√" in the corresponding cell based on your own understanding. Your judgment is critical to our scientific and rigorous preparation of the PPP market transparency index.

Thanks for your help!

Research Group of SUFE

January 8, 2020

In paired comparison, what is the relative importance of the two factors to the "total transparency index"?																		
	Comparison of importance																	
Disclosure in due time	9	8	7	6	5	4	3	2	1	2	3	4	5	6	7	8	9	Immediate disclosure

In paired comparison, what is the relative importance of the two factors to the "disclosure in due time"?																		
	Comparison of importance																	
Identification stage	9	8	7	6	5	4	3	2	1	2	3	4	5	6	7	8	9	Preparation stage
Identification stage	9	8	7	6	5	4	3	2	1	2	3	4	5	6	7	8	9	Procurement stage
Preparation stage	9	8	7	6	5	4	3	2	1	2	3	4	5	6	7	8	9	Procurement stage

In paired comparison, what is the relative importance of the two factors to the "immediate disclosure"?																		
	Comparison of importance																	
Identification stage	9	8	7	6	5	4	3	2	1	2	3	4	5	6	7	8	9	Preparation stage
Identification stage	9	8	7	6	5	4	3	2	1	2	3	4	5	6	7	8	9	Procurement stage
Identification stage	9	8	7	6	5	4	3	2	1	2	3	4	5	6	7	8	9	Implementation stage
Preparation stage	9	8	7	6	5	4	3	2	1	2	3	4	5	6	7	8	9	Procurement stage
Preparation stage	9	8	7	6	5	4	3	2	1	2	3	4	5	6	7	8	9	Implementation stage
Procurement stage	9	8	7	6	5	4	3	2	1	2	3	4	5	6	7	8	9	Implementation stage

Appendix Ⅱ Interim Measures for the Administration of Information Disclosure for Public-Private Partnership Integrated Information Platform

Circular on Issuing the *Interim Measures for Administration of Information Disclosure for Public-Private Partnership Integrated Information Platform*

(Cai Jin [2017] No. 1)

The financial offices (bureaus) of all provinces, autonomous regions, municipalities directly under the Central Government and cities specifically designated in the state plan, the Financial Bureau of Xinjiang Production and Construction Corps, and the Financial Supervision Commissioner Offices of the Ministry of Finance at all provinces, autonomous regions, municipalities directly under the Central Government and cities specifically designated in the state plan,

In order to further carry out the related requirements of the *Circular of the General Office of the State Council on Forwarding the Guiding Opinions of the Ministry of Finance, the National Development and Reform Commission and the People's Bank of China on Promoting the Public-Private Partnership Model in the Public Service Sectors* (Guo Ban Fa [2015] No.42), strengthen and standardize the information disclosure of Public-Private Partnership ("PPP") projects, cause various parties to the PPP projects to act in good faith and strictly honor their agreements, protect the public's right to know and promote fair competition and regulated development of the PPP market, we hereby formulate the *Interim Measures for the Administration of Information Disclosure for*

*Public-Private Partnership Integrated Information Platfor*m, which are issued to you for your implementation.

Ministry of Finance
January 23, 2017

Interim Measures for the Administration of Information Disclosure for Public-Private Partnership Integrated Information Platform

Chapter I General Provisions

Article 1 In order to strengthen and standardize the information disclosure of Public-Private Partnership ("PPP") projects, cause various parties to the PPP projects to act in good faith and strictly honor their agreements, protect the public's right to know and promote fair competition and regulated development of the PPP market, the *Interim Measures for the Administration of Information Disclosure for Public-Private Partnership Integrated Information Platform* (the "Measures") are hereby formulated in accordance with the Budget Law of the People's Republic of China, the Government Procurement Law of the People's Republic of China, the Circular of the General Office of State Council on Forwarding the Guidelines of the Ministry of Finance, the National Development and Reform Commission and the People's Bank of China on Promoting the Public-Private Partnership Model in the Public Service Sectors (Guo Ban Fa [2015] No.42) and other related provisions.

Article 2 The Measures apply to the disclosure of information about the PPP projects within the territory of the People's Republic of China that have been included in the PPP integrated information platform.

Article 3 PPP project information disclosure shall be conducted in the principles of objectiveness, fairness, timeliness and convenience.

Article 4 Local finance departments at all levels (hereinafter referred to as the "finance departments") will, in conjunction with the related departments of the government at the same level, promote, guide, coordinate and supervise the PPP project information disclosure work within their respective administrative region and carry out the following work in combination with local realities:

1. collect and sort out the PPP project information;

2. enter into, maintain and update the PPP project information via the PPP integrated

information platform;

3. organize to prepare the annual work report of their government-level PPP project information disclosure;

4. make available the PPP project information in other channels at the same time in accordance with laws and regulations and actual needs; and

5. other efforts related to the PPP project information disclosure.

Relevant government departments, project implementing organizations, corporate partners or PPP project company and other PPP project participants shall provide the PPP project information in a truly, complete, accurate and timely manner.

Chapter Ⅱ Contents Subject to Disclosure

Article 5 The PPP project information to be disclosed during the project identification phase includes:

1. summary of the implementation program, including: basic information of the project (including the project cooperation scope, cooperation period, project output specification, performance standards and other basic information), risk allocation framework, operation mode, transaction structure (including financing structure, return mechanism and relevant supporting arrangements), contracts, regulatory framework, selection of the purchase mode;

2. the value-for-money evaluation report that has been examined and approved by the finance departments and the competent industry authority, including: qualitative evaluation indicators and weights, scoring standards, scoring results; main indicators, methods, processes and results (including PSC value, PPP value), etc. (if any) for the purpose of quantitative evaluation; conclusions on whether value-for-money evaluation is passed or not;

3. the financial affordability assessment report that has been examined and approved by the finance departments, including: liabilities of fiscal expenditure of each year and total expenditure liabilities, total liabilities of fiscal expenditure of the PPP projects implemented by the government at the same level in current year and that of the PPP projects to be implemented for various years, and ratios of them in the general public budget expenditures of various years; measurement basis, key factors and indicators of the financial affordability assessment as well as others; and conclusions on whether the financial affordability assessment is passed or not;

4. Other basic information, including: proposals for new or renovated or expanded projects and approval documents, feasibility study report (including planning permits, siting opinions, land pre-review opinion, environmental impact assessment report and other supporting documents) and approval documents, design documents and approval documents (if any); historical materials of construction and operation maintenance of stocked public assets as well as the asset evaluation report issued by a third party and the employees placement scheme, claim and debt disposal programs, land disposal programs and others (if any) that may be involved in the transfer of stocked assets or equity.

Article 6 The PPP project information to be disclosed during the project preparatory phase includes:

1. the authorization documents of the government, including the authorization granted to the executive agency, the governments signing the PPP project contract, the government's investment representatives (if any) and others;

2. the examined and approved project implementation program (including the approval documents of the people's government at the same level with respect to the implementation programs), including: basic information of the project (including the project cooperation scope, cooperation period, project output specification, performance standards and other basic information), risk allocation framework, operation mode, transaction structure (including financing structure, return mechanism and relevant supporting arrangements), contracts and core boundary conditions; regulatory framework; selection of the purchase mode;

3. the value-for-money evaluation report that has been verified based on the examined and approved project implementation program, if any; and

4. the financial affordability assessment report that has been verified based on the examined and approved project implementation program, if any.

Article 7 The disclosure of information in the procurement process shall comply with the provisions on government procurement and other provisions, and the PPP project information to be disclosed shall include:

1. prequalification announcements (including prequalification application documents) and supplementary announcement (if any);

2. project procurement documents, including notes to competitors, PPP project contract (draft), review methods (including composition of the review group, the number of review experts and the producing way thereof, the review rules, etc.);

3. addenda (if any);

4. concluding observations with respect to the review of prequalification and response documents;

5. the list of prequalification experts, review experts and the working group of negotiation about confirmation;

6. announcement of pre-bid winners and transaction results;

7. the announcement of the bid-winning and transaction results and the letter of acceptance;

8. the authorization documents of the government updated and adjusted during the procurement process (if any), including the authorization granted to the executive agency, the governments signing the PPP project contract, the government's investment representatives (if any) and others; and

9.the document of the people's government at the same level on consent to sign the PPP project contracts, and the signed PPP project contract, listing main output specifications and performance indicators, the return mechanism, the price adjustment mechanism and other core provisions.

Article 8 The PPP project information to be disclosed during the project implementation phase includes:

1. registration of the project company (if any), capital subscribed by the shareholders and availability of the capital, increase or decrease of the capital (if any), qualifications of the project company (if any);

2. name of the financing institution, amount of funds raised for the project, the financing structure and particulars on the financing delivery;

3. review of the project construction permits, construction progress, quality and cost and others made based on the related agreements under the PPP project contracts;

4. the operation of corporate partners or the project company (especially major business or financial risks that may seriously affect the normal operation of the corporate partners or the project company) and satisfaction of the operational performance;

5. the project company's performance monitoring report, interim evaluation report, major changes or termination of the project, project pricing and previous price adjustments;

6. the financial report of the project company, including payment for the project, the government subsidy granted to the project, and the assets and liabilities of the project

company and others;

7. cost monitoring and review of the project company, alteration of PPP project contracts or signing of supplementary agreements;

8. major breach of contract and withdrawal of performance bond, handling of public complaints, etc.;

9. provisions or decisions made by the government at the corresponding level or its functional departments that may have a significant impact on the project;

10. major disputes, litigations or arbitrations with respect to the project or of the parties directly related to the project (mainly the contracting parties to the PPP project contracts), except those forbidden according to the relevant judicial proceedings; and

11. the directory of the PPP projects at the same level, pilot library thereof and changes to the projects as well as the budget, implementation and settlement situations of governments for the PPP projects as approved by the people's congresses at the same level.

Article 9 The PPP project information to be disclosed during the project transfer phase includes:

1. composition of the transfer working group, transfer procedure, transfer standards and other transfer programs;

2. list of the assets or equity or interests to be transferred, assessment report on the assets or equity to be transferred (if applicable), scheme on performance test, and the release of various security or interests on the assets or facilities to be transferred;

3. detection results on satisfaction of the transfer standards for project facilities; and

4. post evaluation reports (including evaluation for the project output, cost effectiveness, regulatory effectiveness, sustainability, PPP model applications, etc.), as well as the subsequent operation manner.

Chapter Ⅲ Manner of Information Disclosure

Article 10 PPP project information can be disclosed immediately or in due time.

Article 11 To make disclosure immediately refers to the automatic disclosure of the related information as stipulated by the Measures via the PPP integrated information platform made by the finance departments, in concert with the related departments, the project implementing organizations and others according to the different stages of the PPP projects and the corresponding entry time. The contents and requirements of the instant disclosure are detailed in the appendix to the Measures.

Article 12 To make disclosure in due time refers to the disclosure of the relevant information as stipulated in the Measures by the finance departments, in concert with the related departments when the project enters into a specific stage or reaches a specific condition rather than automatic disclosure upon the entry of the relevant information. Except as otherwise provided in the Measures, the information during the project identification, preparation and procurement processes will be disclosed by the finance departments in conjunction with the relevant departments at any time within six months after the entry into the implementation phase of the project; The information during the implementation phase will be made available to the public by the finance departments in conjunction with the relevant departments at any time before April 30 of the year following the determining or completion of matters corresponding to the information. The information not made available to the public after the expiration of the foregoing period of time will be opened to the public automatically. The contents and requirements of making disclosure in due time are detailed in the appendix to the Measures.

Article 13 The PPP project information made available to the public according to the Measures may be inquired on the official website of China Public Private Partnerships Center (www.cpppc.org). Information on government procurement of PPP projects shall be published at the media designated by the finance department of a people's government above provincial level.

Chapter Ⅳ Supervision and Administration

Article 14 The Ministry of Finance will evaluate and supervise the disclosure of the PPP project information all over the country, and the provincial finance department is responsible for the supervision and management of the PPP project information to be disclosed in the said province. Where the finance departments at lower level do not enter into the PPP project information that shall be made available to the public on a truly, complete, accurate and timely basis, the finance departments at higher level shall order them to make corrections within a time limit; if they refuse to make corrections or the circumstances are serious, they will be criticized.

Article 15 The relevant government departments, project implementation agencies, corporate partners or PPP project company and other PPP project information providers shall be responsible for the authenticity, completeness, accuracy and timeliness of the information provided. Once the information provided is untrue, incomplete, inaccurate and not provided timely, the PPP project information provider shall take the initiative to amend, supplement or take other effective remedial measures in a timely manner. If the provider of the PPP project information is confirmed with related materials produced by the finance departments or stakeholders not providing information in accordance with the provisions or falls under other improper circumstances, the finance departments may order it to correct within a time limit; if it refuses to correct without justifiable reasons, the finance departments can weed out the project from the project library. The project being weeded out may not be included into the PPP integrated information platform within one year since the date on which it is weeded out.

Article 16 The finance department shall, in conjunction with the relevant government departments, complete the annual report on the disclosure of information about the PPP projects implemented by the government at the same level for the previous year before February 28 each year, submit it to the finance department at the provincial level, which will report the information to the Ministry of Finance before March 31 each year after making summarization. The report shall include:

1. circumstances on disclosure of the PPP project information on an instant basis and made in due time;

2. major issues occurred during the disclosure of the PPP project information and improvements thereof; and

3. other matters that need to be reported.

Article 17 The personnel of the finance departments will be subject to corresponding liabilities according to the *Civil Servant Law, the Law on Administrative Supervision, the Regulations on the Penalties and Sanctions against Illegal Financial Conducts* and other related provisions of the State if they abuse their power, neglect of duty, play favoritism and commit irregularities and have any other violations during the supervision and management of the PPP project information disclosure; if they are suspected of constituting a crime, they will be transferred to judicial organs.

Article 18 Citizens, legal persons or other organizations may provide feedbacks to the PPP project information disclosure situation through the PPP integrated information platform, and the relevant information provider shall verify the same and handle it in a timely manner.

Chapter Ⅴ Supplementary Provisions

Article 19 The PPP integrated information platform consisting of three parts, i.e. project library, institution library and document library, refers to the PPP integrated information management and release platform for the whole country established by the Ministry of Finance according to the *Circular on Regulating the Operation of the Public-Private Partnership (PPP) Integrated Information Platform* (Cai Jin [2015] No.166).

Article 20 In the event that the PPP project information disclosure involves state secrets, trade secrets, personal privacy, intellectual property rights, which may endanger national security, public safety, economic security and social stability or harm legitimate rights and interests of the citizens, legal persons or other organizations, it will be handled in accordance with relevant laws and regulations.

Article 21 The Measures will come into force as of March 1, 2017.

Requirements for Information Disclosure of PPP Projects

Stage	Contents to be disclosed	Manner of disclosure	Time limit	Information provider
Identification of projects	Introduction to the project, the cooperation scope, the cooperation term, the operation mode, selection of the mode of purchasing social capital	Immediate disclosure	Within ten working days from the date of completion of the implementation programs	Project initiator
	Transaction structure (including financing structure, return mechanism and relevant supporting arrangements), project output specification and performance standards, risk allocation framework, contracts and regulatory system	Disclosure in due time	Within six months after entering into the implementation phase	Project initiator
	Value-for-money qualitative evaluation indicators and weights, scoring standards, scoring results	Immediate disclosure	Within ten working days after the report is finalized	
	Conclusions on whether value-for-money evaluation is passed or not (including opinions of the finance departments in concert with industry departments)	Immediate disclosure	Within ten working days after the issue of approval documents with respect to the implementation programs	

(continued)

Stage	Contents to be disclosed	Manner of disclosure	Time limit	Information provider
Identification of projects	Value-for-money evaluation report that has been examined and approved (including the approval documents issued by the finance departments)	Disclosure in due time	Within six months after entering into the implementation phase	
	Financial expenditure liabilities of the project and those of the PPP projects implemented and to be implemented in the year and annual budget arrangements, and the ratio of expenditure for all the PPP projects out of the budget in each year in the expenditure of the general public budget	Immediate disclosure	Within ten working days after the issue of approval documents with respect to the implementation programs	
	Measurement basis, key factors and indicators of the financial affordability assessment	Immediate disclosure	Within ten working days after the report is finalized	
	Conclusions on whether the financial affordability assessment passes or not	Immediate disclosure	Within ten working days after the issue of approval documents with respect to the implementation programs	
	Financial affordability assessment report that has been examined and approved (including the approval documents issued by the finance departments)	Disclosure in due time	Within six months after entering into the implementation phase	
	Proposals for new or renovated or expanded projects and approval documents	Disclosure in due time	Within six months after entering into the implementation phase	Implementing organization
	Feasibility study report (including a full set of supporting documents) and approval documents, design documents and approval documents (if applicable)	Disclosure in due time	Within six months after entering into the implementation phase	Implementing organization

(continued)

Stage	Contents to be disclosed	Manner of disclosure	Time limit	Information provider
Identification of projects	Asset evaluation report with respect to the stocked public assets or equity, and various programs and others (if applicable) that may be involved in the transfer of stocked assets or equity	Disclosure in due time	Within six months after entering into the implementation phase	Implementing organization
Preparation for projects	Authorized documents of the government, including the authorization of the parties to the implementing agency, the contracting parties of the PPP project contract, the government's investment representatives (if applicable), etc.	Immediate disclosure	Within ten working days after authorization	Local government at the same level
	Introduction to the project, the cooperation scope, the cooperation term, the operation mode, selection of the mode of purchasing social capital	Immediate disclosure	Within ten working days after entering into the procurement procedures	Implementing organization
	Transaction structure (including financing structure, return mechanism and relevant supporting arrangements), project output specification and performance standards, risk allocation framework, core boundary conditions, contracts and regulatory system	Disclosure in due time	Within six months after entering into the implementation phase	Implementing organization
	Government's approval documents with respect to the implementation programs	Immediate disclosure	Within ten working days after the issue of approval documents	Implementing organization
	Project implementation program as examined and approved and amendments thereto	Disclosure in due time	Within six months after entering into the implementation phase	Implementing organization
Procurement of projects	Prequalification announcements (including prequalification application documents)	Immediate disclosure	Within ten working days after the issue of the prequalification announcement	Implementing organization

(continued)

Stage	Contents to be disclosed	Manner of disclosure	Time limit	Information provider
Procurement of projects	Project procurement documents, addenda (if any)	Disclosure in due time	Within six months after entering into the implementation phase	Implementing organization
	Concluding observations with respect to the review report of prequalification and response documents, including the list of prequalification experts and review experts	Disclosure in due time	Within six months after entering into the implementation phase	Procurement authority
	List of the working group of negotiation about confirmation	Disclosure in due time	Within six months after entering into the implementation phase	Implementing organization
	Announcement of pre-bid winners and transaction results, the announcement of the bid-winning and transaction results and the letter of acceptance;	Immediate disclosure	As agreed according to the law and the procurement documents	Executive agency, procurement authority
	Signed PPP project contracts	Disclosure in due time	Within six months after entering into the implementation phase	Implementing organization
	Key terms of PPP project contract, listing main output specifications, return mechanism for performance indicators, and the price adjustment mechanism	Immediate disclosure	Within ten working days after the project contract is approved by the people's government	Executive agency and project company
	Government's responsibility confirmation documents for the expenditure of the project or the update or adjustment documents (if applicable) of the people's congress at the same level (or the NPC Standing Committee) including the financial expenditure liability of the project into budgets which span two years	Disclosure in due time	Within six months after entering into the implementation phase	Implementing organization
	Government's authorization documents (if any) for the adjustment and updates during the project procurement process	Immediate disclosure	Appendices to the project contract approved by the people's government within ten working days will be made	Implementing organization

(continued)

Stage	Contents to be disclosed	Manner of disclosure	Time limit	Information provider
Implementation of projects	Registration of the project company, capital subscribed by the shareholders and availability of the capital, increase or decrease of the capital (in applicable)	Immediate disclosure	Upon incorporation and within ten working days after the capital fund is obtained	Project company
	Financing limit, key terms and closing conditions	Disclosure in due time	Before April 30 of the year following the determining or completion of matters corresponding to the information	Project company
	Review of the project construction permits, construction progress, quality and cost and others made based on the PPP project contracts	Immediate disclosure	According to the PPP project contracts; if the PPP project contracts do not make any provisions, prior to April 30 in the next year after the end of corresponding activities	Executive agency and project company
	Annual operation of private capital partners or the project company and satisfaction of the operational performance	Immediate disclosure	According to the PPP project contracts; if the PPP project contracts do not make any provisions, prior to April 30 in the next year after the end of corresponding activities	Project company
	Project company's performance monitoring report, interim assessment report, major changes or termination of the project, project pricing and previous adjustments	Immediate disclosure	According to the PPP project contracts; if the PPP project contracts do not make any provisions, prior to April 30 in the next year after the end of corresponding activities	Implementing organization
	Cost monitoring and review of the project company, alteration agreements on the PPP project contracts or supplementary agreements	Disclosure in due time	Before April 30 of the year following the end of corresponding activities	Implementing organization Project company

(continued)

Stage	Contents to be disclosed	Manner of disclosure	Time limit	Information provider
Implementation of projects	Related contents of the financial report of the project company, including payment for the project, the government subsidy granted to the project, and the assets and liabilities of the project company and others	Disclosure in due time	Before April 30 of the year following the end of corresponding activities	Project company
	Major breach of contract and withdrawal of performance bond, handling of public complaints, etc.	Immediate disclosure	Within ten working days upon occurrence	Implementing organization
	Provisions or decisions made by the government at the corresponding level or its functional departments that may have a significant impact on the project	Immediate disclosure	Within ten working days after the issue of provisions and decisions	Implementing organization
	Major disputes, litigations or arbitrations with respect to the project or the parties directly related to the project	Immediate disclosure	Except as otherwise provided in the Measures, within ten working days upon occurrence	Project company
	Directory of the PPP projects at the same level, pilot library thereof and changes to the projects as well as the budget, implementation and settlement situations of governments for the PPP projects as approved by the people's congresses at the same level	Immediate disclosure	Disclosed or quarterly disclosed as required by the law (if any)	
Transfer of projects	Composition of the transfer working group, transfer procedures, transfer standards, and other transfer programs	Immediate disclosure	Within ten working days after the transfer program is determined	Implementing organization
	List of the assets or facilities or interests to be transferred, assessment report on the assets or equity to be transferred (if applicable), scheme on performance test	Immediate disclosure	Within ten working days after the list or report is finalized or after the end of the test	Implementing organization

(continued)

Stage	Contents to be disclosed	Manner of disclosure	Time limit	Information provider
Transfer of projects	Release of various security or interests on the assets or facilities to be transferred (if applicable)	Immediate disclosure	Within ten working days after the corresponding release	Executive agency and project company
	Detection results on the satisfaction of the transfer standards for project facilities	Immediate disclosure	Within ten working days after the issue of detection results	Implementing organization
	Post assessment report and the subsequent operation mode of the project	Immediate disclosure	Within ten working days after the post evaluation report is finalized or the subsequent operation manner of the project is determined	Implementing organization

Appendix Ⅲ List of PPP Information Disclosure and Regulatory Management Systems

No.	Issued on	Document No.	Document	Issued by
1	2013.12.19	No. 74 Decree of Ministry of Finance	Measures for the Administration of Government Procurement in No-bid Procurement Model	Ministry of Finance
2	2014.09.23	Cai Jin [2014] No.76	Circular on Issues Concerning the Promotion and Application of the Public-Private Partnership Model	Ministry of Finance
3	2014.11.29	Cai Jin [2014] No.113	Circular on Issuing the Operational Guidelines for Public-Private Partnership Model (Trial)	Ministry of Finance
4	2014.11.30	Cai Jin [2014] No.112	Circular on Issues Concerning the Implementation of the Demonstration Projects of Public-Private Partnership	Ministry of Finance
5	2014.12.30	Cai Jin [2014] No.156	Circular on Regulating the Contract Management of Public-Private Partnership	Ministry of Finance
6	2014.12.31	Cai Jin [2014] No.215	Circular on Issuing the Administrative Measures for Government Procurement under Public-Private Partnership Projects	Ministry of Finance
7	2014.12.31	Cai Jin [2014] No.214	Circular on Issuing the Interim Measures for the Administration of Competitive Consultation of Government Procurement	Ministry of Finance

(continued)

No.	Issued on	Document No.	Document	Issued by
8	2015.02.13	Cai Jian [2015] No.29	Circular on Promoting Public-Private Partnership Projects in Municipal Public Utilities	Ministry of Finance&&Ministry of Housing and Urban-Rural Development
9	2015.03.10	Fa Gai Tou Zi [2015] No.445	Circular on Relevant Work Concerning the Promotion of the Development Financial Support for Public-Private Partnership	National Development and Reform Commission
10	2015.04.07	Cai Jin [2015] No.21	Circular on Issuing the Guidelines for the Financial Affordability Assessment of the Public-Private Partnership Projects	Ministry of Finance
11	2015.05.19	Guo Fa Ban [2015] No.42	Notice of the General Office of the State Council on Forwarding the Guideline of the Ministry of Finance, the National Development and Reform Commission, and the People's Bank of China on the Promotion of Public-Private Partnership (PPP) Model in Public Service Sector	The General Office of the State Council
12	2015.06.25	Cai Jin [2015] No.57	Circular on Further Effectively Implementing the Demonstration of Public-Private Partnership Projects	Ministry of Finance
13	2015.12.18	Cai Jin [2015] No.166	Circular on Regulating the Operation of the Public-Private Partnership (PPP) Integrated Information Platform	Ministry of Finance
14	2015.12.18	Cai Jin [2015] No.167	Circular on Issuing Guidelines for Value-for-money Evaluation of PPP (Trial)	Ministry of Finance
15	2016.01		The Public-Private Partnership Law of the People's Republic of China (Exposure Draft)	Ministry of Finance
16	2016.05.28	Cai Jin [2014] No.112	Circular on Further Effectively and Jointly Implementing Public-Private Partnerships	National Development and Reform Commission, Ministry of Finance

(continued)

No.	Issued on	Document No.	Document	Issued by
17	2016.10.20	Cai Jin [2016] No. 92	Circular on Issuing the Interim Measures for the Administration of Finance for Public-private Partnership Projects	Ministry of Finance
18	2016.12.21	Fa Gai Tou Zi [2016] No.2698	Circular on Relevant Work Concerning the Promotion of Asset Securitization of PPP Projects in Infrastructure Sector	National Development and Reform Commission
19	2016.12.30	Cai Jin [2016] No. 144	Administrative Measures of the Ministry of Finance for the Public-Private Partnership (PPP) Expert Database	Ministry of Finance
20	2017.01.23	Cai Jin [2017] No.21	Circular on Issuing the Interim Measures for Administration of Information Disclosure for Public-Private Partnership Integrated Information Platform	Ministry of Finance
21	2017.03.22	Cai Jin [2017] No.8	Circular on Issuing the Interim Measures for the Administration of PPP Consulting Agency Database	Ministry of Finance
22	2017.10.19		Guidelines for Qualification for Asset-backed Securities' Listing and Information Disclosure in PPP Projects	Shanghai Stock Exchange
23	2017.11.10	Cai Ban Jin [2017] No.92	Circular on Regulating Project Database of the National PPP Integrated Information Platform	Ministry of Finance
24	2019.03.07	Cai Jin [2019] No.10	Guide of the Ministry of Finance on Promoting the Regulated Development of Public-Private Partnership	Ministry of Finance
25	2020.03.16	Cai Jin [2020] No.13	Guideline for Public-Private Partnership (PPP) Project Performance Management	Ministry of Finance

Appendix Ⅳ Ranking of Cities with Over 20 Projects in PPP Market Transparency Index

Ranking	City	Project quantity	Immediate disclosure	Disclosure in due time	Overall index
1	Xuancheng, Anhui	34	85.19	83.57	84.56
2	Dehong, Yunnan	20	89.76	74.45	83.79
3	Shijiazhuang, Hebei	37	85.25	81.48	83.78
4	Binzhou, Shandong	25	88.73	75.95	83.75
5	Siping, Jilin	20	87.02	78.09	83.54
6	Hotan, Xinjiang	20	87.74	76.91	83.52
7	Zibo, Shandong	28	88.78	73.51	82.82
8	Aksu, Xinjiang	66	85.02	79.36	82.81
9	Dezhou, Shandong	44	86.27	77.07	82.68
10	Lincang, Yunnan	25	85.42	78.21	82.61
11	Dongguan, Guangdong	108	84.61	79.15	82.48
12	Dali, Yunnan	38	87.73	74.05	82.39
13	Zhaotong, Yunnan	21	85.61	77.23	82.34
14	Liaocheng, Shandong	29	87.56	74.12	82.32
15	Changji, Xinjiang	31	82.86	80.86	82.08
16	Rizhao, Shandong	56	85.07	77.35	82.06
17	Jinan, Shandong	46	85.65	76.15	81.94
18	Weifang, Shandong	93	85.33	76.26	81.79
19	Yantai, Shandong	39	84.42	77.57	81.75

(continued)

Ranking	City	Project quantity	Immediate disclosure	Disclosure in due time	Overall index
20	Cangzhou, Hebei	46	83.53	78.87	81.71
21	Xingtai, Hebei	39	86.79	73.73	81.70
22	Honghe, Yunnan	46	84.58	77.10	81.66
23	Baoding, Hebei	37	81.88	81.29	81.65
24	Jining, Shandong	82	86.87	73.42	81.62
25	Tangshan, Hebei	52	85.68	75.16	81.58
26	Changchun, Jilin	50	85.19	75.63	81.46
27	Bortala, Xinjiang	48	84.40	76.79	81.43
28	Chengde, Hebei	56	84.35	76.82	81.41
29	Yuxi, Yunnan	57	83.42	78.25	81.41
30	Lanzhou, Gansu	22	83.94	77.36	81.38
31	Yongzhou, Hunan	23	83.54	77.95	81.36
32	Zhuzhou, Hunan	30	83.70	76.91	81.05
33	Baoshan, Yunan	31	85.14	74.51	80.99
34	Taizhou, Jiangsu	28	83.06	77.61	80.94
35	Bayannur, Inner Mongolia	25	84.34	75.54	80.91
36	Putian, Fujian	28	83.52	76.67	80.85
37	Heze, Shandong	74	85.00	74.34	80.85
38	Yiyang, Hunan	29	83.74	76.27	80.83
39	Chaoyang, Liaoning	23	83.57	76.45	80.79
40	Weihai, Shandong	27	84.02	75.63	80.75
41	Xilingol League, Inner Mongolia	30	86.96	70.98	80.72
42	Xiangtan, Hunan	21	83.45	75.76	80.45
43	Xinxiang, Henan	44	79.49	81.66	80.34
44	Bijie, Guizhou	65	81.29	78.21	80.09
45	Lijiang, Yunnan	20	85.80	71.15	80.09
46	Handan, Hebei	36	83.00	75.50	80.07
47	Linyi, Shandong	76	82.79	75.34	79.88
48	Qujing, Yunnan	42	83.64	73.94	79.86
49	Luzhou, Sichuan	27	85.86	70.34	79.81
50	Yulin, Guangxi	31	79.10	80.75	79.74

(continued)

Ranking	City	Project quantity	Immediate disclosure	Disclosure in due time	Overall index
51	Changsha, Hunan	43	82.68	75.10	79.72
52	Chizhou, Anhui	21	78.46	81.61	79.69
53	Shangqiu, Henan	36	83.89	73.04	79.66
54	Hengshui, Hebei	32	83.09	74.23	79.64
55	Nanjing, Jiangsu	90	83.41	73.22	79.43
56	Nanning, Guangxi	29	80.51	77.70	79.41
57	Hulunbeier, Inner Mongolia	34	83.90	72.39	79.41
58	Lu'an, Anhui	41	80.58	77.44	79.35
59	Changde, Hunan	38	84.14	71.54	79.23
60	Huai'an, Jiangsu	41	82.18	74.53	79.20
61	Qianxinan, Guizhou	34	84.32	70.88	79.08
62	Dalian Liaoning	34	82.28	73.71	78.94
63	Yangjiang, Guangdong	26	81.56	74.01	78.62
64	Jingmen, Hubei	33	82.28	72.82	78.59
65	Guangzhou, Guangdong	24	82.87	71.88	78.59
66	Pingdingshan, Henan	59	78.66	77.97	78.39
67	Hefei, Anhui	20	78.53	77.94	78.30
68	Heyuan, Guangdong	24	83.07	70.82	78.29
69	Meizhou, Guangdong	23	81.45	73.21	78.23
70	Bengbu, Anhui	30	77.65	78.90	78.13
71	Kunming, Yunnan	54	79.86	75.26	78.06
72	Xi'an, Shaanxi	83	82.72	70.78	78.06
73	Xuchang, Henan	29	77.48	78.86	78.02
74	Dongying, Shandong	33	80.59	73.83	77.95
75	Pu'er, Yunnan	26	79.10	75.94	77.87
76	Chuxiong, Yunnan	44	80.09	74.35	77.85
77	Jilin City, Jilin	23	80.75	72.93	77.70
78	Hanzhong, Shaanxi	29	80.15	73.82	77.68
79	Guiyang, Guizhou	51	80.90	72.46	77.61
80	Zhaoqing, Guangdong	27	78.87	75.57	77.58
81	Nanchong, Sichuan	35	79.71	73.79	77.40

(continued)

Ranking	City	Project quantity	Immediate disclosure	Disclosure in due time	Overall index
82	Weinan, Shaanxi	31	80.83	72.01	77.39
83	Xuzhou, Jiangsu	58	78.38	75.77	77.36
84	Ili, Xinjiang	24	80.14	72.98	77.34
85	Jiaxing, Zhejiang	22	81.89	70.05	77.27
86	Haozhou, Anhui	34	77.52	76.74	77.21
87	Zhengzhou, Henan	56	76.62	77.82	77.09
88	Fuyang, Anhui	62	76.94	77.32	77.09
89	Suzhou, Anhui	42	77.81	75.80	77.03
90	Yichang, Hubei	37	78.76	74.14	76.96
91	Wenshan, Yunnan	28	81.09	70.45	76.94
92	Kaifeng, Henan	34	76.83	77.06	76.92
93	Chuzhou, Anhui	36	78.27	74.69	76.88
94	Tongren, Guizhou	26	79.95	72.05	76.87
95	Ningbo, Zhejiang	49	79.30	72.89	76.80
96	Shaoyang, Hunan	22	76.81	76.66	76.75
97	Tongchuan, Shaanxi	21	80.29	71.03	76.68
98	Hangzhou, Zhejiang	66	81.91	68.31	76.61
99	Anyang, Henan	45	78.96	72.80	76.56
100	Chongzuo, Guangxi	24	80.72	69.96	76.52
101	Zunyi, Guizhou	114	80.60	69.91	76.43
102	Yichun, Jiangxi	48	81.19	68.99	76.43
103	Anqing, Anhui	48	75.90	77.06	76.35
104	Changzhi, Shanxi	37	80.78	69.27	76.29
105	Shantou, Guangdong	29	81.09	68.63	76.23
106	Zhoukou, Henan	47	78.80	72.07	76.18
107	Lvliang, Shanxi	49	83.20	65.12	76.15
108	Xiangxi, Hunan	50	78.32	72.31	75.98
109	Ningde, Fujian	63	77.57	73.46	75.97
110	Liupanshui, Guizhou	50	78.68	71.62	75.93
111	Luoyang, Henan	57	76.50	74.87	75.86
112	Lishui, Zhejiang	62	80.46	68.63	75.85

(continued)

Ranking	City	Project quantity	Immediate disclosure	Disclosure in due time	Overall index
113	Jiuquan, Gansu	20	82.13	65.93	75.82
114	Jinzhong, Shanxi	50	80.43	68.57	75.81
115	Puyang, Henan	42	76.45	74.68	75.76
116	Huzhou, Zhejiang	45	79.80	69.18	75.66
117	Zhanjiang, Guangdong	26	76.52	74.24	75.63
118	Chenzhou, Hunan	38	76.01	74.83	75.55
119	Jiaozuo, Henan	31	75.01	76.25	75.49
120	Yueyang, Hunan	25	77.34	72.10	75.30
121	Chifeng, Inner Mongolia	56	76.57	73.30	75.29
122	Nanchang, Jiangxi	20	78.72	69.84	75.26
123	Yancheng, Jiangsu	26	76.36	73.50	75.25
124	Shuozhou, Shanxi	23	80.84	66.48	75.24
125	Huanggang, Hubei	27	80.64	66.69	75.20
126	Pingxiang, Jiangxi	30	81.51	65.33	75.20
127	Urumqi, Xinjiang	64	79.76	68.02	75.18
128	Shiyan, Hubei	23	78.18	70.46	75.17
129	Bazhong, Sichuan	44	76.09	73.52	75.09
130	Sanmenxia, Henan	23	74.85	75.25	75.01
131	Chengdu, Sichuan	55	77.84	70.55	74.99
132	Wenzhou, Zhejiang	83	77.48	70.86	74.90
133	Jiangmen, Guangdong	40	80.57	65.62	74.74
134	Tongling, Anhui	21	79.66	66.95	74.71
135	Zhumadian, Henan	69	75.71	73.13	74.70
136	Suqian, Jiangsu	43	77.57	69.72	74.51
137	Anshun, Guizhou	28	72.82	77.14	74.50
138	Leshan, Sichuan	32	75.86	72.30	74.47
139	Datong, Shanxi	29	77.92	68.70	74.33
140	Qingdao, Shandong	74	79.21	66.56	74.27
141	Shaoguan, Guangdong	25	76.36	70.95	74.25
142	Guangyuan, Sichuan	36	74.64	73.22	74.09
143	Huaihua, Hunan	23	74.60	73.11	74.01

(continued)

Ranking	City	Project quantity	Immediate disclosure	Disclosure in due time	Overall index
144	Yangzhou, Jiangsu	27	77.04	68.85	73.85
145	Hengyang, Hunan	25	80.85	62.73	73.78
146	Longyan, Fujian	26	72.70	75.46	73.78
147	Jiujiang, Jiangxi	23	81.72	61.34	73.77
148	Qiandongnan, Guizhou	49	77.90	67.06	73.68
149	Linfen, Shanxi	58	77.65	67.46	73.67
150	Nanping, Fujian	26	73.61	73.53	73.58
151	Nanyang, Henan	71	72.83	74.74	73.58
152	Quanzhou, Fujian	66	75.25	70.88	73.54
153	Xinzhou, Shanxi	37	78.86	64.68	73.33
154	Huizhou, Guangdong	44	73.74	72.14	73.12
155	Liangshan, Sichuan	44	75.59	69.14	73.08
156	Ma'anshan, Anhui	20	74.24	71.11	73.02
157	Yinchuan, Ningxia	25	75.52	69.05	72.99
158	Loudi, Hunan	33	74.86	69.99	72.96
159	Shaoxing, Zhejiang	31	74.96	69.79	72.94
160	Yibin, Sichuan	62	72.38	73.71	72.90
161	Xiaogan, Hubei	31	75.87	68.07	72.83
162	Xinyang, Henan	52	70.07	76.12	72.43
163	Xianning, Hubei	34	79.19	61.69	72.36
164	Fuzhou, Fujian	48	71.96	72.98	72.36
165	Chongqing	43	77.48	64.01	72.23
166	Zhangzhou, Fujian	60	74.60	68.15	72.08
167	Sanming, Fujian	22	74.89	67.55	72.03
168	Quzhou, Zhejiang	40	76.37	65.07	71.96
169	Huangshi, Hubei	23	77.31	63.31	71.85
170	Erdos, Inner Mongolia	33	78.68	60.35	71.53
171	Dazhou, Sichuan	28	72.63	69.28	71.32
172	Shenyang, Liaoning	26	75.47	64.36	71.14
173	Jingzhou, Hubei	29	79.12	58.29	71.00
174	Taiyuan, Shanxi	34	78.12	59.83	70.98

(continued)

Ranking	City	Project quantity	Immediate disclosure	Disclosure in due time	Overall index
175	Taizhou, Zhejiang	67	71.44	70.14	70.93
176	Ji'an, Jiangxi	23	75.83	62.97	70.81
177	Enshi, Hubei	35	74.52	64.56	70.63
178	Wuhan, Hubei	67	74.45	64.09	70.41
179	Ganzhou, Jiangxi	95	74.46	63.89	70.34
180	Neijiang, Sichuan	25	67.73	74.27	70.28
181	Fuzhou, Jiangxi	36	76.76	58.29	69.56
182	Mianyang, Sichuan	30	69.43	69.23	69.35
183	Xiangyang, Hubei	44	71.46	65.88	69.28
184	Bayingolin, Xinjiang	30	76.15	58.39	69.22
185	Liuzhou, Guangxi	27	71.42	65.53	69.12
186	Yuncheng, Shanxi	34	74.68	58.71	68.45
187	Tianjin	49	74.70	58.24	68.28
188	Hami, Xinjiang	27	76.06	54.52	67.66
189	Beijing	70	71.29	61.56	67.49
190	Guang'an, Sichuan	20	72.90	57.76	66.99
191	Harbin, Heilongjiang	30	70.94	60.71	66.95
192	Suining, Sichuan	22	68.93	62.48	66.42
193	Qiannan, Guizhou	53	70.55	59.30	66.16
194	Zigong, Sichuan	23	67.59	62.79	65.72
195	Qingyuan, Guangdong	23	77.89	46.52	65.66
196	Shangrao, Jiangxi	38	72.17	54.12	65.13
197	Jinhua, Zhejiang	39	67.77	51.02	61.24
198	Haikou, Hainan	52	57.54	58.35	57.86

Postscript

The *2019 China PPP Market Transparency Report* was prepared by the Research Group of PPP Research Center under the China Public Finance Institute at Shanghai University of Finance and Economics (SUFE). The Research Group was led by associate professor Fang Fang, Party Secretary of the School of Public Economics and Administration, SUFE, with core members including associate professor Zong Qingqing and PhD candidate Shen Yanyan, both at the School of Public Economics and Administration, SUFE. Based on the PPP Market Transparency Index prepared in 2017 and 2018, the Research Group has carried out investigation, analysis and evaluation concerning the information disclosure landscape of the Chinese PPP market by the end of 2019. During the evaluation, the Research Group has managed to maintain the stability of the index system and index compilation methods, thus ensuring the comparability of PPP market transparency results in 2019 with those in 2017 and 2018. Meanwhile, the information disclosure of PPP projects in 2019 has also been put in comparison with that in the previous years. The Group hopes that its work could accurately and objectively reflect the information disclosure status of the Chinese PPP market, thereby contributing to the healthy and sustainable development of the PPP in China.

The successful completion of the research project relies on the strong support and assistance of other organizations. First of all, Asian Development Bank, China Public Finance Institute at SUFE, and School of Public Economics and Administration at SUFE have provided valuable financial support for the approval and smooth implementation of the project. Second, China Public Private Partnerships Center (CPPPC) provided vigorous support. Finally, such institutions as the School of Public Economics and Administration and Research Office of SUFE have secured the smooth progress of our research. Zhang Liao, Chairman of Jumbo Consulting; Lu Zhixiang, Chief Financial Officer of YMCI East and South China Business Unit; Zhao Shikun, Managing Director of China Lustre United Consulting Uc Company; Liang Guoyong, Economic Affairs Officer of the United Nations Conference on Trade and Development; Tian Hui, General Manager of Shanghai Branch of China Reform Holdings Corporation Ltd.; Zhou Tao, Vice President of Shanghai Branch of China Construction Bank; professor Zhou Yahong, Dean of School of Economics, SUFE; professor Liu Xiaochuan, Executive Dean of the China Institute of Public Finance, SUFE; professor Fan Ziying, Deputy Dean of the Institute of Public Finance and Director of PPP Research Center, SUFE, among other experts, have also offered valuable opinions, which contributed to the completion of the research. We would like to hereby express our gratitude to the institutions and specialists above. However, it needs to be stated again that this Report, prepared independently by the Research Group, represents the academic opinions of the Research Group and doesn't represent the official opinions of such institutions above.

Finally, acknowledgments to the graduates and undergraduates of Shanghai University of Finance and Economics, including Chen Lituo, Chen Xiao, Ding Qinxian, Gao Jiawen, Gong Zhiqiang, Huang Lipeng, Huang Xiang, Liang Yawen, Sheng Lingyu, Shi Jia, Xiang Xiyue, Xu Zhaopei, Xue Zongyue, Yan Shuhui, Yu Jiujiu, Zeng Jing, Zhang Xiaoying, Zhou Yunqin, and Zhu Junyi, who have participated in the data collection and consolidation of the project.

At the end, the Research Group would like to express our sincerest thanks to all parties for their support and assistance. We also welcome experts and practitioners from all walks of life to put forward valuable opinions and suggestions with regard to our work, with a view to formulating PPP market transparency index in a more scientific and rigorous manner in the future. Please contact our members for more details:

Zong Qingqing (email: zong.qingqing@mail.sufe.edu.cn)

PPP

2019

中国 PPP 市场透明度报告

上海财经大学 PPP 研究中心

上海财经大学出版社

图书在版编目(CIP)数据

2019中国PPP市场透明度报告/上海财经大学PPP研究中心著.—上海:上海财经大学出版社,2020.12
ISBN 978-7-5642-3178-1/F.3178

Ⅰ.①2… Ⅱ.①上… Ⅲ.①政府投资-合作-社会资本-研究报告-中国-2019 Ⅳ.①F832.48 ②F124.7

中国版本图书馆CIP数据核字(2020)第217218号

责任编辑 江 玉
封面设计 张克瑶

2019中国PPP市场透明度报告

著 作 者:上海财经大学PPP研究中心
出版发行:上海财经大学出版社有限公司
地 址:上海市中山北一路369号(邮编200083)
网 址:http://www.sufep.com
电子邮箱:webmaster@sufep.com
经 销:全国新华书店
印刷装订:江苏凤凰数码印务有限公司
开 本:787mm×1092mm 1/16
印 张:19.75
字 数:319千字
版 次:2020年12月第1版
印 次:2020年12月第1次印刷
定 价:138.00元

2019

中国PPP市场透明度报告

课题委托单位

亚洲开发银行

课题组顾问

刘小川

上海财经大学中国公共财政研究院执行院长　教授

Ko Wang

Professor and Dean's Chair of Real Estate and Infrastructure
Johns Hopkings Carey Business School

课题组成员

方　芳　　宗庆庆　　沈言言

本课题得到了亚洲开发银行的资助，也得到了中国政府有关部门的支持，但本报告不代表上述机构的观点，所有与报告内容有关的责任都由课题组承担。

内容提要

PPP是Public-Private Partnerships的英文首字母缩写，译为政府和社会资本合作。当前，中国的PPP模式已经不仅仅是政府的一种市场化投融资手段，更是一次全面的、系统的公共服务供给市场化社会化改革举措，因而各界对PPP的发展都寄予厚望，希望PPP能起到引领财政体制机制改革、助力公共事业全面深化改革的作用。在这一背景下，PPP项目的规范化管理就显得尤为重要，其中PPP项目及时、完善的信息公开又是PPP项目规范化管理的基础。2017年以来，财政部连续发布的多份文件都涉及了PPP项目的信息公开工作，特别是2017年初发布的《政府和社会资本合作（PPP）综合信息平台信息公开管理暂行办法》（财金〔2017〕1号），详细规定了PPP项目信息公开的各方面要求。进入2018年后，PPP项目的退库清理成为PPP管理的重心之一，2 000多个不符合管理规范的PPP项目被清理退库，同时也有不少新增项目加入PPP管理库中。进入2019年后，伴随着更多的PPP项目进入执行阶段，如何有效推动PPP项目适时公开信息的管理工作显得愈发重要。同时，公众对提高PPP项目信息质量的呼声也越来越高。2020年3月31日，财政部发布《政府与社会资本合作项目绩效管理操作指引》，全方位建立了完整的PPP绩效考核体系，明确了责任主体，将信息真实、公开、透明、质量纳入具体的考核细则。

在此背景下，上海财经大学PPP研究中心课题组继过去连续两年对截至年底的PPP项目信息公开工作进行评估后，又对截至2019年12月31日的中国PPP项目的最新信息公开状况进行了详细的评估。具体而言，课题组对2020年底财政部PPP管理库的9 398个项目的信息公开工作进行了详细评估，编制了一套“2019中国PPP市场透明度指数”。该指数囊括75个指标字段,并分为即时公开透明度指数、适时公开透明度指数,以及识别阶段、准备阶段、采购阶段和执行阶段等各阶段的透明度分指数。课题组采用层次分析法和专家打分法相结合的方法对指数进行合成:对于分指数下面的具体指标,按照专家对其重要程度的判定,设置不同的分值;而在分指数合成总指数当中,则采用同类指数编制过程中常用的层次分析法,以保证指数编制方法的可靠性。最终,通过对指数具体结果的统计分析,课题组得到以下几个主要发现:

第一,2019年全国PPP市场透明度总指数为76.19,较2018年略有提高。截至2019年12月31日,全国PPP市场透明度总指数为76.19(满分100,下同),与2018年的75.25相比提高了1左右。其中即时公开透明度指数为79.14,相比2018年(77.61)提高了1.5,而适时公开透明度指数为71.57,与2018年(71.55)几乎持平。进一步对PPP项目的异质性分析表明,PPP项目透明度指数没有明显的行业差异,示范项目和非示范项目的透明度指数也差别不大;项目发起时间则显著影响了项目透明度指数,项目发起时间越晚,项目越为透明。

第二,2019年PPP市场透明度指数相比2018年产生跨期差异的重要原因在于评估对象的变动。首先,进入执行阶段项目数占比大幅增加导致2019年PPP项目透明度降低。其次,通过分解退出效应、存量效应和进入效应来看,透明度指数较差的项目被退库,继续在库的项目改进了自己的信息公开工作,再加上新增项目比存量项目指数也要稍高一些,这些因素共同推动了2019年PPP市场透明度指数的提升。

第三,不同省份PPP市场透明度指数差异有所扩大,梯队层次明显。大多数省份的透明度指数集中在70～80之间,形成第二梯队。排名前5位的省份PPP市场透明度指数超过80,构成了第一梯队。排在末尾的6个省份PPP市场透明度指数不足70,属于第三梯队。就具体排名而言,透明度排名第一的是甘肃(81.97),排名第二的是河北(81.29),排名第三的是吉林(80.52),排名第四的是山东(80.2),排名第五的是云南(80.17)。对比2018年的排行榜可以发现,PPP项目信息透明度工作进步最大的省份是江苏(77.69)和广东(77.20),两省在全国的排名较2018年均上升了17位,在2019年榜单中分列第九位和第十二位。

第四,超过半数的城市PPP市场透明度指数较2018年有所提高,剩余城市PPP市场透明度指数有所下降。课题组挑选了46个PPP项目数量较多(入管理库的项目超50个）的城市，对其PPP信息公开工作进行了分析。通过和2018年的PPP市场透明度指数对比可以发现，部分地级以上城市2019年的指数较2018年是大幅上升的，尤其是新疆阿克苏，其2019年总指数较2018年上升了15.39，紧随其后的是广东东莞，较2018年上升了13.62。不过，同时也可以发现，很多地级以上城市2019年的PPP市场透明度指数较2018年有所降低，尤其是贵州黔南和海南海口，2019年的总指数较2018年下降最多，分别下降了13.10和12。2019年PPP市场透明度指数排在前5位的城市为：新疆阿克苏（82.81）、广东东莞（82.48）、山东日照（82.06）、山东潍坊（81.79）和山东济宁（81.62）。

第五，PPP中介机构信息公开指数跨期差异不大，中介机构透明度指数得分与其资历、业务量正相关。课题组分析了PPP中介机构的信息公开现状，主要得到以下几个发现：中介机构信息透明度指数平均为75.20，而在二级指数中，中介机构参与的项目信息公开得分较高，但部分中介机构网站主动公开相关信息的工作不理想，与2018年相比意愿进一步降低。进一步的分析还发现，中介机构的信息透明度指数与中介机构参与的PPP项目数量和中介机构存续年龄具有明显的正相关关系。

在指数的编制和分析过程中，课题组也提炼出了进一步改进PPP信息公开工作的一些政策建议，例如，增加PPP项目信息公开时效性的考核，完善“不适用”类信息和临时性重大事项信息公开的管理，加强PPP项目重点信息公开的监督检查力度，进一步明确PPP信息公开的责任主体和具体分工，等等。我们希望通过进一步完善PPP信息公开和规范管理的制度来进一步提高PPP市场的信息透明度，进而助推整个PPP市场的规范化发展。

目录

1

导　论

1.1 PPP的概念内涵与操作流程

1.1.1 PPP含义

PPP是Public Private Partnerships的英文首字母缩写，直译为政府和社会资本合作。PPP是社会资本参与基础设施和公用事业项目投资运营的一种制度创新，不同的国际组织对其均有自己不尽相同的定义。例如，亚洲开发银行认为，PPP是指为开展基础设施建设和提供公共服务，公共部门和私营部门之间可能建立的一系列合作伙伴关系。联合国发展计划署认为，PPP是指政府、营利性企业和非营利性组织基于某个项目而形成的相互合作关系，在这种关系中，政府并不是把项目的责任全部转移给私营部门，而是由参与合作的各方共同承担责任和融资风险。欧盟委员会认为，PPP是公共部门和私人部门之间的一种合作关系，其目的是为了提供传统上由公共部门提供的公共项目或服务。世界银行则认为，PPP是私营部门和政府机构间就提供公共资产和公共服务签订的长期合同，而私营部门须承担重大风险和管理责任。而根据中国政府的定义，政府和社会资本合作模式是指政府通过特许经营权、合理定价、财政补贴等事先公开的收益约定规则，引入社会资本参与城市基础设施等公益性事业投资和运营，以利益共享和风险共担为特征，发挥双方优势，提高公共产品或服务的质量和供给效率。中国政府对PPP模式的定义与其他国际组织定义的差异主要体现在“社会资本”和“私人资本”上，在中国，社会资本覆盖范围更广，除了私人资本、境外资本等之外，还包括国有企业资本等。

综合上述几个定义，可以认为，广义上，PPP就是指政府和社会资本充分发挥各自优势，为提供公共产品或服务而建立的合作伙伴关系，这些合作通常集中于基础设施及公共服务领域。在PPP模式的合作中，政府一般采取竞争性方式选择具有投融资、运营管理能力的社会资本，双方按照平等协商原则订立合同，由社会资本提供公共服务，政府依据公共服务绩效评价结果向社会资本支付对价。具体而言，PPP通常模式是由社会资本主要负责基础设施和公用事业的项目设计、建设、运营和维护工作，承担商业和财务风险，通过政府购买、使用者付费或其他回报机制获得合理投资回报；政府主要负责公共服务及基础设施质量和价格监管，保护消费者利益，以保证公共利益最大化，并承担政策法律风险。PPP最初主要是在基础设施领域产生的制度创新，随后逐渐发展并覆盖大多数公共产品或服务领域，包括交通、能源、水利、水务等经济基础设施和科技、环保、教育、文化、体育、卫生、旅游、社会福利等社会基础设施。

1.1.2 PPP操作流程

财政部于2014年11月下发《政府和社会资本合作操作指南》，对PPP项目的全生命周期的操作规范进行了规定，对PPP项目的设计、融资、建造、运营、维护至终止移交的各环节操作流程进行了全方位规范。PPP项目操作流程可分为项目识别、项目准备、项目采购、项目执行和项目移交五个阶段，具体如图1－1所示。而财政部于2017年初发布的《政府和社会资本合作（PPP）综合信息平台信息公开管理暂行办法》（财金〔2017〕1号，以下简称“1号文”）中对PPP项目信息公开的管理指引，也是按照这五个阶段分别规定的，因此，区分这五个阶段也是PPP市场透明度指数编制工作中的重要中间步骤。

图1－1 PPP项目操作流程

此外，2017年11月，财政部印发《关于规范政府和社会资本合作（PPP）综合信息平台项目库管理的通知》（财办金〔2017〕92号），对PPP项目的流程管理进一步优化，实行分类管理，将PPP项目按阶段分为项目储备清单和项目管理库。项目储备清单内的项目重点用于孵化和推介，项目管理库内的项目则要接受严格监管，确保全生命周期规范运作。对照之前的五阶段划分，储备清单主要对应识别阶段，是地方政府部门有意愿采用PPP模式的备选项目，但由于尚未完成物有所值评价和财政承受能力论证等的审核，严格而言还不能称之为PPP项目，因而属于储备库；管理库则囊括准备阶段、采购阶段、执行阶段和移交阶段，是严格按照相关管理办法进行全生命周期管理的PPP项目。

1.2 PPP市场透明度的概念内涵

就字面上的理解，信息透明度是指一个市场、公司或项目的信息公开程度。不过具体到本报告所聚焦的PPP市场透明度，则特指各责任主体（主管部门、政府授权合作方、社会资本方、中介机构等）对PPP项目信息公开的程度。从理论上讲，整个PPP市场的信息公开程度还包括项目管理方式的公开、政策文件的公开、项目各参与方的信息公开，如目前已有的PPP专家库、机构库等当中包含的丰富的信息，但限于数据可得性等原因，本报告中的PPP市场透明度主要指PPP项目的信息公开程度，并在此基础上汇总形成各类透明度指数。从横向看，我们主要构建了省份、城市以及行业等透明度指数。从纵向看，我们主要构建了透明度总指数、即时公开透明度指数、适时公开透明度指数以及分阶段指数。除了PPP项目信息公开程度外，本报告还专门构建分析了PPP中介机构信息透明度，将其作为专门的一章。

PPP是一个市场化的公共服务供给机制，需要与市场化相适应的管理手段和服务能力，提升PPP市场透明度就是其中重要一环。经过三年多的系统推进，PPP信息公开工作取得积极成效。全国PPP综合信息平台已成为各地强化项目管理、推进项目对接、推动项目落地的重要工具。当前，我国正加速推进PPP项目信息和政务服务信息公开，不断提升PPP管理透明度。

特别是在2017年1月，财政部金融司印发1号文，即《政府和社会资本合作（PPP）综合信息平台信息公开管理暂行办法》（财金〔2017〕1号），进一步明确PPP项目信息公开的责任主体，细化公开内容、时点和方式，确保及时充分披露入库PPP项目的基本情况、实施方案、评价论证报告、采购文件、项目合同等关键信息，并要求示范项目率先公开，确保项目在阳光下运作，强化政府监管和社会监督，推动项目规范实施。因此，该文件也是本报告评估中国PPP市场透明度的主要依据：达到该文件各项信息公开要求的PPP项目，即为信息透明度高的项目，反之，若对于该文件要求披露的信息，PPP项目没有披露，则就是信息透明度低的项目。而且为了保证评估的客观、公平，凡不在该文件要求范围内的相关信息，课题组均暂不将其纳入评估范围。这是因为课题组的数据也来自财政部PPP中心的信息平台，而该信息平台的设计依据主要就是该1号文。

1.3 PPP信息公开的必要性与意义

第一，改善营商环境，鼓励社会资本参与公共事业。通常而言，在政府和社会资本的合作当中，政府天然处于强势地位，因此，社会资本往往对与政府的合作有顾虑。PPP更是一种社会资本先期投入、分期收回的长期投资模式，诚信政府对社会资本的参与至关重要。因此，提高PPP市场透明度有助于打消社会资本方参与PPP项目的顾虑，营造公平、公正的市场环境。同时，提高PPP市场透明度也有助于强化政府和企业的契约精神，铲除腐败土壤，维护廉洁高效的政府形象。

第二，促进社会和谐，增强民众的关注与信心。作为一项公共事业，而不是商业项目，PPP与民众的切身利益密切相关。一方面，PPP项目一般是为普通民众提供的公共产品与服务，建设和运行的质量直接关系到民众的切身利益；另一方面，PPP项目要么最终需要纳税人的税收来买单，要么需要使用者来付费，因而也直接关系到民众利益。因此，加大PPP信息公开力度，有助于社会公众更方便地关注、监督PPP市场和PPP项目，促进社会公众的理解和配合，也为相关工作的推进营造和谐氛围。

第三，提升供给效率，增强公共产品绩效管理。PPP项目主要应用于基础设施等公共产品与服务上，这些项目一般具有信息不对称性强、定价难等特征，因此，加强PPP项目信息公开工作，有助于各领域的专业人士科学严谨地评估PPP项目中的定价基准、财政承受能力和收费标准等问题，有助于提高公共产品与服务的科学定价。同时PPP市场透明度的提高也有助于缓解公共产品建设和运行当中的信息不对称问题，铲除内幕交易的土壤，实现国有资产的保值增值，维护纳税人和消费者的权益。最后，完善的信息公开也有助于化解地方债务风险和金融风险。

第四，提升治理水平，构建新型公共管理模式。PPP是一种市场化、社会化的公共产品与服务的供给管理模式，旨在通过改革创新，打破垄断，引入竞争机制，利用市场的专业化和创新能力，丰富公共产品与服务的供给，提高公共产品与服务的供给质量，满足人们不断增长的多样化的公共产品与服务的需求。因此，加大PPP项目信息公开对提升治理水平和构建新型公共管理模式具有重要的现实意义。早在20世纪八九十年代，我国在基础设施建设领域就开始尝试公私合作模式，但由于制度建设缺位，导致项目"异化变形"。为了解决这些问题，在本轮推广PPP的过程中，行业主管部门从制度建设入手，按照"顶层设计+配套政策+操作指引"三位一体的思路，制定了覆盖PPP全生命周期的制度体系。完善的信息公开就是这一制度体系中不可或缺的一部分，主管部门可以以PPP信息披露为抓手，敦促地方政府以及PPP项目各个参与方更规范地参与PPP项目，进而共同促进这一新型公共管理模式的不断完善。

第五，促进PPP发展，推动全面深化改革进程。在公共服务领域推广运用PPP，是全面深化改革的一项重要任务，是推进供给侧结构性改革的一项重要举措，是实施创新驱动、发展新经济的一项重要手段。推动PPP市场发展充分体现了依法治国和发挥市场在资源配置中的决定性作用以及更好发挥政府作用的核心精神。PPP市场的发展，推动了整个行政体制、财政体制和投融资体制的改革。因此，通过提高PPP市场透明度带来的PPP市场规范化发展，对于其他改革事业也有很大的借鉴价值。当前，中国PPP市场的信息披露工作在同类政府事务中处于领先地位，甚至在全球都处于领先地位。深入评估分析和总结PPP市场信息公开工作取得的成绩和经验，可以为其他改革事业提供有益借鉴。

第六，营造国家形象，展示中国制度自信。PPP项目各国都有所涉历，多个国际组织也都非常关注各国的PPP市场。中国的PPP项目在经过多年的探索之后，形成了自己的模式和风格，在很多方面都有所创新。总结分析PPP市场透明度，对于塑造中国政府开放、高效的形象，提高在国际PPP市场上的影响力和话语权，具有很大的帮助。而且，基础设施也是"一带一路"倡议中的重要组成部分，通过信息公开推动

PPP规范化，有助于PPP的中国模式在“一带一路”国家和地区的推广，在输出产品和技术的同时，也输出中国的软实力。

1.4 中国PPP信息公开实践历程

自2013年我国大力推广PPP项目以来，根据党中央、国务院的部署，财政部先后出台了《政府和社会资本合作（PPP）综合信息平台信息公开管理暂行办法》（财金〔2017〕1号）、《关于规范政府和社会资本合作（PPP）综合信息平台项目库管理的通知》（财办金〔2017〕92号）和《关于进一步规范全国PPP综合信息平台项目信息管理工作的通知》（财政企函〔2018〕2号）等文件。此外，财政部统筹推进PPP改革，推进PPP项目信息公开的工作。

第一，建立了全国政府和社会资本合作（PPP）综合信息平台。2015年，财政部在国家“互联网+”行动计划指导下，构建了一个覆盖全国各地区、涉及19大领域、贯穿项目实施全过程、服务主体全覆盖的PPP综合信息平台。首先，建立了贯通“中央-省-市-县”各级财政部门的PPP项目信息采集和管理的一条通道。其次，包括了信息披露和线上管理两大平台，用来发布PPP政策法规、工作动态、项目合作、知识分享以及信息跟踪管理等，而且还满足了项目管理、交易撮合、信息服务三大功能。最后，涵盖了项目库、专家库、机构库和资料库四大核心应用数据库，其中，项目库用于收集和管理全国PPP项目的关键信息和资料，专家库和机构库用于收集和管理专家、咨询机构、社会资本、金融机构等各参与方信息，资料库用于收集和管理PPP相关政策法规、工作动态、指南手册、培训材料和经典案例等信息。

第二，建立信息披露机制。明确了PPP项目信息公开的责任主体、各阶段公开信息内容和具体要求，制定了专家库、机构库管理的规定，明确了PPP专家、咨询机构信息公开的要求。

第三，创新PPP信息披露制度。按月披露PPP项目入库和退库的信息，按季度开展PPP项目信息统计和发布。通过财政部门户网站“PPP专栏”，财政部政府和社会资本合作中心中、英文网站及微信公众号“道PPP”“中国PPP地图”手机客户端等网络媒介，实现PPP政策文件和工作动态的多点发布。目前，我国已经形成定期披露、全面披露、多方式披露的PPP项目信息公开格局。

在各方面的关心支持和共同努力下，PPP信息公开工作取得积极成效。项目库、机构库、专家库的社会影响力和认可度不断提高，已成为各地强化项目管理、推进项目对接、推动项目落地的重要抓手。项目库季报被视为PPP市场的“沪深指数”。金融机构甚至为信息公开程度更高的示范项目开辟了信贷支持的“绿色通道”。据统计，截至2019年12月末，PPP综合信息平台收录的管理库项目累计9 440个，储备清单项目2 922个。PPP专家库入库专家达到497人，涵盖政策、法律、财务、咨询、行业、学术等各领域的高级人才，成为服务全国PPP发展的“专业智库”。网站、微信公众号等已成为PPP信息的权威发布平台。2020年3月31日，财政部发布《政府与社会资本合作项目绩效管理操作指引》，全方位建立了完整的PPP绩效考核体系，明确了责任主体，将信息真实、公开、透明、质量纳入具体的考核细则。这意味着PPP绩效管理政策的实施将更加精准有效地提升信息公开的质量。

PPP信息公开对中国PPP发展产生了积极作用。世界银行发布的2018年度《PPP基础设施采购报告》从PPP准备、采购、合同管理和民间自提项目四个维度，对135个经济体的PPP政策法规建设进行了打分评价。报告指出，中国搭建了PPP基础制度框架，规范了物有所值评价、财政承受能力论证等关键环节的操作方法，制定了采购文件、工程进度等重要信息的公示制度，营造了良好的政策环境。在分数构成上，中国PPP采购得分82分（高收入经济体平均得分77分，中上收入经济体平均得分64分），位居全球前列；合同管理得分76分（高收入经济体平均得分58分，中上收入经济体平均得分57分）；PPP准备得分61分（高收入经济体平均得分63分，中上收入经济体平均得分48分）；民间自提项目得分54分（高收入经济体平均得分66分，中上收入经济体平均得分63分）。

PPP市场信息公开工作取得的成绩和经验需要总结，同时也要深入剖析有待进一步完善的内容。本评估报告旨在通过编制指数的方式，对PPP市场的透明度工作进行经验总结，分析其成绩和不足。而严谨、公正的市场透明度评估，有赖于评估方法的科学性，具体到本报告，就体现在PPP市场透明度指标体系和指数编制方法的设计上，这将是本报告第2章讨论的重点。

1.5 中国PPP市场发展基本概况①

按照《关于规范政府和社会资本合作综合信息平台运行的通知》(财金〔2015〕166号)要求,财政部建立了全国政府和社会资本合作(PPP)综合信息平台及项目库。本报告对PPP项目信息公开的评估就是基于该信息平台上所能获取的数据,因此,在本节,我们首先根据该平台上的数据,对中国PPP市场的基本情况进行简述。

1.5.1 全国管理库PPP项目情况和阶段分布

截至2019年末,管理库项目累计9 440个,同比增加786个,增长9.1%;累计投资额14.4万亿元,同比增加1.2万亿元,增长9.1%,覆盖31个省份及新疆兵团和19个行业领域;落地项目累计6 330个,投资额9.9万亿元,落地率67.1%,比2018年末上升12.9个百分点;开工项目累计3 708个,投资额5.6万亿元,开工率58.6%,比2018年末上升10.9个百分点;管理库准备、采购、执行阶段项目数分别为1 409个、1 701个、6 330个,投资额分别为2.0万亿元、2.5万亿元、9.9万亿元(如图1-2所示),目前无移交阶段项目。

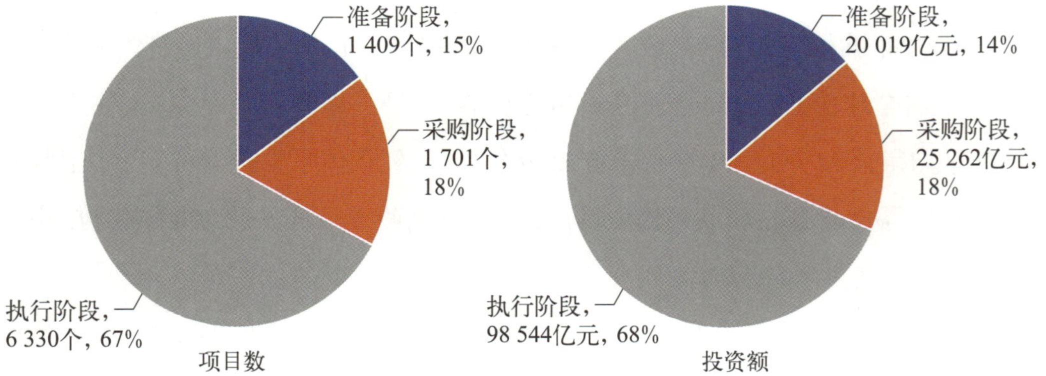

图1-2 2019年末管理库各阶段项目情况

① 本部分的数据和分析要点主要来自财政部政府和社会资本合作中心发布的全国PPP综合信息平台项目管理库2019年年报。由于采样截止日期和数据缺失等原因,我们后文中纳入指数编制的样本与本部分的样本并不严格对应。

2019年，PPP市场由过去的重数量和速度向重质量转变。全年新入管理库项目1 434个，同比减少2 640个，下降64.8%；新入库项目投资额2.2万亿元，同比减少3.6万亿元，下降62.1%。每月新入库项目数和投资额波动不定，如图1-3所示。各地清退项目648个，涉及投资额8 023亿元。由于管理库内存量项目结构调整导致投资额变化，因而新入库项目投资额减去退库项目投资额与净入库项目投资额不一致。

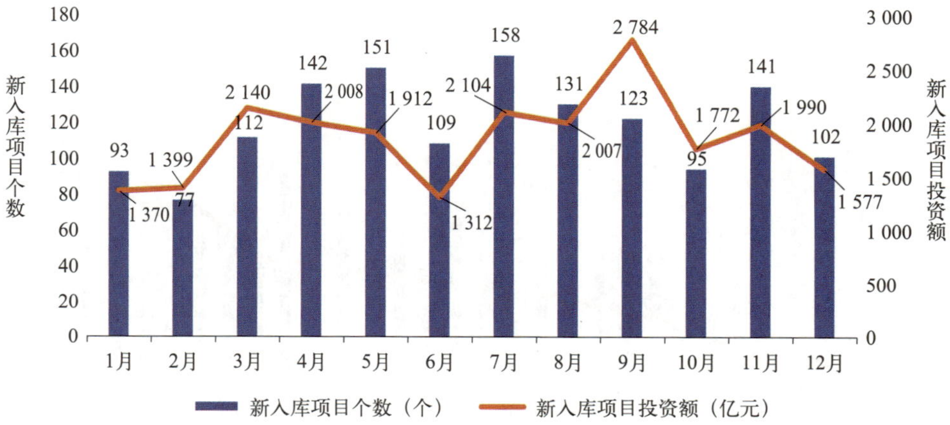

图1-3 2019年1 434个新入库项目按月分布情况

全年净入库项目（即2019年末比2018年末新增在库项目）786个，同比减少731个，下降48.2%；净入库项目投资额1.2万亿元，同比减少1.2万亿元，下降50.0%。1—12月每月净入库项目数及投资额波动不定，如图1-4所示。

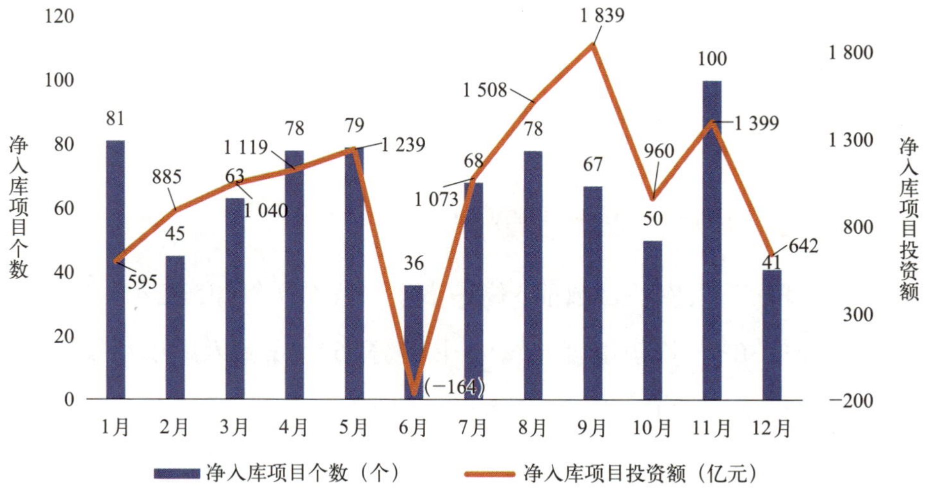

图1-4 2019年管理库每月净入库项目数和投资额

1.5.2 管理库项目地区分布情况

2019年各地新入库项目数排名前5位的分别是河南143个、广东103个、江西80个、山东（含青岛）80个、山西75个；新入库项目投资额排名前5位的是河南2 243亿元、四川1 797亿元、贵州1 752亿元、天津1 511亿元、重庆1 507亿元。2019年新入库项目数、投资额地区分布如图1-5所示。

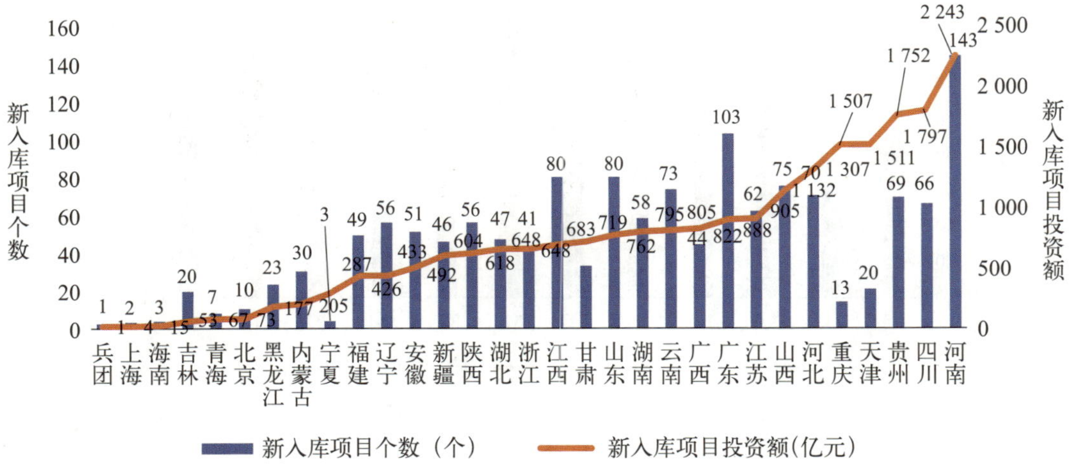

图1-5 2019年新入库项目数、投资额地区分布

截至2019年末，按累计项目数排序，管理库前5位是山东（含青岛）768个、河南753个、四川559个、广东519个、贵州516个，合计占入库项目总数的33.0%。按累计投资额排序，管理库前5位是贵州1.2万亿元、云南1.1万亿元、四川1.0万亿元、浙江9 767亿元、河南9 664亿元，合计占入库项目总投资额的36.8%。截至2019年末，管理库各地项目数、投资额情况分别如图1-6和图1-7所示。

1.5.3 管理库项目行业分布情况

2019年管理库新入库项目数前5位是市政工程629个、交通运输174个、生态建设和环境保护130个、城镇综合开发95个、教育62个；新入库项目投资额前5位是交通运输8 633亿元、市政工程5 298亿元、城镇综合开发2 779亿元、生态建设和环境保护1 471亿元、林业749亿元。2019年新入库项目数、投资额行业分布如图1-8所示。

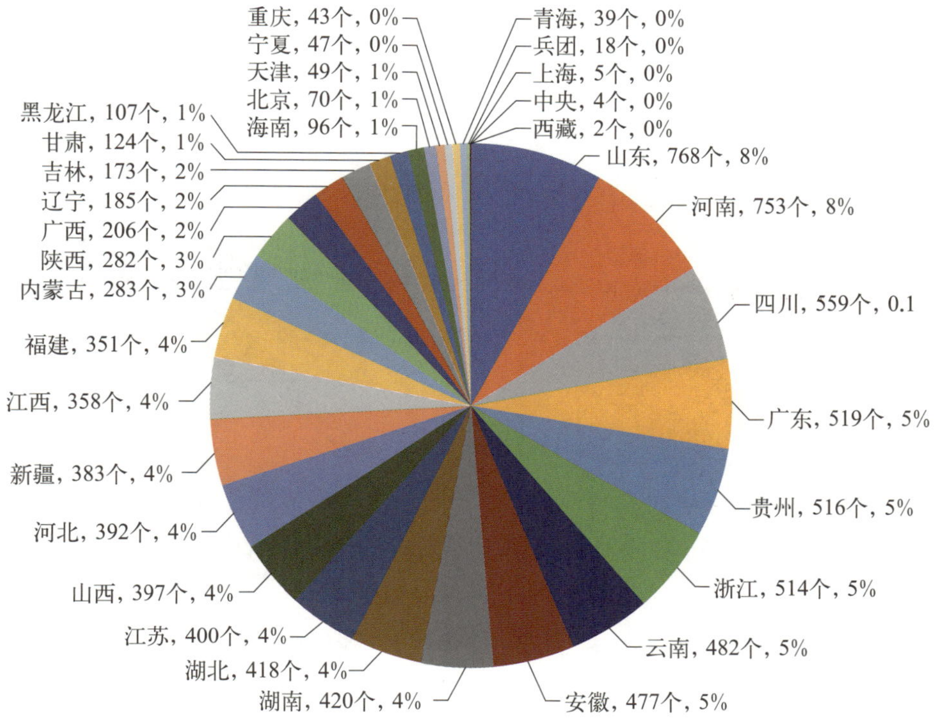

图1-6　截至2019年末各地管理库项目数

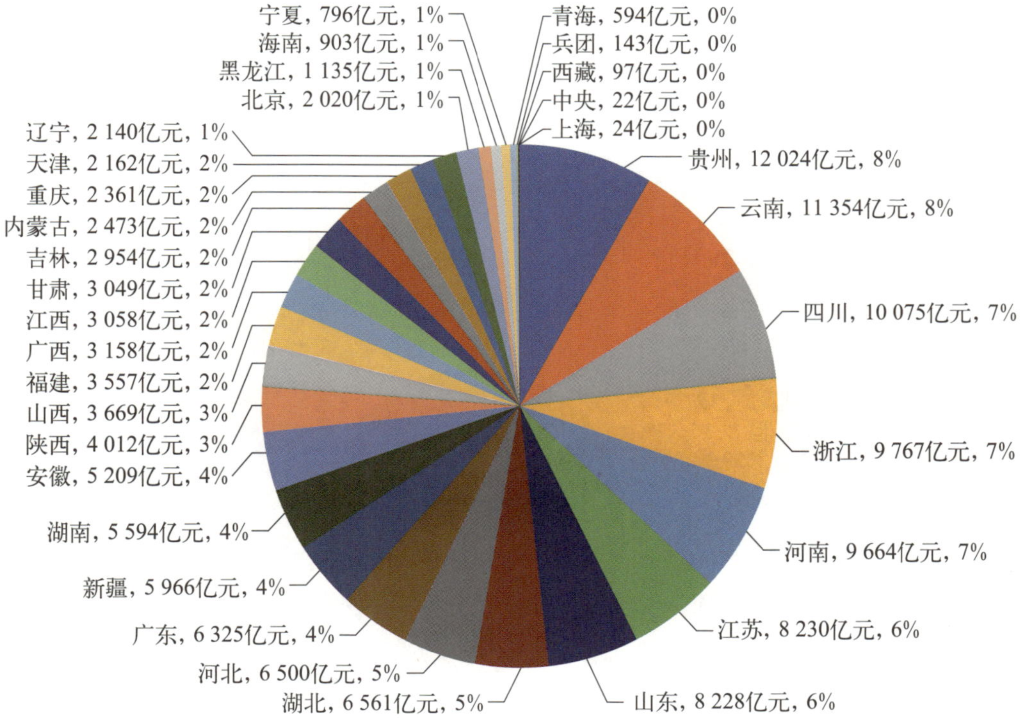

图1-7　截至2019年末各地管理库项目投资额

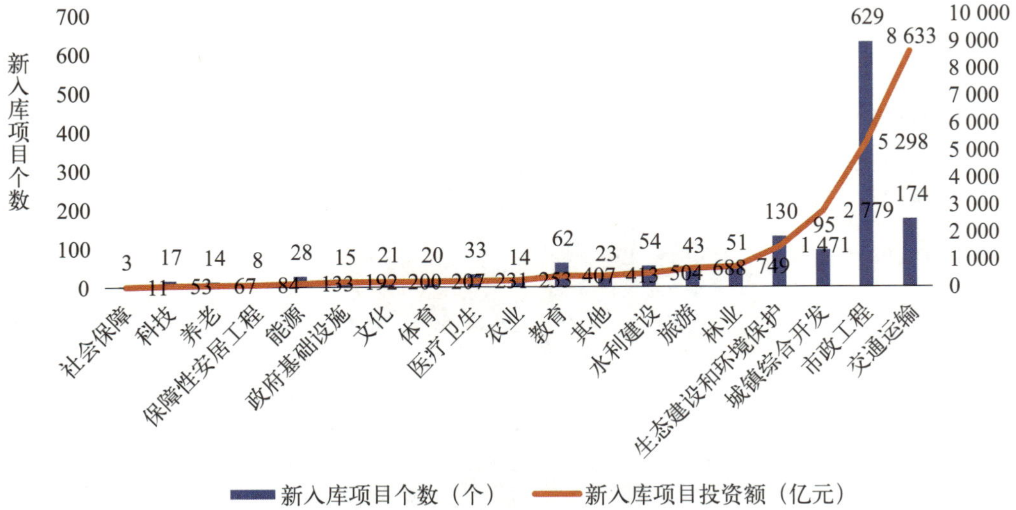

图1-8　2019年新入库项目数、投资额行业分布

截至2019年末，管理库各行业累计PPP项目数、投资额如图1-9和图1-10所示。其中，项目数前5位是市政工程3 793个、交通运输1 317个、生态建设和环境保护924个、城镇综合开发611个、教育447个，合计占管理库项目总数的75.2%；项目投资额前5位是交通运输4.6万亿元、市政工程4.2万亿元、城镇综合开发2.0万亿元、生态建设和环境保护9 988亿元、旅游4 666亿元，合计占管理库总投资额的84.2%。

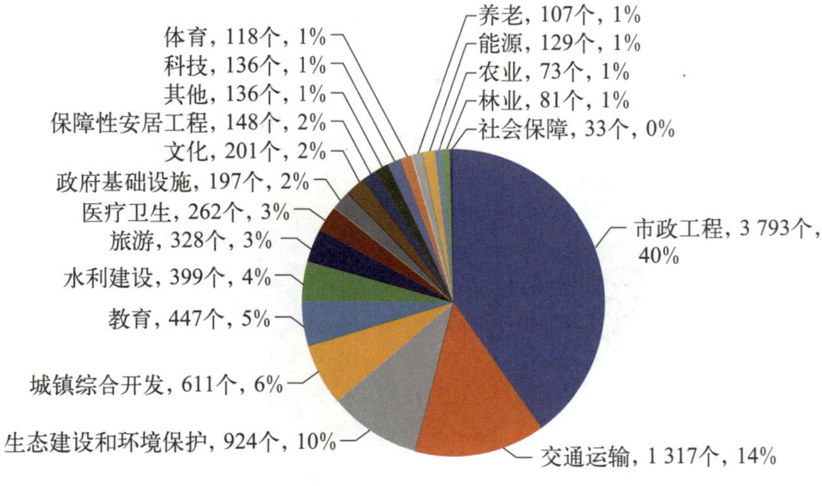

图1-9　截至2019年末管理库项目数行业分布

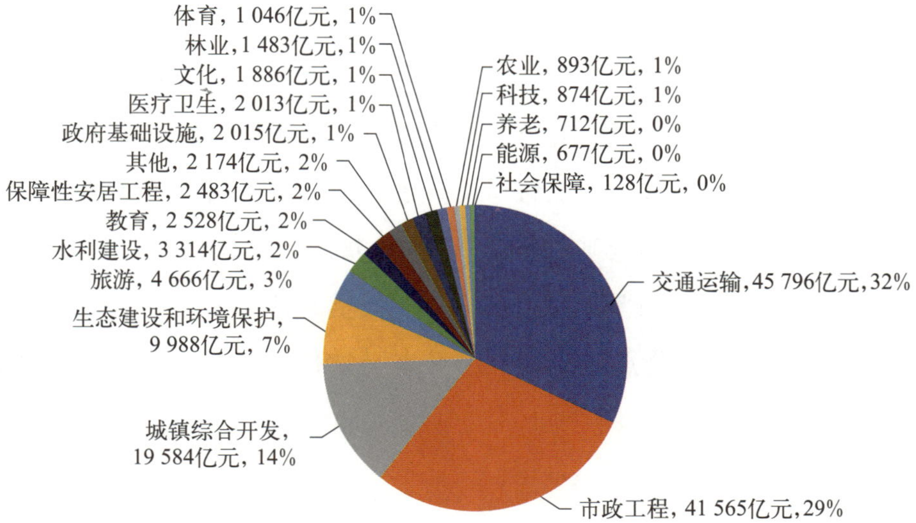

图1-10 截至2019年末管理库项目投资额行业分布

1.5.4 签约落地项目情况

2019年，管理库落地项目1 639个，投资额2.7万亿元，项目个数比2018年减少323个，投资额增加584亿元，上升2.3%。

截至2019年末，落地率67.1%，同比上升12.9个百分点。2018年12月末至2019年12月末管理库项目落地率变化如图1-11所示。

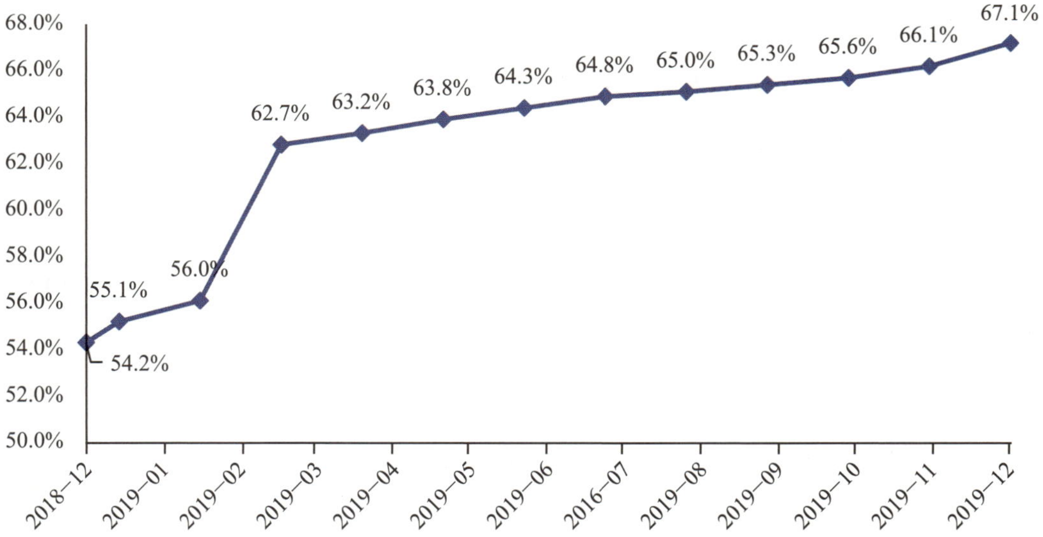

图1-11 2018年12月末至2019年12月末管理库落地率变化

1.5.5 开工项目情况

2019年，开工项目1 471个，比2018年增加393个；投资额2.4万亿元，比2018年增加8 768亿元，上升56.4%，有了大幅增长。截至2019年末，累计开工项目3 708个，投资额5.6万亿元，分别占落地项目的58.6%和56.7%。

开工率，即开工项目与落地项目数之比。截至2019年末，开工率为58.6%，比2018年末上升10.9个百分点。2018年12月末至2019年12月末开工率变化如图1-12所示。

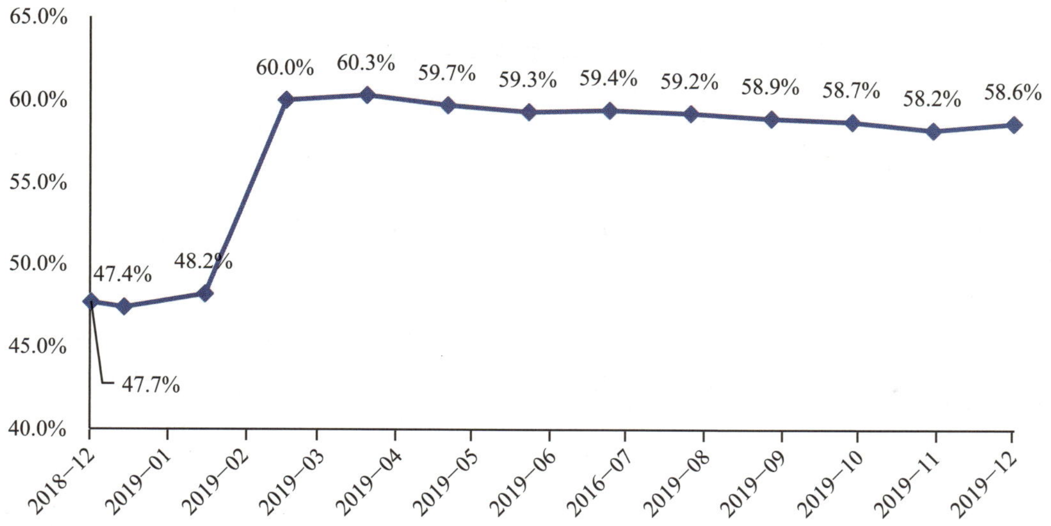

图1-12　2018年12月末至2019年12月末开工率变化

1.5.6 管理库项目按回报机制分布情况

按照三种回报机制统计，2019年使用者付费类项目净入库3个，投资额3 142亿元，占净入库项目投资额的25.9%；可行性缺口补助（即政府市场混合付费）类项目净入库697个，投资额9 925亿元，占净入库项目投资额的81.8%；政府付费类项目净入库86个，投资额净减932亿元，占净入库项目投资额的−7.7%。

截至2019年末，累计使用者付费类项目629个，投资额1.4万亿元，分别占管理库的6.7%和9.6%；累计可行性缺口补助类项目5 418个、投资额9.7万亿元，分别占管理库的57.4%和67.1%；累计政府付费类项目3 393个，投资额3.3万亿元，分别占管理库的35.9%和23.2%，如图1-13和图1-14所示。

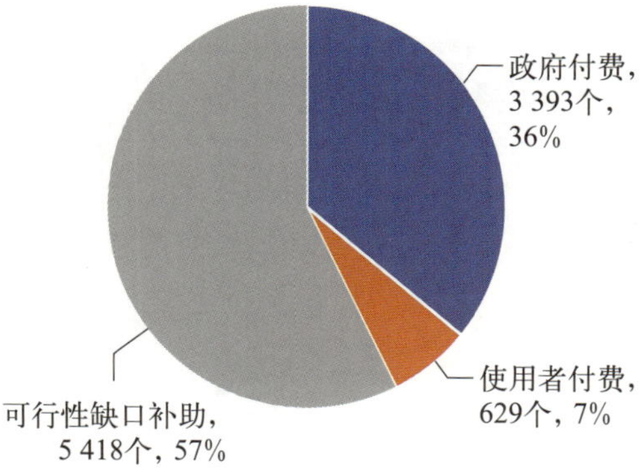

图1-13 2019年末管理库项目数按回报机制分布

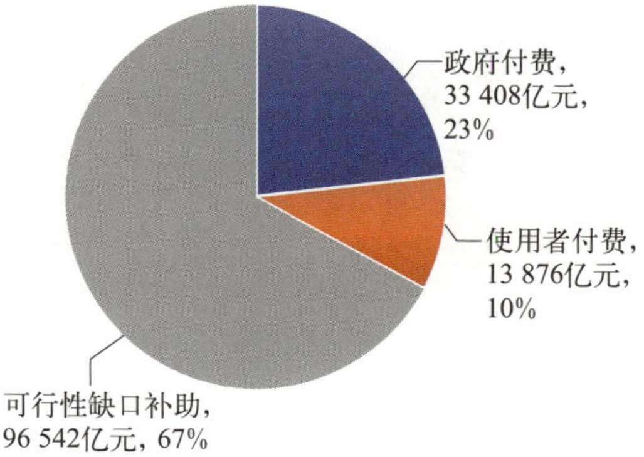

图1-14 2019年末管理库项目投资额按回报机制分布

2

指标体系与计算方法

2.1 指标体系构建

2.1.1 指标体系基本原则

指标体系是否科学、合理，直接关系到指数编制的质量和结果评估的可靠性。为此，设定的指标体系必须客观合理地、尽可能全面地反映影响PPP信息透明度的所有因素，同时也要考虑到数据的可获得性、可靠性等。要建立一套既科学又可执行的PPP市场透明度评价指标体系，必须遵照一定的原则。因此，课题组首先明确了PPP透明度评价指标体系构建中应该坚持的几个原则，主要包括层次性原则、共通性原则、连续性原则等。

（1）层次性原则。层次性指的是指标体系自身的多重性。由于PPP信息内容涵盖的多层次性，指标体系也必须由多层次结构组成，才能反映出各层次的特征。同时，各个要素相互联系构成一个有机整体，能从项目的不同阶段、不同层次反映PPP市场透明度的总体情况。具体而言，参考PPP相关信息公开管理办法的精神，PPP市场透明度的指标体系可以分为总指数、分阶段二级指标以及底层具体指标三个层次，由此透明度指数可以分为总指数，以及识别阶段、准备阶段、采购阶段、执行阶段和移交阶段五个阶段的分指数等。当然，考虑到不同项目可能处于不同的阶段，因而并不是每一个项目的透明度指数都完整囊括这五个阶段。

（2）共通性原则。课题组评价的是每一个PPP项目的信息公开透明度，由于项目会存在一些特有的信息，因而基于可比性的考虑，课题组主要选取那些适用于全体项目样本的指标。那些不是对所有项目均适用的指标，如“设计文件及批复文件”“项目采购阶段调整、更新的政府方授权文件”“增减资情况”等，课题组暂时没有将其纳入指标体系，但会在报告末尾对完善该类指标信息披露工作的管理办法提供一些政策建议。

（3）连续性原则。本次编制的指数是课题组第三次评估PPP市场的透明度，因而指标体系不仅要反映2019年我国PPP项目信息披露的实际情况，而且还要考虑到其与2017年和2018年的衔接，保持指数的连续性，当然也要考虑到未来可能的变更。换言之，指标体系应具备较强的动态适应性。课题组希望可以通过长期追踪的方式，对我国PPP市场的信息公开状况进行持续性评估。

（4）突出性原则。指标的选择要尽量全面，但同时也应该区别主次和轻重，要突出重点。对于某些特别重要的指标，要尽量多地选择相关字段。同时，课题组通过专家问卷调查的方式，对比较重要的指标设置高分，对不太重要的信息设置低分。例如物有所值评价方面、财政承受能力论证方面，可以赋予比那些基本项目信息等更重要的分数值。

（5）公正性原则。作为一个政策效果评估的报告，PPP市场透明度报告发布后，预期会对不同的地区和项目产生一定的影响。因此，透明度指数报告必须坚持公平、公正的原则，做到一视同仁，坚持成绩和问题都点到、都说透。既要如实展示不同地区、不同类型的PPP项目信息公开的客观状况，同时也要尽可能讲清楚导致各地区和行业等PPP市场透明度指数结果出现差异的各类原因，特别是那些客观、外生的原因，要尽量做到公正公允。

（6）时点性原则。本次评估的是截止到2019年12月31日财政部PPP综合信息平台管理库里所有的项目信息披露情况，属于存量概念，即评估的对象是截至这个时点所有PPP项目历史累加的信息披露情况。囿于数据的可获得性，课题组的评估没有涉及这些信息披露的具体时间等动态特征，例如，部分指标作为适时公开指标，理论上课题组除了可以评估其是否披露外，还可以评估其披露的及时性，这也是信息披露工作的重要评价方面，然而课题组无法获得相关指标披露具体时点等细节信息，因而这方面的信息就暂时无法纳入课题组的指标体系。

2.1.2 指标体系设计依据

（1）设计依据。评估PPP市场的信息公开现状，首要的依据就是相关政策文件。2017年1月23日，财政部正式发布《政府和社会资本合作（PPP）综合信息平台信息公开管理暂行办法》（即1号文），这是主管部门对PPP项目信息披露工作的主要操作指南。各地的PPP项目信息披露工作均是按照该文件执行的。因此，1号文的政策细则便是课题组设计PPP市场透明度指标体系时最主要的依据。课题组设计的指标体系主要来自该1号文的要求，1号文当中没有要求的信息，原则上就不进入课题组的指标体系，这样处理是为了使指标体系对不同地区而言是公平公正的。

（2）数据来源。根据主管部门财政部政府和社会资本合作中心的规定，各地的PPP项目均要在财政部政府和社会资本合作中心网站首页开设的PPP综合信息平台系统中进行入库和公布。考虑到数据来源的一致性，课题组选择该PPP综合信息平台系统作为主要数据来源。因此，本报告中指标设置的主要依据是1号文，数据来源则主要为财政部PPP综合信息平台系统。当然，由于1号文正式实施的时间还不长，因而还存在一些需要完善的地方，比如很多字段在1号文当中是要求披露的，但目前在PPP官方披露网站上并没有展示，从而无法纳入指标体系中，只能在未来PPP官方信息网站上披露的信息增加后再进一步完善相关指标体系。最后，由于财政部PPP综合信息平台上披露的个别字段的说法略有调整，因而在这次评估中也对相关指标进行了同步更新。

（3）评估对象。财政部办公厅于2017年11月10日发布《关于规范政府和社会资本合作（PPP）综合信息平台项目库管理的通知》，要求在全国PPP综合信息平台项目库基础上构建储备库和管理库。该文认为："储备库是指识别阶段项目，是地方政府部门有意愿采用PPP模式的备选项目，但尚未完成物有所值评价和财政承受能力论证的审核。管理库是指准备、采购、执行和移交阶段项目。"结合PPP主管部门的政策意见，课题组将分析对象限定在至少已经进入准备阶段的项目，即已经进入管理库中的项目。此外，课题组也剔除了个别在PPP综合信息平台中无法查询到的项目。最终纳入课题组分析对象的样本共计9 398个，与2018年相比有一定的增加。

（4）获取方式。课题组以政府和社会资本合作中心网站可获取数据为基础①，同时参考2017年1号文中的要求来筛选及获取指标，并对其进行归类。经过课题组的

① 财政部PPP中心也向课题组直接提供了部分数据。课题组对此表示感谢。

整理，指标体系共包含80个指标字段，其中有5个指标因为种种原因未纳入本年度的透明度指标体系（我们将在2.1.4小节详细解释相关原因），因而课题组评估2019年中国PPP市场透明度时共使用了75个指标字段，并对其进行了逐个提取，包括网站直接阅读提取和下载PDF文件阅读提取等方式。

值得注意的是，在75个字段中，有33个指标的信息需要阅读相应PDF文件后方可提取，然而课题组在人工阅读后发现，其中存在“伪造”的样本：一些项目显示某个指标上传了PDF附件，但实际上只是一个空白文件或虚假文件，这是因为依据系统规定，该PDF 文件是必填项，如不上传，整个项目就无法上网入库，也无法进行下一步操作，因此，为了整个项目信息的入库工作，一些项目选择了上传一个虚假的或空白的PDF文件。为了甄别并在未来减少这些“虚假上传”的行为，保障评估工作的科学和公平，课题组对所有项目的所有PDF文件进行了细致的人工核实，并对这些“虚假上传”行为进行“惩罚”。具体而言，对于33个PDF文件指标，课题组设置的得分细则为：上传文件且为真，可以赋值为1；没有上传文件，赋值为0；上传文件但为假文件，则赋值为−1。此外，还有部分文件字段上传不够全面，对于这种情形，课题组将其赋值为0.5。

2.1.3　指标体系具体构建

根据1号文的要求，PPP项目的有些信息应该即时公开，而有些信息则可以适时公开。其中，即时公开的指标很容易处理，但适时公开指标则比较棘手，原因是课题组需要界定什么时候公开算是“适时”，而课题组无法获得项目进入某个阶段的具体时间或该信息何时就应该被披露等信息。不过，按照1号文的规定，多数适时公开都是指“进入执行阶段的6个月内公开”，因此，为了克服这一难题，课题组延续2017年和2018年评估的做法，决定选择2019年6月底进入执行阶段的项目作为适时公开的分析对象，这样对于在2019年6月底之前已经进入执行阶段的项目，如果截至2019年12月31日仍未公开对应的信息，课题组就可以判定该项目没有“适时”公开相应信息，换句话说，适时公开的工作做得不到位。

不过，这样处理后，即时公开信息对应的研究样本和适时公开信息对应的研究样本就完全不同了。具体而言，截至2019年12月底进入管理库的总样本有9 398个，这些样本都可以作为即时公开透明度的评估样本；但在2019年6月底以前进入执行阶段的样本只有5 162个，这些样本将作为适时公开透明度的评估样本。对于单个项目而言，有些项目同时包含了即时公开和适时公开的信息，有些项目则仅包含即时公开的信息，无法放在一个框架下来评估。因此，对于单个项目的信息透明度而言，PPP信息透明度指数就包含两个独立的指标，一个是即时公开透明度指数，另一个是适时公开透明度指数。不过考虑到最终主要在地区和行业领域等层面上对PPP市场透明度进行评估分析，因此，在总指数计算上，课题组将通过层次分析法对即时公开透明度指数和适时公开透明度指数进行赋权，在省份、行业等层面上合成一个PPP市场透明度的总指数。

即时公开透明度指数和适时公开透明度指数下面均包括分阶段指数和具体指标两个层次。PPP项目一般分为五个阶段：识别阶段、准备阶段、采购阶段、执行阶段和移交阶段，但我国目前还没有进入移交阶段的PPP项目，因此，无论是即时公开透明度指数还是适时公开透明度指数，都暂不包含这一阶段。此外，由于对适时公开的指标，执行阶段也缺少合适的指标字段，因而适时公开透明度指数也不包含执行阶段的信息。由此，最终即时公开透明度指数包含识别阶段、准备阶段、采购阶段和执行阶段四个阶段，适时公开透明度指数则包含识别阶段、准备阶段和采购阶段三个阶段。

最终的指标体系层级如图2-1所示，即时公开透明度指数和适时公开透明度指数的具体指标体系则分别如表2-1和表2-2所示。

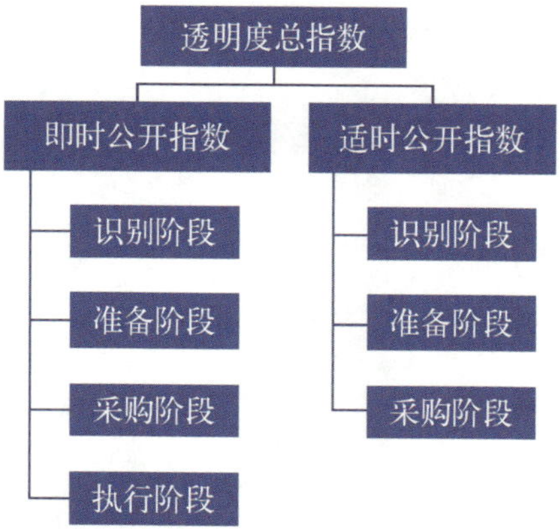

图2-1　PPP透明度指标体系层级

表2-1 PPP即时公开信息透明度指数指标体系

一级指标	具体指标	备注
识别阶段	项目总投资	
	拟合作期限	
	二级行业	
	项目运作方式	
	回报机制	
	项目发起时间	
	发起类型	
	发起人名称	
	项目概况	
	负责实施方案编制的机构名称	
	负责实施方案编制机构联系人	
	负责实施方案编制机构的联系电话	
	项目联系人	
	项目联系电话	
	财政联系人	
	财政联系电话	
	项目用地总面积	
	计划开发年度	
	实施方案描述	
	实施机构	
	实施机构联系人	
	实施机构联系人电话	
	采购社会资本方式的选择	
	项目合作范围（识别）	
	物有所值定性评价指标及权重、评分标准、评分结果	
	物有所值评价通过与否的评价结论（含财政部门对报告的审核意见）	

（续表）

一级指标	具 体 指 标	备注
识别阶段	本项目以及年度全部已实施和拟实施的PPP项目财政支出责任数额及年度预算安排情况，以及每一年度全部PPP项目从预算中安排的支出责任占一般公共预算支出比例情况	
	财政承受能力论证的测算依据、主要因素和指标	
	通过财政承受能力论证与否的结论	
准备阶段	拟引入社会资本投资额	
	政府拟出资额	
	审核通过实施方案的政府名称	
	政府方授权文件，包括对实施机构、PPP项目合同的政府方签约主体、政府方出资代表等的授权	
	本级政府对实施方案审核通过时间	
	政府对实施方案的审核通过文件	
采购阶段	项目资格预审公告（含资格预审申请文件）	
	预中标及成交结果公告；中标、成交结果公告及中标通知书	
	项目本级行业主管部门对拟签署PPP合同的审核意见	
	项目本级财政部门对拟签署PPP合同的审核意见	
	项目本级法制部门对拟签署PPP合同的审核意见	
	项目本级人民政府是否批准了拟签署的PPP合同	
	批准日期	
	项目本级人民政府对PPP项目合同中约定的政府跨年度财政支出责任纳入中期财政规划的审核意见	
	审核日期	
执行阶段	项目公司名称	
	项目公司成立时间	
	项目公司注册资金	
	项目公司经济性质	
	股东认缴	

（续表）

一级指标	具 体 指 标	备注
执行阶段	本级人民政府对政府方出资代表的授权	
	重大违约及履约担保的提取请款，对公众的处理情况等	—
	本级政府或其职能部门作出的对项目可能产生重大影响的决定	—
	项目或项目直接相关方重大纠纷、涉诉或涉仲情况	—
	本级PPP项目目录、本机PPP项目示范点库及项目变化情况、本级人大批准的政府对PPP项目的财政预算、执行及决算情况等	—
	本级人民政府对政府方出资代表的授权	
移交阶段	移交工作组的组成、移交程序、移交标准等移交方案	—
	移交资产或设施或权益清单、移交资产或权益评估报告、性能测试方案	—
	移交项目资产或设施上各类担保或权益限制的解除情况	—
	项目设施移交标准达标测试结果	—
	项目后评价报告，以及项目后续运作方式	—

注："—" 表示暂不适用，最终未纳入本年度透明度指数的指标体系，但未来随着数据系统的完善和数据可获得性的增强，可能会纳入指标体系。

表2-2 PPP适时公开信息透明度指数指标体系

一级指标	具 体 指 标	备注
识别阶段	物有所值评价报告及批复附件	
	财政承受能力论证报告及批复附件	
	新建或改扩建项目建议书及批复文件	
	可行性研究报告	
	设计文件及批复文件	
	存量公共资产或权益的资产评估报告	
准备阶段	物有所值评价完成时间	
	财政承受能力论证完成时间	
	审核通过的项目实施方案及修正案	

（续表）

一级指标	具 体 指 标	备注
采购阶段	资格预审：公告时间	
	资格预审：预审时间	
	项目采购：公告时间	
	采购结果：响应文件评审时间	
	采购结果：结果确认谈判时间	
	采购结果：政府审核时间	
	采购结果：合同签署时间	
	采购结果：合同公布时间	
	采购结果：合同公布媒体	
	合同签订的项目投资额	
	采购文件	
	资格预审专家评审结论性意见及资格预审专家名单	
	响应文件专家评审结论性意见及评审专家名单	
	确认谈判工作组成员名单	
	PPP项目合同附件	
	本级政府支出责任确认文件	
执行阶段	融资额度、融资主要条件及融资交割情况	—
	项目施工许可证、建设进度、质量及造价等与PPP项目合同的符合性审查	—
	社会资本或公司的年度运营情况及绩效达标情况	—
	项目公司绩效监测报告、中期评估报告、项目重大变更或终止情况、项目定价及历次调价情况	—
	项目公司成本监审、所有的PPP合同修订协议或补充协议	—
	项目公司财务报告相关内容，包括项目收费情况，项目获得的政府补贴情况，项目公司资产负债情况	—

注：“—”表示暂不适用、最终未纳入本年度透明度指数的指标体系，但未来随着数据系统的完善和数据可获得性的增强，可能会纳入指标体系。

2.1.4 其他核心问题说明

(1)关于没有纳入指标体系的字段的说明。有部分政府和社会资本合作中心网站上可获取的指标没有纳入2019年透明度指数指标体系中(详情请参看表2-1和表2-2),主要包括以下几种情形:第一,部分指标不是对所有项目均适用。如"项目采购阶段调整、更新的政府方授权文件""增减资情况"等,不是对所有项目均适用,不属于强制披露的范围。第二,缺失判断是否进入适时披露的时间节点。部分指标披露时点的要求为事件发生次年4月30日之前,由于不知道是否发生了该事件或何时发生,如执行阶段的多个指标"项目公司成本监审情况""PPP合同修订协议或补充协议"等,因而这些指标暂时也无法纳入评估范围。第三,无信息时无法判断相关事件是否发生。对于临时性重大事项,如"重大违约及履约担保的提取情况,对公众投诉的处理情况等",要求10日内公开,但相关信息没有披露时无法判断该事件究竟是没有发生,还是发生了没有披露,因而暂时也无法纳入评估范围。当然,对于这些问题,通过项目信息管理系统的完善,未来有可能可以纳入评估范围,我们将在报告中给出课题组的一些思考与建议。

(2)本报告主要评估是否进行了信息披露,而不是信息披露内容的"质量"。本报告评估的主要内容是PPP项目的信息披露工作,包括这些信息披露的完整程度、重要程度等的区分,但除了明显造假外,课题组的评估不涉及其披露的具体内容的"质量"和"优劣"。具体而言,对于一项指标,一个项目公开披露了其相关信息,在课题组的评估中就是得分的,但该信息中反映的具体工作可能做得很好,也可能做得很差,这暂时不在课题组的评估范围内。例如,对于财政承受能力论证报告的PDF文件,作为一个非常重要的信息,课题组通过人工核查的方法,一一核实其披露情况,同时专家打分中也可能对其赋予较高的分值,这些都是评估中要考虑的因素。至于财政承受能力论证报告做得是否规范、科学,论证是否充分,结论是否可靠等内容,则不在课题组的评估范围内。因为从逻辑上讲,即便这份财政承受能力论证报告不太规范,或者质量不高,但只要有关责任方选择了真实公开披露该报告,那在信息披露工作上就是得分的。当然,未来课题组会考虑超越"信息透明度评估"的范畴,对这些重点报告中所反映的某地或某领域PPP工作的规范性进行重点的专题评估。

2.2 指数计算方法

2.2.1 计算方法简介

在多指标综合评价中，权重确定直接影响评价的结果。确定权重的方法有很多，根据计算权重时原始数据的来源不同，大体上可分为主观赋权法和客观赋权法两大类。主观赋权法主要是由专家根据经验主观判断而得到，如Delphi法、层次分析法（The Analytic Hierarchy Process，AHP）、专家打分法等，这类方法能纳入权威专家对不同指标之间的相对重要程度的考量，但客观性稍差。客观赋权法主要是依据各指标的具体数值计算而得到，它不依赖于人的主观判断，因而客观性较强，但不一定能科学反映不同指标之间的相对重要程度，也不一定能满足决策者的主观要求。客观赋权法这类方法的代表有主成分分析法和变异系数法等。主观赋权法和客观赋权法各有优劣，本项目最终选择的是主观赋权法。具体而言，在计算各准则层指标对上层目标的权重时，课题组使用层次分析法；而在计算各具体指标对上一层准则层的权重时，课题组则选择了专家打分法。①

2.2.2 层次分析法

层次分析法是一种系统分析与决策的综合评价方法，它可以较合理地解决定性问题定量化的处理过程。层次分析法的主要特点是通过建立层次结构，把人们的判断转化为若干因素两两之间重要性的比较，从而把难以量化的定性判断转化为可操作的定量判断。

在所构建的层次分析模型中，通过调查判断，形成判定矩阵。当检验判定矩阵通过一致性检验时，则可以接受判定矩阵，并计算得出各指标的权重值；若该一致性检验未通过，则意味着判定矩阵的元素值需要调整，直至通过一致性检验为止。具体

① 课题组在计算各具体指标对上一层准则层的权重时，还使用了变异系数法，结果发现变异系数法与专家打分法得出的结果非常一致。最终选择专家打分法是因为这一方法更能够体现包括行业主管部门、高校学者、社会资本方在内的社会各界对不同指标重要性的看法与态度，而不是仅仅依赖于不同指标之间的统计特征，更有利于各个地区发现PPP信息披露工作中存在的问题并有针对性地改进。

地，层次分析法的实施步骤如下：

第一步，建立层次结构模型。通过对影响PPP信息透明度各因素的深入分析，将有关各因素按从属关系分解成若干层次，最上层为目标层，中间层为准则层，具体的指标在最下层。本报告的层级结构模型如图2-1所示。

第二步，构建判定矩阵。构建判定矩阵，比较两两具体指标之间的相对重要性。根据本项目构建的PPP项目透明度层级示意图，共涉及两个分类指数，因而涉及三个判定矩阵，分别是总指数判定矩阵（判定即时公开透明度指数和适时公开透明度指数在合成PPP市场透明度总指数时的相对重要性）、即时公开透明度指数判定矩阵（判定识别阶段、准备阶段、采购阶段和执行阶段的分指数在合成即时公开透明度指数时的相对重要性）和适时公开透明度指数判定矩阵（判定识别阶段、准备阶段和采购阶段的分指数在合成适时公开透明度指数时的相对重要性）。

一般地，假设比较n个因素c_1，c_2，…，c_n对上一层因素的影响，判定矩阵要求每次两两比较两个因素对上一层因素的相对重要性，这一相对重要性通常用数值1～9来体现，以构成判定矩阵的每个元素赋值c_{ij}（数值的含义如表2-3所示，一般由具备丰富经验的专家来选择）。全部比较结果构成“成对比较矩阵”，也称为“正互反矩阵”。

表2-3　判定矩阵标度含义

标度c_{ij}	定　义	含　义
1	同等重要	c_i和c_j的影响相同
3	稍微重要	c_i比c_j的影响稍强
5	较强重要	c_i比c_j的影响强
7	强烈重要	c_i比c_j的影响明显地强
9	极端重要	c_i比c_j的影响绝对地强
2、4、6、8	两相邻判断的中间值	c_i与c_j的影响之比在上述两个相邻等级之间
1/2…1/9	倒数	c_i与c_j的影响之比为上面α_{ij}的互反数

$$C=\begin{pmatrix} c_{11} & c_{12} & \cdots & c_{1n} \\ c_{21} & c_{22} & \cdots & c_{2n} \\ \vdots & \vdots & \vdots & \vdots \\ c_{n1} & c_{n2} & \cdots & c_{nn} \end{pmatrix}$$

$C=(c_{ij})_{n\times n}, c_{ij}>0, c_{ji}=\dfrac{1}{c_{ij}}, c_{ii}=1$。

若正互反矩阵C满足$c_{ij}\times c_{jk}=c_{ik}$,则称C为完全一致性矩阵。

第三步,计算判定矩阵的最大特征值及其特征向量。在运用判定矩阵确定各指标权重时,实际上就是求解判定矩阵的特征向量。通过解正互反矩阵的最大特征值,可求得相应的特征向量,经归一化后即为权重向量。

$$CW=\lambda_{\max}W$$

第四步,一致性检验。首先,计算该n阶判定矩阵的一致性指标值CI。

$$CI=\frac{\lambda_{\max}-n}{n-1}$$

其次,计算平均随机一致性指标RI。从1～9及其倒数中随机抽取数字构成n阶正互反矩阵,计算其最大特征值;重复1 000次,得到1 000个随机正互反矩阵的最大特征值,再计算1 000个最大特征值的均值k;计算平均随机一致性指标。

$$RI=\frac{k-n}{n-1}$$

最后,计算一致性比率CR,并验证是否一致。

$$CR=\frac{CI}{RI}$$

当$CR<0.1$时,一般认为矩阵A的不一致程度在容许范围之内,可以用其特征向量作为权向量,否则需对判定矩阵进行修正(重复第二步和第三步),直至CR小于0.1

为止。

第五步，计算权重向量。将通过一致性检验的判定矩阵最大特征值所对应的特征向量进行归一化即可得到该层各因素对上层因素的权重大小。

根据这一方法，课题组邀请了包括高校学者代表（3位）、政府主管部门代表（3位）、社会资本方代表（3位）以及中介咨询机构代表（2位）在内的共11位业内权威专家进行三个判定矩阵的填写，并随后通过前文所述的层次分析法计算出各阶段的具体权重，最后求得不同专家所赋权重的平均数。附件一给出了专家判定矩阵调查表。表2-4则给出了根据专家判定矩阵计算出的权重表。其中，即时公开透明度指数方面，识别阶段、准备阶段、采购阶段和执行阶段的分指数在合成即时公开透明度指数时的权重分别为0.19、0.19、0.4和0.22；在适时公开透明度指数方面，识别阶段、准备阶段和采购阶段的分指数在合成适时公开透明度指数时的权重分别为0.25、0.30和0.45；而在将适时公开透明度指数和即时公开透明度指数加总合成PPP市场透明度总指数时，根据专家填写的判定矩阵计算出两者的权重分别是0.61和0.39。

表2-4 透明度指数专家判定矩阵权重表

即时公开透明度指数		适时公开透明度指数		总指数权重	
阶 段	权 重	阶 段	权 重	分指数	权 重
识别阶段	0.19	识别阶段	0.25	适时公开	0.39
准备阶段	0.19	准备阶段	0.30	即时公开	0.61
采购阶段	0.4	采购阶段	0.45	—	—
执行阶段	0.22	—	—	—	—

2.2.3 具体指标权重计算方法

以上AHP层次分析法确定了中间各层级相对其上一层级的权重大小，还需要确定最下层（即各具体指标）对其上一层的权重大小，对此，课题组使用了专家打分法。

具体而言，根据上文所讨论的内容，特别是其中的"突出性原则"，课题组将通过专家打分的方法，对其中的具体指标进行打分。经过专家打分后，不同的具体指标就相当于包含了一定的权重。课题组将不同的具体指标划分为"一般""重要"和"特别重要”三种程度，分别用1分、2分和3分来表示，然后交由专家对不同的指标进行赋分。数值越高，代表该具体指标相对越重要。课题组同样邀请了包括高校学者代表、政府主管部门代表、社会资本方代表以及中介咨询机构代表在内的共11位专家进行打分。表2-5和表2-6给出了专家打分的具体结果。需要进一步说明的是，上述不同指标的具体得分都是在某阶段内相互对比的，而不是直接进行全部指标间的对比。为清晰展示这一点，我们在表2-5和表2-6中列出了得分所对应的在本阶段内的具体权重。

表2-5 即时公开透明度指数具体指标专家打分结果

所属阶段	具 体 指 标	得分	权重
识别阶段	项目总投资	2.455	4.4
	拟合作期限	2.273	4.1
	二级行业	1.091	1.9
	项目运作方式	2.182	3.9
	回报机制	2.909	5.2
	项目发起时间	1.636	2.9
	发起类型	1.455	2.6
	发起人名称	1.182	2.1
	项目概况	2.000	3.6
	负责实施方案编制的机构名称	1.909	3.4
	负责实施方案编制机构联系人	1.364	2.4
	负责实施方案编制机构的联系电话	1.364	2.4
	项目联系人	1.455	2.6
	项目联系电话	1.455	2.6
	财政联系人	1.455	2.6
	财政联系电话	1.455	2.6
	项目用地总面积	2.000	3.6
	计划开发年度	2.000	3.6

（续表）

所属阶段	具 体 指 标	得分	权重
识别阶段	采购社会资本方式的选择	2.455	4.4
	实施方案描述	2.364	4.2
	实施机构	1.455	2.6
	实施机构联系人	1.455	2.6
	实施机构联系人电话	1.364	2.4
	项目合作范围（识别）	2.182	3.9
	物有所值定性评价指标及权重、评分标准、评分结果	2.545	4.5
	物有所值评价通过与否的评价结论（含财政部门对报告的审核意见）	2.636	4.7
	本项目以及年度全部已实施和拟实施的PPP项目财政支出责任数额及年度预算安排情况，以及每一年度全部PPP项目从预算中安排的支出责任占一般公共预算支出比例情况	2.818	5.0
	财政承受能力论证的测算依据、主要因素和指标	2.636	4.7
	通过财政承受能力论证与否的结论	2.455	4.4
准备阶段	拟引入社会资本投资额	2.182	18.2
	政府拟出资额	2.273	18.9
	审核通过实施方案的政府名称	1.727	14.4
	政府方授权文件，包括对实施机构、PPP项目合同的政府方签约主体、政府方出资代表等的授权	2.000	16.7
	本级政府对实施方案审核通过时间	1.727	14.4
	政府对实施方案的审核通过文件	2.091	17.4
采购阶段	项目资格预审公告（含资格预审申请文件）	2.364	11.2
	预中标及成交结果公告；中标、成交结果公告及中标通知书	2.545	12.1
	项目本级行业主管部门对拟签署PPP合同的审核意见	1.909	9.1
	项目本级财政部门对拟签署PPP合同的审核意见	2.000	9.5
	项目本级法制部门对拟签署PPP合同的审核意见	1.909	9.1
	项目本级人民政府是否批准了拟签署的PPP合同	2.455	11.6
	批准日期	2.455	11.6

（续表）

所属阶段	具 体 指 标	得分	权重
采购阶段	项目本级人民政府对PPP项目合同中约定的政府跨年度财政支出责任纳入中期财政规划的审核意见	2.727	12.9
	审核日期	2.727	12.9
执行阶段	项目公司名称	1.636	15.6
	项目公司成立时间	1.545	14.8
	项目公司注册资金	1.818	17.4
	项目公司经济性质	1.455	13.9
	股东认缴	2.000	19.1
	本级人民政府对政府方出资代表的授权	2.000	19.1

表2-6 适时公开透明度指数具体指标专家打分结果

一级指标	具 体 指 标	得分	权重
识别阶段	物有所值评价报告及批复附件	3.000	18.0
	财政承受能力论证报告及批复附件	3.000	18.0
	新建或改扩建项目建议书及批复文件	2.333	14.0
	可行性研究报告	2.667	16.0
	设计文件及批复文件	2.677	16.1
	存量公共资产或权益的资产评估报告	3.000	18.0
准备阶段	物有所值评价完成时间	1.556	33.3
	财政承受能力论证完成时间	1.556	33.3
	审核通过的项目实施方案及修正案	1.556	33.3
采购阶段	资格预审：公告时间	1.778	5.5
	资格预审：预审时间	1.667	5.2
	项目采购：公告时间	1.889	5.9
	采购结果：响应文件评审时间	1.556	4.8
	采购结果：结果确认谈判时间	1.889	5.9

（续表）

一级指标	具 体 指 标	得分	权重
采购阶段	采购结果：政府审核时间	1.778	5.5
	采购结果：合同签署时间	1.778	5.5
	采购结果：合同公布时间	1.889	5.9
	采购结果：合同公布媒体	1.444	4.5
	合同签订的项目投资额	2.556	8.0
	采购文件	2.889	9.0
	资格预审专家评审结论性意见及资格预审专家名单	2.111	6.6
	响应文件专家评审结论性意见及评审专家名单	2.111	6.6
	确认谈判工作组成员名单	1.222	3.8
	PPP 项目合同附件	2.556	8.0
	本级政府支出责任确认文件	3.000	9.3

2.2.4 指数合成计算过程

在多指标体系综合评价中，合成是指通过一定的算式将多个指标对事物不同方面的评价值综合在一起，以得到一个整体性的评价。可用于合成的数学方法很多，常见的合成模型有加权算术平均合成模型、加权几何平均合成模型、加权算术平均和加权几何平均联合使用的混合合成模型。三种模型都有各自的特点和适用场合，并没有优劣之分。在综合比较了三种合成方法之后，课题组选用了加权算术平均合成模型。加权算术平均合成模型的公式如下：

$$d = \sum_{i=1}^{n} w_i d_i$$

其中，d 为综合指数，w_i 为各评价指标归一化后的权重，d_i 为单个指标的评价得分，n 为评价指标的个数。具体指数合成时，是由下往上逐层汇总而成，先计算各层分组指数，然后由各层分组指数加权汇总得到综合指数（逐层级的计算过程详见第 4 章）。

具体而言，课题组首先通过网站读取方式获取各个具体指标的披露情况并赋值（共四种可能的取值，分别是：1代表公开且无明显造假行为，0代表没有公开，0.5代表部分公开，−1代表“虚假”公开）。之后根据专家打分法再将这些具体指标的得分加总，计算出某个阶段（比如适时公开的识别阶段等）的得分率（百分制）。随后，在此基础上再根据用层次分析法得出的权重，将不同阶段的分指数合成为即时公开透明度指数或适时公开透明度指数。最后，对即时公开透明度指数和适时公开透明度指数按照层次分析法得出的权重进行加权，计算出PPP市场透明度总指数。

根据课题组的指标体系设计和指数计算方法，理论上某项目的透明度总指数（或者分阶段指数）的满分可以达到100分，表示课题组设计的指标均得到了正确、完整的公开。最低分可以少于0分，即出现负分，表示该项目公布的信息中存在较多的虚假信息。0分则表示课题组设计的指标在该项目中均没有得到公开，也可能表示该项目公开了一些指标但同时也虚假公开了另外一些指标导致成绩被“抹杀”了，经过课题组“惩罚”后，近似等于所有指标均没有公开，当然这一情况也很不容易出现，特别是对于很多指标合成后的总指数。

需要强调的是，在计算总指数时，由于有些项目没有完整的五个业务阶段，因此，为保证指数的稳定性，课题组通过权重归一化使得相对权重保持一致。例如，在即时公开透明度指数的计算中，识别、准备、采购和执行四个阶段的权重分别为0.19、0.19、0.40和0.22，但某个项目只有前三个阶段，那么这三个阶段的权重就分别为：

识别阶段=0.19/(0.19+0.19+0.4)=0.244，

准备阶段=0.19/(0.19+0.19+0.4)=0.244，

采购阶段=0.4/(0.19+0.19+0.4)=0.512。

3

指数基本结果与总体分析

3.1 样本数据基本情况

3.1.1 样本概况

根据前文的介绍，课题组将PPP透明度指数编制分为即时公开透明度指数和适时公开透明度指数两部分。其中，即时公开透明度指数涉及9 398个项目样本，较2018年增加了762个；适时公开透明度指数则涉及5 162个项目，较2018年增加了1 612个。此外，在2019年的9 398个总样本当中，处于准备阶段、采购阶段和执行阶段的项目分别有1 398个、1 678个和6 322个。从图3-1可以看出，相对于2018年而言，2019年的项目样本中进入执行阶段的样本占比大幅上升，从54%提升到67%，而处于准备阶段和采购阶段的样本占比则均有所下降。

经历了2018年的规范整顿后①，PPP项目进入了规范有序推进阶段，因而2019年的项目总数相比上一年变动不大，退库比例也不再像上一年那样高②。在下文中我们

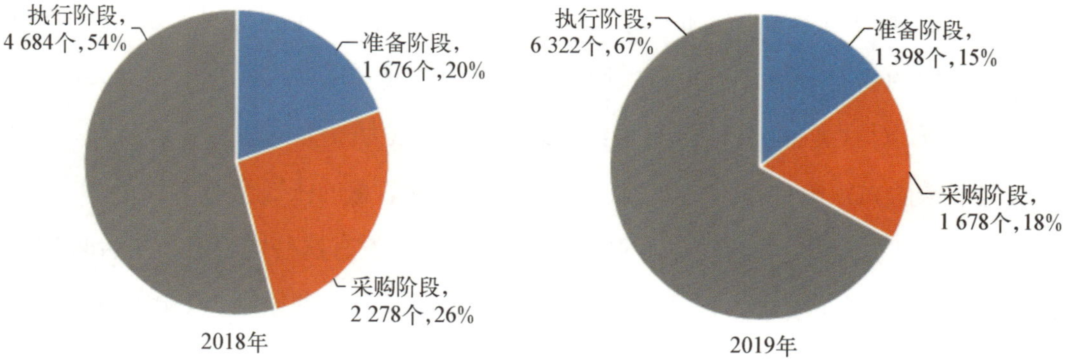

图3-1 2018年和2019年项目样本阶段分布

---

① 2018年PPP管理中的一大任务就是将不合格的PPP项目清理退库。详见《关于规范政府和社会资本合作（PPP）综合信息平台项目库管理的通知》（财金〔2017〕92号文）以及《关于进一步加强政府和社会资本合作（PPP）示范项目规范管理的通知》（财金〔2018〕54号文）。

② 根据我们后文的测算，2019年PPP项目管理库退库比例大约为9.97%，即2018年底的8 640个项目中有大约9.9%的项目（861个项目）并不在2019年底的项目管理库中。这一数据远低于2018全年38.75%的退库比例。

将发现2019年透明度总指数与2018年相比变动很小。尽管如此，我们还是会在本章第3.4小节重点讨论2019年相对2018年PPP透明度得分变化的原因。

3.1.2 指标构建

在上一章有关指标体系的介绍中，我们已经知道本指数共包含75个指标字段，基本来自中心网站，对于其中的33个指标字段，课题组需要从政府和社会资本合作中心网站上进行人工读取，主要目的是核实其真实性。在这些指标的构建中，对42个直接从网站或政府和社会资本合作中心获取的数据，课题组直接对其进行0和1的赋值，即某项目公布了该项指标，就赋1分，没有公布这些指标，就赋0分。而对于从政府和社会资本合作中心网站人工采集的指标，课题组对其打分更加细化：完整公布该指标信息，赋1分；部分公布，为0.5分；没有公布，为0分；显示公开了该信息（如有PDF附件）但为假文件或错误文件，则设为−1分，以示惩戒。

对部分公开和错误公开的样本，这里需要再稍作解释。所谓部分公布，主要是指该指标信息实际上包含了多个信息，但只公布了其中的一部分。例如，对于“物有所值定性评价指标及权重、评分标准、评分结果”，如果只公布了评分标准，或者只公布了评分结果，就只给0.5分。再如，对于物有所值评价报告、财政承受能力论证报告，文件要求是公布“物有所值评价报告及本级行业主管部门会同财政部门的审核通过意见”以及“财政承受能力论证报告及本级财政部门的审核通过意见”等，有些项目只公布其中的物有所值评价报告或财政承受能力论证报告，没有公布批复文件，或者情况相反，对这类情况，课题组也给0.5分。而赋值为−1分的所谓错误公开，主要情形为上传的PDF附件是空白文档、错误文档，以及信息的张冠李戴等情形。不过，对于极少一部分附件，虽然没有实质内容，但对为什么没有这些内容进行了合理化解释，例如项目在政策要求之前就已经运行，根据不溯及既往的原则，课题组不认定这种解释文件为错误公开，以免产生“误伤”。

这里以适时公开的“物有所值评价报告及本级行业主管部门会同财政部门的审核通过意见”为例，来说明课题组手工数据采集的基本情况。如图3−2所示，在5 162个适时公开评估样本中，完整公开“物有所值评价报告及本级行业主管部门会同财政部门的审核通过意见”的样本有4 164个，部分公开的有390个，没有公开的有

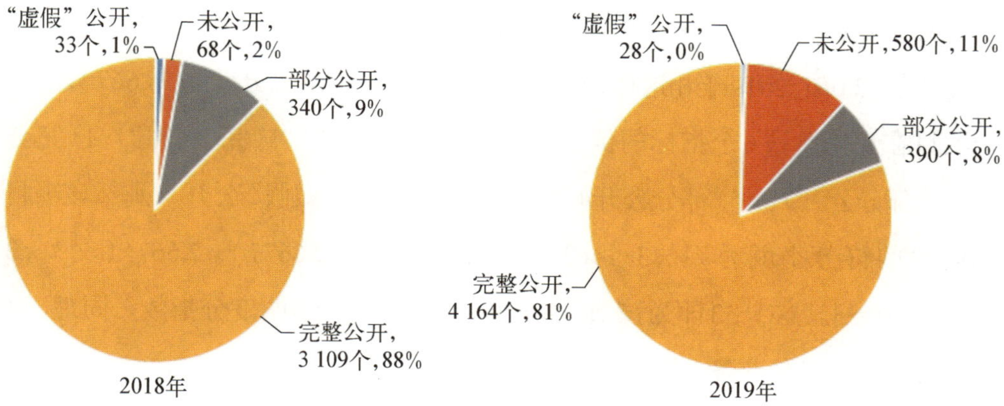

图3-2 物有所值评价报告及附件披露情况

580个，公开但文件为假文件、错误文件的样本有28个。与2018年相比，该指标完整公开率从88%大幅降低到2019年的81%，虚假公开比率从1%降为0.54%，未公开比率从2%大幅上升至11%。

最后，这些具体指标的公开程度得分再乘以上一章关于具体指标相对重要程度的专家评分，即可得到该指标的具体分数，进而可以逐级计算得到全国或某地区的PPP市场透明度指数。

3.2 全国总指数计算

3.2.1 指数合成

计算得到各指标的具体得分后，我们就可以计算出某个PPP项目在某阶段的得分率（标准化为100），这也就是透明度指数在该阶段的分指数。我们首先以适时公开透明度指数中的识别阶段为例进行说明，这个阶段包含6个信息，分别为"物有所值评价报告及本级行业主管部门会同财政部门的审核通过意见""财政承受能力论证报告及本级财政部门的审核通过意见""新建或改扩建项目建议书及批复文件""可行性研究报告或资金申请报告或申请核准项目的报告，及相关主管部门对上述报告的批复、批准或核准等文件；存量公共资产的资产评估报告""设计文件及批复文件"和"存量公共资产或权益的资产评估报告及存量资产或权益转让时所可能涉及到的各类方案等”。这6个指标在专家评分过程中的得分分别为3分、3分、2.333分、2.667分、2.667分和3分，这样，在适时公开的识别阶段总分就是16.667分。假如某个项目在识别阶段6个指标的信息公开中分别被判定为1（完全公开）、1（完全公开）、0.5（部分公开）、0.5（部分公开）、0（未公开）和−1（“虚假”公开），那么该项目在识别阶段的得分率就为[1×3+1×3+0.5×2.333+0.5×2.667+0×2.667+(−1)×3]/16.667×100=33。这个33即为该项目在适时公开阶段的透明度分指数。同理，可得到即时公开和适时公开各个阶段的透明度分指数。

表3-1给出了不同阶段的即时公开透明度指数，从中我们可以看出，在9 398个即时公开透明度评估对象中，识别阶段、准备阶段、采购阶段和执行阶段的平均指数分别为89.71、84.48、73.61和71.17。相对而言，在识别阶段和准备阶段，PPP项目信息披露相对较为理想，采购阶段和执行阶段的信息公开则相对差一些。从管理机制而言，识别阶段和准备阶段的信息大多是PPP项目入库时就必须提交的相关信息，由于入库时主管部门审查较严，因而指数普遍较高，但进入采购阶段和执行阶段后的项目，信息是否按照要求及时上传到PPP综合信息平台，并不妨碍项目工作的往前推进，信息公开的监管工作缺乏强硬抓手，从而导致采购阶段和执行阶段的指数较低。此外，与2018年比较，采购阶段和执行阶段的指数均有较大的增幅，但识别阶段和准备阶段的指数则有小幅度的下降。

表3-1 不同阶段的即时公开透明度指数

阶 段	2019年			2018年		
	样本量	均 值	标准差	样本量	均 值	标准差
识别阶段	9 398	89.71	4.38	8 636	94.36	6.63
准备阶段	9 398	84.48	25.39	8 636	91.45	18.78
采购阶段	8 000	73.61	21.19	6 962	61.88	43.02
执行阶段	6 322	71.17	28.86	4 684	60.59	30.75

表3-2给出了即时公开各个阶段透明度指数的具体分布，从中可以看出一些信息公开较好的项目在某些阶段指数可以达到100，但一些信息公开工作不到位的项

目在某阶段的指数可能出现负值。我们在前文已经多次介绍过，这是因为部分项目上传的PDF文件附件有假文件、错误文件等，而被课题组进行了“扣分”惩罚。我们关注这些“异常”项目，对其进行特别处理，是希望这样能够敦促相关责任部门尽快改进这些方面的工作，补齐短板，推动PPP项目规范化管理。不过，相对而言，我们更关注大多数项目的信息公开情况，因为大多数项目的信息透明度指数结果才代表了整个PPP市场的信息透明程度。因此，我们在表3-2中也给出了不同阶段透明度分指数的25%和75%两个分位数对应的具体数值。对比2019年和2018年即时公开各阶段透明度指数分布可以看出：2019年的即时公开识别阶段信息公开工作要略逊于2018年，因为不论是上四分位数还是下四分位数，2019年的指数均低于2018年。2019年即时公开准备阶段透明度指数的最小值和25分位数分别为−34.09和66.67，两项数值都远远低于2018年的−19.7和91.67。这表明在那些指数较低的项目上，2019年的即时公开准备阶段信息公开工作相对而言非常糟糕，远远不如2018年；而在那些指数较高的项目上，这两年的即时公开准备阶段信息公开工作没什么差异，因为这两年的75分位分值和最大值完全相同。从采购阶段看，在那些指数较低的项目上，2019年的即时公开信息工作明显优于2018年，2019年25分位数高达74.14，但2018年这一数值仅为9.93。最后我们考察执行阶段，这两年的25分位数几乎一样，差别不大，但在最小值方面，2019年的0要远远高于2018年−38.26。总体来看，细致考察指数分布得到的结论与表3-1一致，在即时公开方面，2019年识别阶段和准备阶段的信息公开工作比2018年要逊色一些，不过采购阶段和执行阶段的信息公开工作要明显优于2018年。

表3-2 即时公开各阶段透明度指数的分布

阶 段	2019年				2018年			
	最小值	25分位	75分位	最大值	最小值	25分位	75分位	最大值
识别阶段	58.44	88.64	92.21	97.56	53.25	91.72	100	100
准备阶段	−34.09	66.67	100	100	−19.7	91.67	100	100
采购阶段	0	74.14	87.07	100	−32.06	9.93	100	100
执行阶段	0	61.74	100	100	−38.26	61.73	83.48	100

表3-3给出了不同阶段的适时公开透明度指数，从中我们可以看出，在5 162个适时公开透明度评估对象中，识别阶段、准备阶段、采购阶段的平均指数分别为44.63、95.81和70.37。在不同阶段的比较上，相对而言，识别阶段较差，而准备阶段的信息公开工作较为理想，我们判断这主要是因为在识别阶段的适时公开信息中，需要公开的主要信息包括物有所值评价报告、财政承受能力论证报告等几个核心文件，对于这些文件，一些项目的信息公开工作做得不太理想。对比2018年的各阶段适时公开透明度指数可以发现，准备阶段这两年的平均指数差别不大，采购阶段2019年平均指数略高于2018年，但识别阶段2019年平均指数比2018年低11。

表3-3　不同阶段的适时公开透明度指数

阶　段	2019年			2018年		
	样本量	均　值	标准差	样本量	均　值	标准差
识别阶段	5 162	44.63	20.03	3 550	55.04	18.34
准备阶段	5 162	95.81	11.66	3 550	94.81	13.46
采购阶段	5 162	70.37	16.18	3 550	65.21	20.60

表3-4给出了适时公开各个阶段透明度指数的具体分布，包括最小值、最大值、上四分位数和下四分位数。从中我们可以看到，在适时公开的信息中，准备阶段和采购阶段的大部分项目的信息公开工作都较好，其中，至少有75%的项目的适时公开准备阶段透明度分指数为100。而识别阶段则较差，25%的项目的适时公开识别阶段透明度指数不足43.97。因此，如果想提高PPP项目适时公开信息的整体透明度，可以将焦点集中于物有所值评价报告、财政承受能力论证报告等几个核心报告的规范、完整披露上，相信补齐短板后能让适时公开透明度指数大幅上升。与2018年适时公开各个阶段透明度指数对比，2019年识别阶段指数略低于2018年，而采购阶段指数高于2018年，这一结果与即时公开的跨期对比结果类似。

表3-4 适时公开各阶段透明度指数的分布

阶 段	2019年				2018年			
	最小值	25分位	75分位	最大值	最小值	25分位	75分位	最大值
识别阶段	−63.96	43.97	52.97	100	−52	52	66	100
准备阶段	0	100	100	100	0	100	100	100
采购阶段	−9.68	62.29	85.12	90.66	−43.25	51.21	80.62	100

3.2.2 总指数结果

在得到各阶段的透明度分指数后，我们就可以按照上一章介绍的用层次分析法得到的各阶段分指数的权重，来合成即时公开透明度指数和适时公开透明度指数。表3－5即为即时公开透明度指数和适时公开透明度指数的总体情况。从中可以看出，即时公开透明度指数和适时公开透明度指数平均数值分别为79.14和71.57。与2018年相比，2019年的这两项指标基本保持平稳，虽然数值上略有提高，但幅度都不大。

表3-5 即时公开和适时公开透明度指数

指 数	2019年			2018年		
	样本量	均 值	标准差	样本量	均 值	标准差
即时公开透明度指数	9 398	79.14	13.95	8 636	77.61	21.46
适时公开透明度指数	5 162	71.57	13.90	3 550	71.55	13.03

最后，在得到即时公开透明度指数和适时公开透明度指数之后，在全国平均意义上，我们还可以按照用层次分析法计算得到的将即时公开透明度指数和适时公开透明度指数合成总指数时的权重，合成全国PPP市场透明度总指数。结论是：截至2019年12月底，全国PPP市场透明度总指数为76.19（$79.14 \times 0.61 + 71.57 \times 0.39$），略高于2018年的75.25。图3－3显示了全国PPP市场透明度总指数、即时公开透明度指数、适时公开透明度指数，以及各阶段透明度分指数的平均结果分布。与前文表3－1到表3－4显示的结果一致，图3－3再一次表

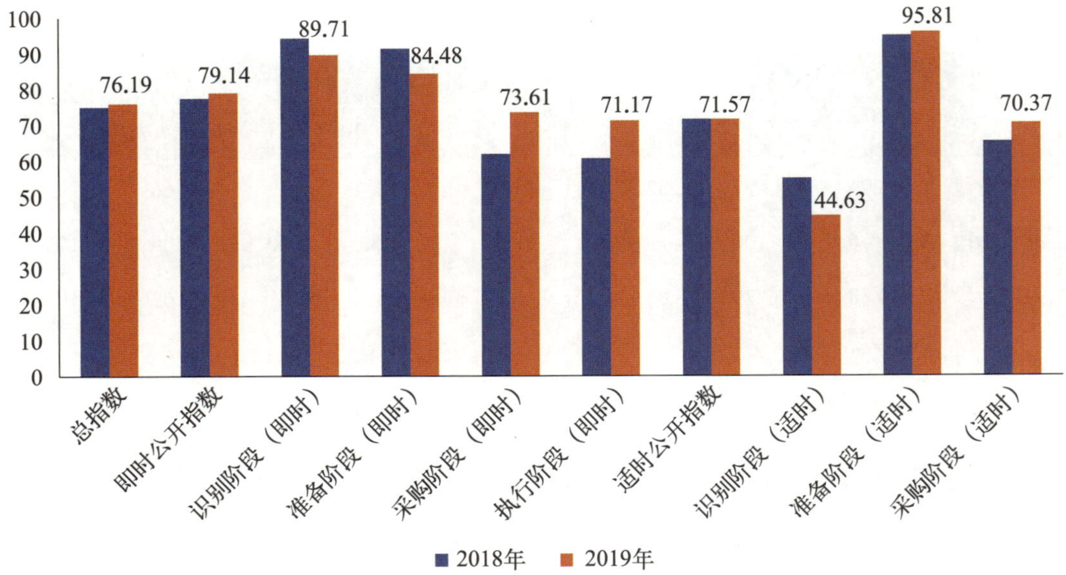

图3-3 全国PPP市场透明度总指数及各阶段指数

明出，2019年指数较2018年的变化主要体现为采购阶段和执行阶段分指数的提高以及识别阶段和准备阶段分指数的下降。

3.3 全国总指数的异质性分析

根据上文的分析，全国PPP市场透明度指数实际上是由全国约9 400个PPP项目的透明度指数平均而得到的。正如在上一节我们所看到的，全国PPP项目透明度平均结果可能掩盖了不同项目的异质性。因此，为了对全国的PPP市场透明度有更深入和直观的展示，在本节，我们主要从不同行业、不同类型等角度，对全国PPP市场透明度进行一些总体层面的分析。在后面的两章里，我们还将从省份和城市层面对各地PPP市场透明度进行更详细的讨论。

3.3.1 不同行业的PPP透明度指数

我们首先来看不同行业的PPP市场透明度指数。从图3-4中我们可以发现，不同行业的PPP市场透明度指数虽然存在一定的差异，但差异数值并不大。例如，分行业透明度总指数最高的为社会保障行业78.47，最低的是林业行业，为72.05，最高和最低仅相差6。去年我们就发现，2018年的透明度指数行业间差异比2017年有所缩小，今年我们可以观察到，行业间差异进一步降低。观察不同行业的即时公开透明度指数和适时公开透明度指数，以及不同阶段的分指数，也有类似发现。因此，总体而言，不同行业PPP项目在信息公开上没有呈现出明显的异质性。这表明不同行业的PPP项目在信息披露工作上并没有特别大的不同，或者说现存的PPP项目信息公开的制度规范具有一定的行业普适性。由于不同行业领域的PPP项目往往由不同的行业主管部门来负责具体的运行管理和监督，因而上述结果也说明不同行业主管部门在PPP项目信息公开的管理上并没有很明显的勤懒之分。此外，从图3-4中还可以观察到，除了体育、教育和养老，其余行业2019年的透明度指数相比2018年均有所提高。

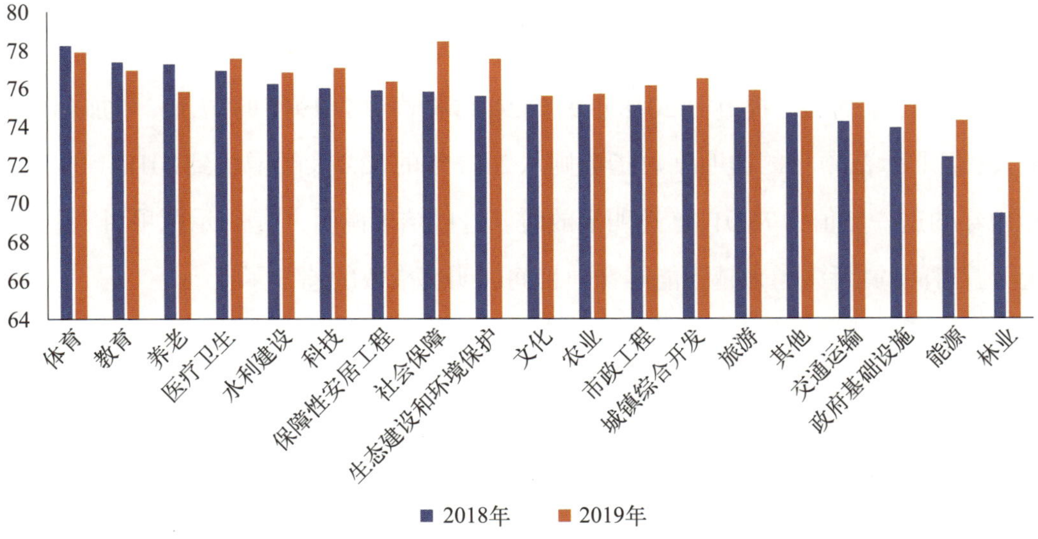

图3-4 分行业PPP市场透明度总指数

3.3.2 示范项目和非示范项目透明度指数

现在我们来分析示范项目和非示范项目在信息公开方面的差异。如图3-5所示，2019年的示范项目和非示范项目的透明度指数相差不大①，示范项目的总体信息

① 2018年的评估显示了类似的结果，即示范项目的透明度总指数与非示范项目的透明度总指数差别很小。

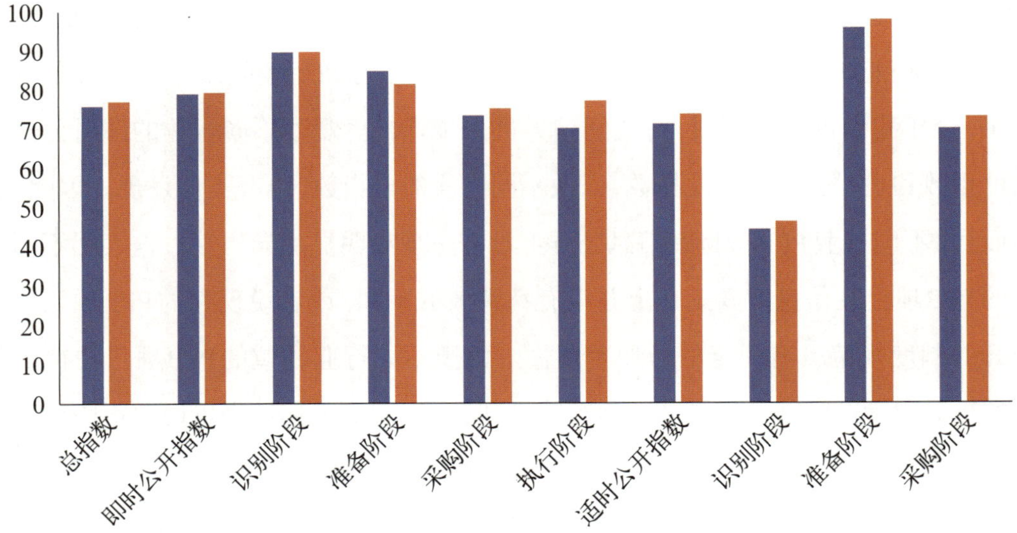

图3-5　2019年示范项目与非示范项目透明度指数

公开程度要略高于非示范项目。总结我们近三年的评估结果，示范项目的透明度总指数从2017年的72.3提高到2018年的74.9，再提高到2019年的77.19，增加幅度并不大；但非示范项目的透明度总指数则从2017年的62.0大幅增长到2018年的75.3，2019年的这一数值为76.01，增速明显放缓。这些结果说明，“是否示范项目”这一变量随着时间的推移，越来越不能解释项目间透明度指数的差异。

3.3.3　项目发起时间与透明度指数

本部分我们进一步考察PPP项目发起时间与PPP透明度指数的关联，以便分析不同PPP项目透明度指数存在较大差异的原因。图3-6汇报了不同年份发起的项目在2018年底和2019年底两次评估中的平均透明度指数。从图3-6中可以清晰地看出，发起时间越晚的PPP项目，信息公开工作做得越到位，从而PPP透明度指数就越高。具体而言，在2019年底，2012年及以前发起的PPP项目透明度指数约为63.1，而2019年发起的项目则为81.2。这一结果在预料之中，原因在于，伴随着项目的推进，项目需要公布的信息也越来越多，要求越来越高。对比2018年底和2019年底的两次评估结果则可以看出，给定相同的发起时间，项目在2018年底的平均透明度指数与2017年底相比差别不大。

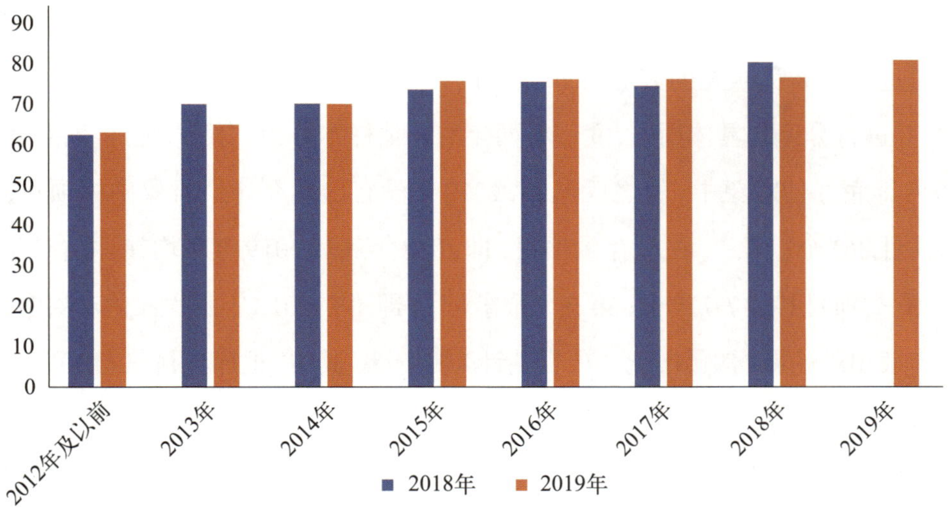

图3-6 不同发起时间的PPP项目透明度指数

3.4 进一步讨论：透明度指数跨期差异分析

从前文可以看到，不论是即时公开透明度指数、适时公开透明度指数还是总指数，2018年底和2019年底两次评估得到的PPP透明度指数存在的跨期差异并不大。进一步进行行业、示范与否以及发起时间维度的异质性分析，同样表明PPP透明度指数存在的跨期差异并不大。尽管如此，我们仍将致力于分析透明度指数跨期差异产生的可能原因。

分析PPP透明度全国指数跨期差异的重要性和政策意义显著，这将有助于我们及时发现PPP项目信息管理工作中的长处与短板，更好地促进PPP项目提质增效。通俗地讲，我们需要了解2019年的PPP信息公开工作与2018年相比，哪些地方改进了，哪些地方存在不足，具体原因是什么。例如，我们在前面第3.2小节就揭示了采购阶段透明度指数的提高与识别阶段透明度指数的降低，可能是驱动PPP透明度指数产生跨期变动的重要原因之一。只不过这两个相反方向的变动在加总成为即时公开透明度指数和适时公开透明度指数后，似乎被相互抵消了。然而，这并不妨碍我们可以给PPP信息监管部门提出“未来一年要继续保持采购阶段信息公开工作方面的良好表现，但要大力改善识别阶段信息公开工作方面的表现”这样极富针对性的建议。

本节我们主要聚焦评估对象本身的变动带来的PPP市场透明度指数跨期变动。我们通过项目名称匹配的方法将2019年的评估对象与2018年的评估对象进行详细对比，并进行分组。具体而言，我们将两年的评估样本分为：第一，退库项目，即包含在2018年底评估对象中，但之后退库，2019年没有出现在评估对象中的项目，此类样本共计861个；第二，在库存量项目，即2018年底和2019年底均在评估对象中的项目，此类项目共计7 779个；第三，新增项目，即不在2018年底的评估对象中，但在2019年底出现的新增项目，此类项目共计1 619个。其中，退库项目仅有2018年的透明度指数，新增项目只有2019年的透明度指数，而在库存量项目则同时有2018年和2019年的透明度指数。对比这三类项目对应的样本量可以很容易地发现：2019年的评估样本相比2018年保持了很大的稳定性，2018年8 640个项目中90%左右的样本在2019年末仍在库，2019年退库和新增项目比例均不高，这在很大程度上能够解释为什么2019年与2018年相比透明度总指数变动不大。

图3-7展示的这几类项目的得分情况进一步证明了这一点。根据图3-7，总体来看，这几类项目的透明度指数情况差别不大。

首先，那些2018年在库且2019年仍在库的项目在2018年的透明度指数高达75.17，但那些在2019年被退库的项目在2018年的透明度指数也不低，达到75.73，甚至还略高于在库存量项目的透明度指数。图3-8则是退库项目和在库存量项目

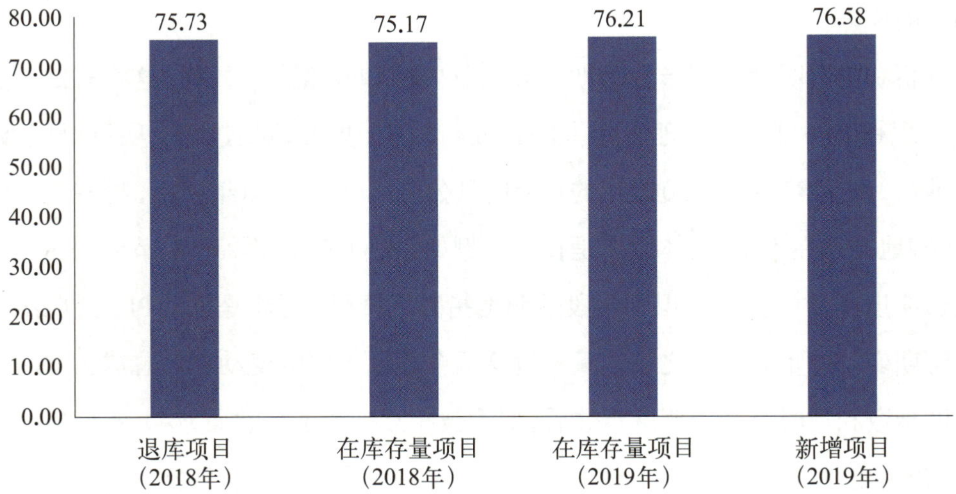

图3-7　不同类型项目透明度得分情况

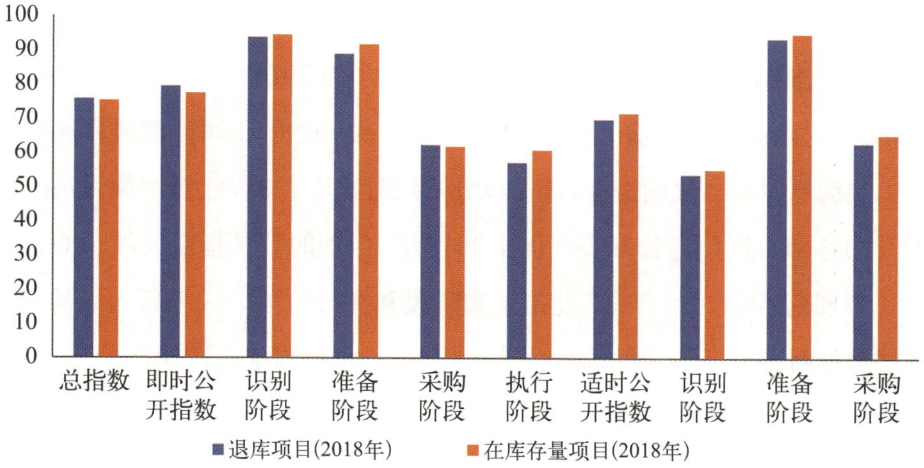

图3-8　2019年退库项目和在库存量项目2018年透明度指数

2018年透明度指数的更详细的展示，从中可以看出，在库存量项目在各阶段的信息公开工作与退库项目没有什么明显差别。

其次，在库存量项目改进了自己的信息公开工作，但并不明显。从图3-9中可以看出，同是在库存量项目，其在2018年的透明度指数为75.17，略微低于2019年的76.21。此外，图3-9则显示，在库存量项目2019年透明度指数优于2018年的主要原因是即时公开采购阶段和执行阶段的指数，以及适时公开采购阶段的指数在2019年得到较大改善，但即时公开识别阶段和准备阶段的指数以及适时公开识别阶段的指数2019年相比2018年下降了，这些发现与我们在本章第3.2小节分析2019年全国

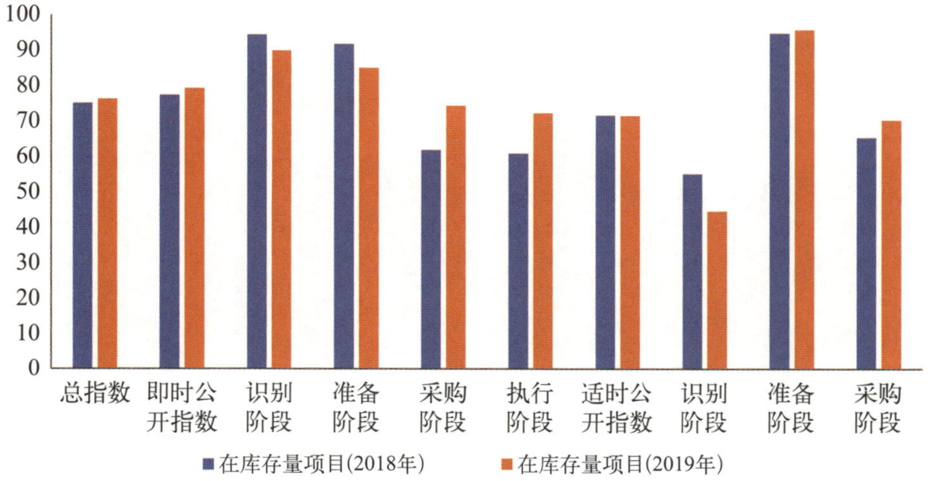

图3-9　2018年和2019年均在库项目的透明度指数

PPP市场透明度指数和2018年差异原因时所得结论基本保持一致。

最后，新增项目透明度指数稍好于在库存量项目2019年的指数，不过差距依然不大。图3-7显示，2019年新增项目透明度指数为76.58，在库存量项目透明度指数为76.21，差别不明显。从图3-10进一步分阶段对比看，2019年新增项目适时公开指数所涉及的各个阶段信息公开表现优于2018年，但即时公开指数所涉及的各个阶段信息公开表现落后于2018年，特别是采购阶段和执行阶段。未来新入库的PPP项目需特别加强即时公开所涉及的信息公开工作，进一步提高信息透明度。

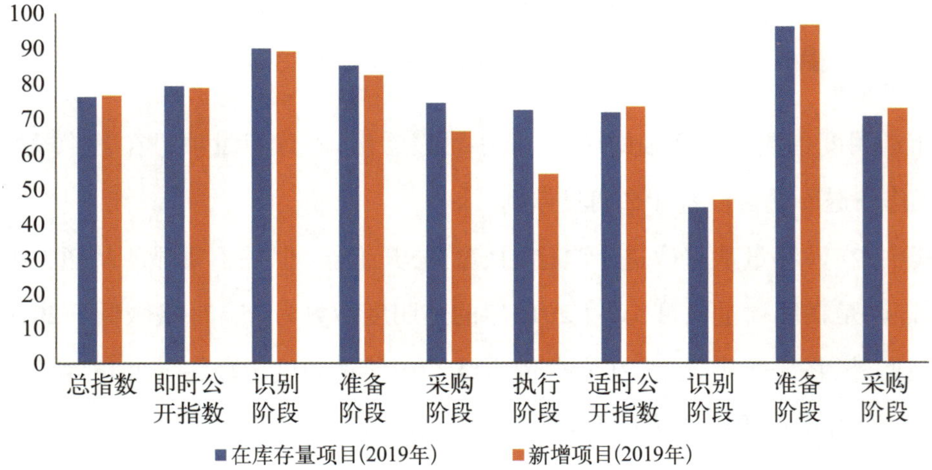

图3-10 在库存量项目与新增项目的2019年透明度指数

4

省级指数的排名与分析

4.1 省级透明度总指数结果分析

4.1.1 省级指数总体排名

上一章介绍了全国层面的2019年PPP市场透明度指数的基本情况，本章主要介绍分省的分析结果。为了得到各省份PPP市场透明度指数，课题组首先基于各个项目的透明度指数计算了各省份即时公开透明度指数和适时公开透明度指数，计算方法是先算出各省份所有项目的即时公开透明度指数和适时公开透明度指数的算术平均，然后按照第二章计算出来的权重合成得出各省份PPP市场透明度指数（即时公开权重为0.61，适时公开权重为0.39）。表4-1给出了2019年32个省级单位（省、直辖市、自治区、新疆生产建设兵团，下同）PPP项目的数量及透明度总指数的具体结果。从中我们可以得到以下几个结论：

第一，总体来看，2019年全国PPP市场透明度总指数省级平均为73.68①，与2018年（75.26）相比略有下降，可能的原因是更多项目进入了执行阶段。2018年适时公开所涉及的仅有3 550个项目，而2019年适时公开涉及项目达到了5 162个，适时公开透明度指数的下降影响了市场透明度总指数的变化。但尽管如此，73.68仍然高于10年来上海财经大学课题组发布的历年财政透明度报告的平均分（2017年各省份财政透明度平均分仅为48.3分），这显示在相关部门的监管下，PPP市场的信息公开工作要领先于其他财政领域。

第二，省级层面的PPP市场透明度指数基本保持在良好水平，绝大多数省份的透明度指数在70～85之间分布。但与2018年相比，各省份PPP市场透明度指数开始出现一定的离散趋势。2018年各省份PPP市场透明度指数均集中在70～80之间，

---

① 这里是各个省份透明度总指数的简单算术平均，所以与前文全国总指数的数值略有不同。

而2019年则有少数省份的PPP市场透明度指数低于70，表明随着PPP项目的持续推进，各省份透明度指数开始逐渐分化。具体排名而言，透明度排名第一的是甘肃（81.97），排名第二的是河北（81.29），排名第三的是吉林（80.52），排名第四的是山东（80.20），排名第五的是云南（80.17）。而西藏、上海、海南、北京、天津则表现相对较差，它们占据了这份榜单的最后5名。对比2018年的排行榜可以发现，PPP项目信息透明度工作进步最大的省份是江苏（77.69）和广东（77.20），两省在全国的排名较上一年均上升了17位，在2019年榜单中分列第九位和第十二位。PPP市场透明度指数排名下降最多的省份是青海，其指数从2018年的78.16下降到了2019年的70.81，虽然只下降了不足8，但由于省份之间指数差距本就很小，因而该省在2019年全国PPP市场透明度指数排名中仅列第二十六位，相较上一年排名下降了24位。新疆生产建设兵团、山东、河北、陕西和黑龙江等省份排名相较上一年均有较大幅度的上升，而新疆兵团、天津、广西和辽宁等省份排名相较上一年均下降明显。

表4-1　2019年省级PPP市场透明度总指数与排名

省　份	2019年项目数量	2019年透明度指数	2019年排名	较上一年排名变化	2018年项目数量	2018年透明度指数
甘肃	124	81.97	1	+3	96	77.63
河北	390	81.29	2	+10	343	76.48
吉林	170	80.52	3	+2	160	77.57
山东	765	80.20	4	+11	755	76.30
云南	481	80.17	5	−2	446	77.91
内蒙古	283	78.07	6	+5	276	76.63
陕西	280	77.94	7	+9	262	76.16
安徽	474	77.84	8	+5	448	76.40
江苏	398	77.69	9	+17	366	73.33
湖南	418	77.64	10	−4	418	77.21
新疆	381	77.48	11	+14	364	73.39
广东	519	77.20	12	+17	439	72.94

（续表）

省 份	2019年项目数量	2019年透明度指数	2019年排名	较上一年排名变化	2018年项目数量	2018年透明度指数
广西	204	77.03	13	−12	170	78.47
河南	752	76.17	14	+6	640	73.90
辽宁	184	75.80	15	−8	134	76.92
山西	396	74.15	16	−7	353	76.90
浙江	513	73.86	17	−3	492	76.33
福建	351	73.80	18	+3	332	73.82
贵州	512	73.76	19	0	512	73.94
四川	557	73.05	20	+4	512	73.47
湖北	417	72.96	21	+1	392	73.79
重庆	43	72.23	22	+1	31	73.64
黑龙江	107	72.09	23	+9	92	71.72
宁夏	47	71.57	24	−7	46	75.51
江西	355	71.52	25	−7	306	74.98
青海	38	70.81	26	−24	32	78.16
兵团	18	69.28	27	−19	19	76.92
天津	49	68.28	28	−18	32	76.81
北京	70	67.49	29	−2	60	73.29
海南	96	62.89	30	+1	99	72.08
上海	5	60.77	31	−3	3	72.98
西藏	1	52.22	32	−2	2	72.61

注：① 本报告表格所涉及的项目数量总体指的是即时公开透明度指数所涉及的9 398个PPP项目，适时公开透明度指数所涉及的5 162个PPP项目是它的一个子集；② “+”表示排名上升，“−”表示排名下降，下同。

4.1.2 即时公开和适时公开省级排名

图4−1和图4−2分别给出了各省份2018年和2019年PPP项目即时公开透明度指数和适时公开透明度指数的分布图。从中我们可以发现：

第一，各省份即时公开透明度指数基本要高于适时公开透明度指数，这一发现与第3章的描述是一致的，再次表明全国各省份PPP项目对适时指标的信息披露工作做得不如即时公开理想。

第二，各省级行政区的透明度总指数、适时公开透明度指数与即时公开透明度指数的省份排名总体是一致的，但也不是完全相同。由于即时公开指数的权重为0.61，而适时公开指数的权重为0.39，不出意外，那些在即时公开透明度方面做得较好的省

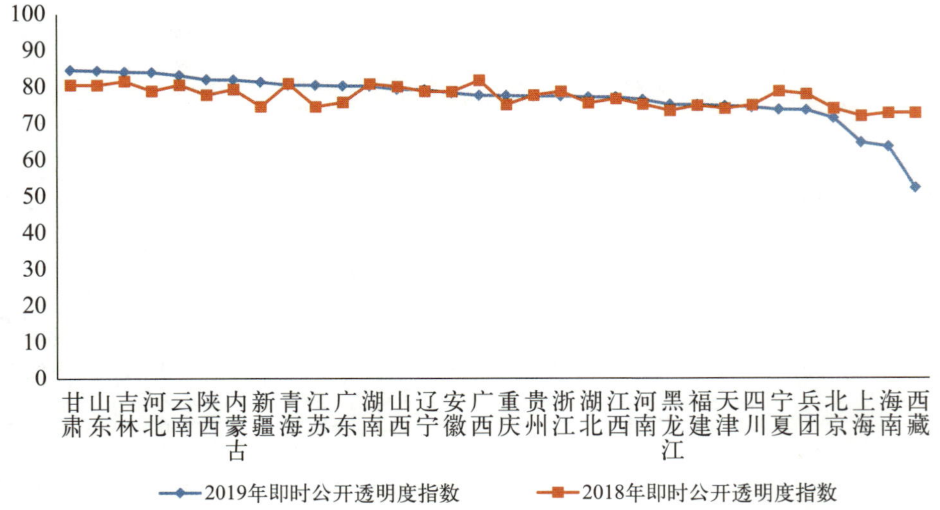

图4-1　2018年和2019年各省份PPP即时公开透明度指数

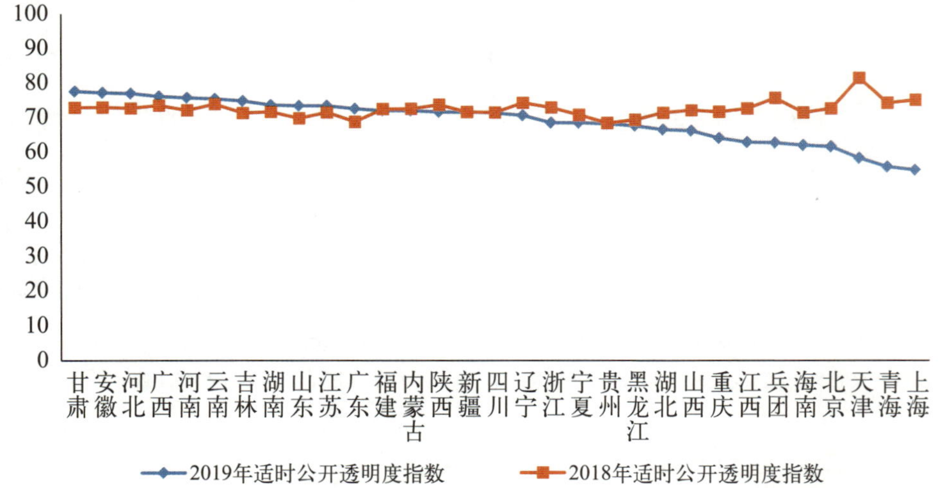

注：其中，西藏由于没有项目涉及适时公布的情况，故无法计算适时公开透明度指数，不参与相关排名。

图4-2　2018年和2019年各省份PPP适时公开透明度指数

份会在总指数上获得一个较好的排名，比如即时公开前5名实际上就是总指数榜单的前5名。尽管如此，即时公开透明度指数和适时公开透明度指数的省份排名之间还存在一定的差异。即时公开透明度指数排名第二位的山东，适时公开透明度指数排名第九位，说明山东在相关信息即时公开方面的工作开展确实较好，但是在适时公开方面的工作较差。而在适时公开透明度指数上排名最末的上海，即时公开透明度排到了倒数第三位，说明上海需要同时加强即时公开和适时公开两方面的工作。两份榜单的差异进一步表明各地区在PPP项目信息公开方面各有优劣，需要取长补短，才能提升整体的透明度，推动PPP项目信息更好地公开。

通过2019年和2018年数据对比可以发现，各省份即时公开透明度指数和适时公开透明度指数的跨期变动没有呈现出显性的规律，表现为有增有减。从即时公开透明度指数变化情况看，有18个省份的即时公开透明度指数上升，14个省份的即时公开透明度指数下降。即时公开透明度指数上升幅度最大的是新疆，从2018年的74.63上升至2019年的81.29，其次是江苏、河北、广东等省份；而即时公开透明度指数下降幅度最大的是西藏，从2018年的72.61下降至2019年的52.22。从适时公开透明度指数变化情况看，有12个省份的适时公开透明度指数上升，19个省份的适时公开透明度指数下降。适时公开透明度指数上升幅度最大的是甘肃，从2018年的72.94上升到2019年的77.66，适时公开透明度指数上升幅度最小的是新疆，从2018年的71.46上升到2019年的71.52，仅上涨0.07；适时公开透明度指数下降幅度最大的是天津，从2018年的81.31下降到2019年的58.24。总体看，伴随着更多的项目进入执行阶段，多数省份出现了适时公开指数得分下降的趋势，这表明多数省份在PPP项目信息适时公开方面的管理工作还需进一步加强。

4.1.3 透明度指数与项目数量关系

在指数编制过程中，有部分专家以及地方财政部门代表人员曾建议我们将各地区管理的PPP数量因素考虑在内，原因是部分省份需要管理的PPP数量较多，可能增大了其监管和督促信息公开的难度从而拉低了PPP市场透明度指数。因此，为了具体考察各地管理的PPP项目数量与该地区PPP市场透明度指数的对应关系，我们使用省份的PPP透明度总指数和项目数量作散点图并进行线性拟合，结果如图4-3

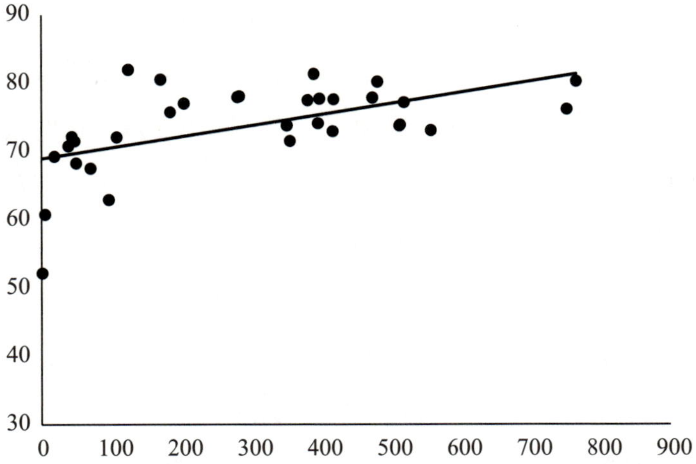

图4-3 省份PPP项目数量与省份PPP市场透明度总指数的散点图

所示。结果表明，省份需要监管的PPP项目数量与该省份PPP市场透明度指数不仅没有明显的负向关系，反而呈现出一定的正相关关系。从统计学意义上讲，“由于管理了太多的PPP项目，所以造成该地区PPP市场透明度指数较低”的猜测似乎并不成立。

人们另一个可能的疑虑在于，部分省份的PPP项目数量过少，统计学意义不大，是否还有必要参与全国排名。课题组的做法是将所有省级单位全部纳入排名榜，没有在排名时人为删除项目数过少的省级单位，以便全面客观地反映当前各省份PPP信息披露工作的现状。这是因为项目数量多少的界限不好界定，不同的读者存在不同标准，如果读者认为某些省级单位项目过少，忽略这一省份的排名信息并不影响对其他省份PPP市场透明度指数相对排名的解读。此外，一个地区项目数量为什么和PPP市场透明度指数呈现正相关，是一个非常有趣也值得讨论的话题，一个可能的原因是，PPP项目数量多的地区，主管部门安排了更多的管理人员或专门的负责人。

4.2 分阶段省级透明度结果分析

4.2.1 即时公开

接下来我们分析各个省份在即时公开和适时公开各个阶段的信息披露工作成

绩。首先，表4-2给出了即时公开和适时公开PPP透明度指数省份排名，并且展示了2019年排名相较上一年的变化。在即时公开方面，甘肃、山东、吉林、河北和云南位列排名前5位，而新疆生产建设兵团、北京、上海、海南和西藏位列排名最后的5位。即时公开透明度指数省份排名上升最多的是新疆，由2018年的第二十五名上升到2019年的第八名；排名下降最多的省份是广西，由2018年的第一名下降到2019年的第十六名，下降了15个名次。在适时公开方面，甘肃、安徽、河北、广西和河南位列排名的前5位，而海南、北京、天津、青海和上海排名最末。适时公开透明度指数省份排名上升最多的是山东，由2018年的第二十八名跃升至2019年的第九名；排名下降最多的是天津和上海，均较上一年下降了28名，2019年分别位列第二十九名和第三十一名。

表4-2　即时公开和适时公开透明度指数省份排名

排名	2019年即时公开透明度指数	较2018年变化	2019年适时公开透明度指数	较2018年变化
1	甘肃	+4	甘肃	+8
2	山东	+4	安徽	+8
3	吉林	−1	河北	+9
4	河北	+6	广西	+4
5	云南	+2	河南	+12
6	陕西	+10	云南	0
7	内蒙古	+2	吉林	+17
8	新疆	+17	湖南	+11
9	青海	−6	山东	+19
10	江苏	+16	江苏	+12
11	广东	+8	广东	+19
12	湖南	−8	福建	+4
13	山西	−5	内蒙古	0
14	辽宁	−3	陕西	−7
15	安徽	−3	新疆	+6

（续表）

排名	2019年即时公开透明度指数	较2018年变化	2019年适时公开透明度指数	较2018年变化
16	广西	−15	四川	+7
17	重庆	+5	辽宁	−13
18	贵州	−1	浙江	−7
19	浙江	−5	宁夏	+8
20	湖北	0	贵州	+11
21	江西	−3	黑龙江	+8
22	河南	−1	湖北	+3
23	黑龙江	+6	山西	−5
24	福建	0	重庆	−4
25	天津	+2	江西	−10
26	四川	−3	兵团	−24
27	宁夏	−14	海南	−1
28	兵团	−13	北京	−14
29	北京	−1	天津	−28
30	上海	+2	青海	−25
31	海南	0	上海	−28
32	西藏	−2		

表4−3给出了2019年度PPP项目即时公开透明度指数以及即时公开所涉及的各个阶段的透明度分指数省份排名。

表4−3　2019年即时公开透明度指数及各个阶段透明度分指数省份排名

排 名	即时公开透明度指数	识别阶段	准备阶段	采购阶段	执行阶段
1	甘肃	西藏	新疆	新疆	云南
2	山东	云南	云南	青海	河北
3	吉林	甘肃	山东	福建	吉林
4	河北	江苏	吉林	陕西	内蒙古

（续表）

排 名	即时公开透明度指数	识别阶段	准备阶段	采购阶段	执行阶段
5	云南	北京	甘肃	山东	湖南
6	陕西	山东	河北	江西	山东
7	内蒙古	新疆	山西	河北	甘肃
8	新疆	吉林	湖北	内蒙古	江苏
9	青海	河北	江西	广东	河南
10	江苏	兵团	广西	江苏	北京
11	广东	河南	内蒙古	吉林	四川
12	湖南	陕西	湖南	安徽	广东
13	山西	青海	青海	甘肃	广西
14	辽宁	广东	陕西	天津	陕西
15	安徽	重庆	江苏	浙江	浙江
16	广西	内蒙古	广东	湖北	宁夏
17	重庆	浙江	贵州	河南	安徽
18	贵州	安徽	河南	宁夏	辽宁
19	浙江	福建	兵团	湖南	重庆
20	湖北	辽宁	辽宁	云南	福建
21	江西	黑龙江	重庆	上海	贵州
22	河南	山西	黑龙江	四川	兵团
23	黑龙江	广西	天津	广西	上海
24	福建	湖南	浙江	重庆	山西
25	天津	湖北	安徽	山西	新疆
26	四川	江西	四川	贵州	湖北
27	宁夏	四川	福建	海南	青海
28	兵团	天津	宁夏	黑龙江	天津
29	北京	宁夏	北京	北京	黑龙江
30	上海	贵州	上海	辽宁	海南
31	海南	海南	西藏	兵团	江西
32	西藏	上海	海南	西藏	西藏

甘肃、山东、吉林和河北在各阶段均表现优异且各阶段也相对稳健，并无明显短板。云南在识别阶段、准备阶段和执行阶段均表现不错，但在采购阶段仅排名第二十名，导致其在即时公开透明度指数排名中只能位列第五，如将来能在执行阶段更好地做好信息披露工作，排名仍有上升的空间。内蒙古在采购阶段和执行阶段表现较好，但是在识别阶段和准备阶段表现较差，从而拉低了其在即时公开透明度指数中的排名。

新疆生产建设兵团、北京、上海、海南和西藏占据了即时公开透明度省级排名的最后5名。其中北京在识别阶段的排名位列第五，但在其他阶段信息披露工作方面的糟糕表现拉低了其即时公开透明度指数排名。西藏在识别阶段的排名位列第一，但是在采购阶段和执行阶段表现很差（均位列倒数第一），这导致其在即时公开透明度指数排名上位列榜单末尾。其余三省份则在各个阶段的信息披露工作均表现不佳。

甘肃在各个阶段的排名都没有十分突出，但最终占据即时公开透明度指数的第一名，而准备阶段和采购阶段排名第一的新疆以及执行阶段排名第一的云南（识别阶段、准备阶段排名第二）几乎在各个阶段的PPP信息透明度指数都要高于甘肃，但在即时公开透明度指数排名上落后于甘肃，这反映了各省份PPP项目的阶段分布对我们的最终结果的确存在着一定程度的影响。如果一个省份处于准备阶段的PPP项目占比较高，且这一阶段的工作做得较为出色，那么该省份很容易获得高分，因为按照第3章所述的算法，原本采购阶段和执行阶段的权重被“归并”到准备阶段和识别阶段中去了。相反，如果一个省份处于准备阶段的PPP项目并不多，那么该省份一旦在采购阶段和执行阶段中的工作略有不足，可能会对最终的透明度总指数产生不利影响。为了更清晰地展示这一问题，表4-4列出了各省份PPP项目按阶段的分布，经过对比很容易发现甘肃处于准备阶段的项目占比要明显高于新疆和云南。当然，需要强调的是，我们这里指出项目分阶段的分布差异，只是为了解读少数省份排名结果及可能的原因，并不是说为了提高PPP市场透明度指数而应该刻意去放缓PPP项目进度。

表4-4 2019年各省份分阶段PPP项目数量

省 份	项目总数量	准备阶段	采购阶段	执行阶段
安徽	474	48	38	388
北京	70	5	3	62

（续表）

省 份	项目总数量	准备阶段	采购阶段	执行阶段
福建	351	45	21	285
甘肃	124	36	32	56
广东	519	49	68	402
广西	204	40	60	104
贵州	512	119	94	299
海南	96	5	8	83
河北	390	54	59	277
河南	752	151	164	437
黑龙江	107	23	15	69
湖北	417	52	92	273
湖南	418	79	77	262
吉林	170	24	29	117
江苏	398	44	68	286
江西	355	51	40	264
辽宁	184	59	46	79
内蒙古	283	27	52	204
宁夏	47	2	5	40
青海	38	8	8	22
山东	765	115	116	534
山西	396	92	132	172
陕西	280	53	41	186
上海	5	1	1	3
四川	557	35	162	360
天津	49	12	9	28
西藏	1	0	1	0
新疆	381	24	44	313
兵团	18	3	5	10

（续表）

省　份	项目总数量	准备阶段	采购阶段	执行阶段
云南	481	86	125	270
浙江	513	45	58	410
重庆	43	11	5	27

4.2.2　适时公开

表4-5给出了2019年度PPP项目适时公开透明度指数以及适时公开所涉及的各个阶段的透明度分指数前十省份榜单。同样可以发现，甘肃和安徽在各个阶段表现抢眼，特别是甘肃在识别阶段排名第一，准备阶段排名第二。广西依靠其在识别阶段的优秀表现，在适时公开透明度指数排名中位列第四。由于采购阶段的信息披露工作重要性最高（根据专家判定矩阵的计算结果，采购阶段权重为0.45），河北和河南凭借在采购阶段较高的指数占据了适时公开透明度指数排名的第三位和第五位。

表4-5　2019年适时公开透明度指数及各个阶段透明度分指数省份排名

排　名	适时公开透明度指数	识别阶段	准备阶段	采购阶段
1	甘肃	甘肃	安徽	河南
2	安徽	广西	甘肃	河北
3	河北	安徽	山东	吉林
4	广西	河北	湖南	云南
5	河南	云南	云南	甘肃
6	云南	吉林	河北	山东
7	吉林	新疆	江苏	安徽
8	湖南	福建	陕西	江苏
9	山东	河南	宁夏	湖南
10	江苏	湖南	广西	广东
11	广东	广东	河南	广西
12	福建	陕西	内蒙古	新疆

（续表）

排　名	适时公开透明度指数	识别阶段	准备阶段	采购阶段
13	内蒙古	四川	重庆	内蒙古
14	陕西	内蒙古	吉林	福建
15	新疆	兵团	辽宁	黑龙江
16	四川	江苏	四川	四川
17	辽宁	浙江	广东	陕西
18	浙江	辽宁	浙江	辽宁
19	宁夏	贵州	福建	贵州
20	贵州	山东	山西	湖北
21	黑龙江	宁夏	贵州	山西
22	湖北	重庆	新疆	宁夏
23	山西	湖北	湖北	浙江
24	重庆	北京	黑龙江	海南
25	江西	山西	江西	江西
26	兵团	江西	海南	北京
27	海南	黑龙江	北京	兵团
28	北京	海南	上海	重庆
29	天津	天津	天津	天津
30	青海	上海	兵团	青海
31	上海	青海	青海	上海

这份榜单的后5名则被海南、北京、天津、青海和上海占据。对比表4-3可以发现，其中北京、上海和海南在即时公开信息披露方面的工作表现也不佳（参看前文分析），即时公开透明度指数也排在末尾，说明这些省份PPP项目信息公开的披露工作亟待加强。

我们使用折线图能更清楚地反映省级单位在适时公开或即时公开各个阶段的具体指数结果。图4-4展示了各个省级单位在即时公开各个阶段的指数结果，对比可以发现：识别阶段和准备阶段信息披露最充分，而采购阶段和执行阶段的指数普遍

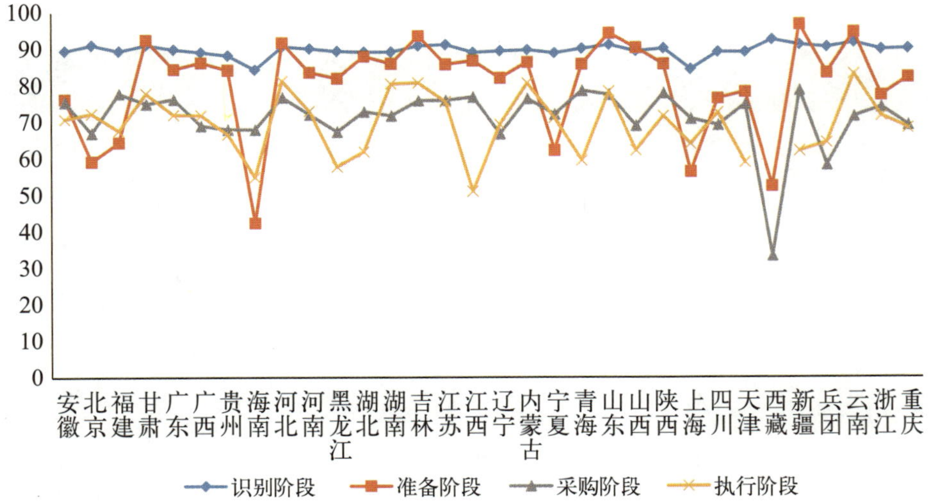

图4-4　2019年各省份即时公开透明度指数各阶段分布

较低。这一结果基本符合预期：识别阶段和准备阶段的很多信息决定了PPP项目能否顺利通过审核，往往更受监管部门和社会参与方的重视，因而指数普遍较高。

图4-5则展示了各个省级单位在适时公开各个阶段的指数结果。与即时公开的情况有所不同，适时公开在识别阶段的信息披露明显不如准备阶段与采购阶段充分。这主要是因为识别阶段涉及两个重要的PDF文件，即“两评”（物有所值评价和财政承受能力论证），课题组对这两份PDF文件 进行了颇为严格的审核，很多项目没有披露或者存在“虚假”披露导致各省份这一阶段的指数普遍相对较低。

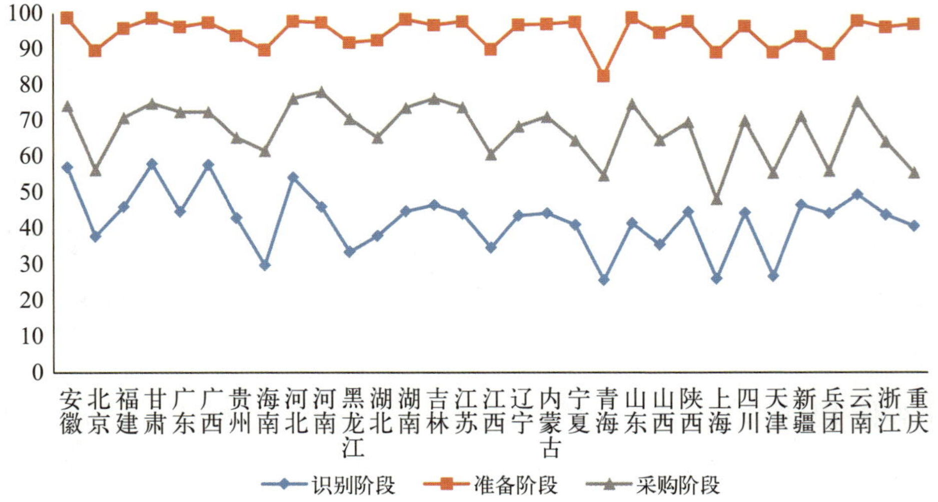

图4-5　2019年各省份适时公开透明度指数各阶段分布

4.3 “两评一案”省级结果分析

所谓“两评一案”，是指“物有所值评价报告及本级行业主管部门会同财政部门的审核通过意见”“财政承受能力论证报告及本级财政部门的审核通过意见”以及“实施方案附件”。“两评一案”在整个PPP项目的识别阶段和准备阶段处于非常重要的地位，也是目前我国PPP项目规范运行必不可少的重要步骤，在很大程度上将决定该PPP项目能否顺利实施。因此，我们在本小节对这几份重点报告的各省份披露情况进行简单总结。

由于“两评一案”涵盖的信息量非常丰富，往往通过长达几十页甚至上百页的PDF文件形式呈现在网站上，供社会各方进行查阅，因此，这三份PDF文件是课题组人工阅读和检查的重点对象。表4-6给出了这三个PDF文件得分的省级单位排序情况。从中可以发现，这三个PDF文件得分排名与适时公开透明度指数排名具有较高的一致性，比如甘肃占据了“财政承受能力论证报告及本级财政部门的审核通过意见”指标的第一名和“物有所值评价报告及本级行业主管部门会同财政部门的审核通过意见”的第二名，正因为其得益于这两项指标的优秀表现，甘肃在适时公开透明度指数排名中位列第一。此外，上海在适时公开透明度指数排名中列在最后一位，主要就是其在这三份文件上的得分排名较差导致的，这表明上海在“两评一案”上的信息披露工作亟待加强。安徽虽然“实施方案附件”项目排名第二，但是“物有所值评价报告及本级行业主管部门会同财政部门的审核通过意见”和“财政承受能力论证报告及本级财政部门的审核通过意见”两项排名较差，因而其适时公开透明度指数排名第二。河北的“两评一案”指标均表现优秀，各项目排名都在前三位，因而其适时公开透明度指数位列第三。广西、河南和云南在“两评一案”中的工作各有优劣，因而分别在适时公开透明度指数排名中位列第四、第五和第六。

表4-6 “两评一案”省级透明度排名

排　名	适时公开透明度指数	物有所值评价	财政承受能力论证	实施方案
1	甘肃	云南	甘肃	广西
2	安徽	甘肃	河北	安徽

（续表）

排　名	适时公开透明度指数	物有所值评价	财政承受能力论证	实施方案
3	河北	河北	湖南	河北
4	广西	河南	云南	江苏
5	河南	陕西	河南	北京
6	云南	广西	陕西	辽宁
7	吉林	内蒙古	内蒙古	新疆
8	湖南	湖南	广西	宁夏
9	山东	安徽	山东	吉林
10	江苏	山东	安徽	湖北
11	广东	福建	福建	浙江
12	福建	江苏	江苏	海南
13	内蒙古	吉林	广东	河南
14	陕西	四川	吉林	甘肃
15	新疆	广东	四川	上海
16	四川	浙江	兵团	福建
17	辽宁	宁夏	宁夏	江西
18	浙江	新疆	浙江	贵州
19	宁夏	兵团	重庆	广东
20	贵州	山西	新疆	陕西
21	黑龙江	辽宁	辽宁	内蒙古
22	湖北	重庆	山西	天津
23	山西	贵州	贵州	湖南
24	重庆	湖北	湖北	黑龙江
25	江西	黑龙江	黑龙江	四川
26	兵团	江西	江西	重庆
27	海南	上海	上海	青海
28	北京	天津	天津	云南

（续表）

排　名	适时公开透明度指数	物有所值评价	财政承受能力论证	实施方案
29	天津	青海	北京	山西
30	青海	北京	青海	山东
31	上海	海南	海南	兵团

未来课题组会考虑做一些专题评估，不仅评估这些关键性指标或核心PDF文件是否披露，还将评估这些报告具体内容的质量，以进一步推动PPP项目更加规范。

5

城市指数的排名与分析

5.1 城市PPP项目分布情况概述

在前面第3章、第4章对全国层面和省级层面的PPP市场透明度指数对比分析的基础上，本章将对中国PPP项目数量相对较多的部分城市的PPP市场透明度情况展开一些分析。在中国338个地级市（自治州、地区、盟等，以下统一都视作“市”）中，已经有326个城市引入了PPP模式（见表5-1），PPP模式推动范围之广，可见一斑。特别是广东、山东、河南、新疆、安徽、云南、辽宁、湖南、广西、江苏、湖北、内蒙古、河北、山西、浙江、江西、陕西、吉林、四川、福建、贵州、宁夏22个省份已经实现了PPP项目地级市的全覆盖。

表5-1 各省份引入PPP模式的城市个数

省份	引入PPP模式的城市个数	城市总数	省份	引入PPP模式的城市个数	城市总数
云南	16	16	江西	11	11
内蒙古	12	12	河北	11	11
吉林	9	9	河南	17	17
四川	21	21	浙江	11	11
宁夏	5	5	海南	2	3
安徽	16	16	湖北	13	13
山东	17	17	湖南	14	14
山西	11	11	甘肃	13	14
广东	21	21	福建	9	9
广西	14	14	贵州	9	9

（续表）

省 份	引入PPP模式的城市个数	城市总数	省 份	引入PPP模式的城市个数	城市总数
新疆	14	14	辽宁	14	14
陕西	10	10	青海	6	8
江苏	13	13	黑龙江	12	13
西藏	1	7			

这些开展PPP项目的城市中，有些拥有较为成熟的PPP市场，有些则刚刚起步。为了使得相关评估分析更具有稳健性、科学性，我们在本次报告中选取了PPP项目数量较多的城市作为分析对象。为了方便画图，我们选择了截至2019年12月31日在PPP综合信息平台项目数量超过50个的46个地级以上城市作为城市层面PPP市场透明度指数具体分析的样本，其中项目数量超过20个的地级以上城市层面的PPP市场透明度指数的结果如附件四所示。这46个具体城市名单包括：新疆阿克苏、广东东莞、山东日照、山东潍坊、山东济宁、河北唐山、吉林长春、河北承德、云南玉溪、山东菏泽、贵州毕节、山东临沂、江苏南京、河南平顶山、云南昆明、陕西西安、贵州贵阳、江苏徐州、河南郑州、安徽阜阳、浙江杭州、贵州遵义、湖南湘西、福建宁德、贵州六盘水、河南洛阳、浙江丽水、山西晋中、内蒙古赤峰、新疆乌鲁木齐、四川成都、浙江温州、河南驻马店、山东青岛、山西临汾、河南南阳、福建泉州、四川宜宾、河南信阳、福建漳州、浙江台州、湖北武汉、江西赣州、北京、贵州黔南、海南海口。

5.2 重点城市指数的基本情况

5.2.1 总指数城市排名

这46个PPP市场发展较为成熟的城市，其2019年PPP市场透明度总指数排名如表5-2所示。排在首位的是新疆阿克苏，指数为82.81，比全国平均水平高6.73；紧随其后的是广东东莞和山东日照，总指数分别达到82.48和82.06。此外，总指数在80以上的城市还有山东潍坊、山东济宁、河北唐山、吉林长春、河北承德、云南玉溪、山东菏泽和贵州毕节，这些都是PPP信息公开工作开展得相对较好的城市。

表5-2 2019年部分城市PPP市场透明度总指数

排名	城 市	2019年项目数量	2019年总指数	较2018年总指数差异	2018年总指数	2017年总指数
1	新疆阿克苏	66	82.81	15.39	67.43	55.89
2	广东东莞	108	82.48	13.62	68.86	79.76
3	山东日照	56	82.06	3.88	78.18	81.07
4	山东潍坊	93	81.79	4.72	77.08	60.76
5	山东济宁	82	81.62	6.93	74.69	78.48
6	河北唐山	52	81.58	5.03	76.55	78.84
7	吉林长春	50	81.46	5.11	76.35	71.10
8	河北承德	56	81.41	3.45	77.96	79.88
9	云南玉溪	57	81.41	3.82	77.59	76.43
10	山东菏泽	74	80.85	3.66	77.19	66.56
11	贵州毕节	65	80.09	4.85	75.24	64.12
12	山东临沂	76	79.88	4.84	75.04	70.63
13	江苏南京	90	79.43	8.25	71.19	64.99
14	河南平顶山	59	78.39	2.96	75.43	66.57
15	云南昆明	54	78.06	0.33	77.73	75.03
16	陕西西安	83	78.06	1.68	76.38	66.28
17	贵州贵阳	51	77.61	−0.53	78.14	59.17
18	江苏徐州	58	77.36	2.77	74.59	54.67
19	河南郑州	56	77.09	5.51	71.58	60.58
20	安徽阜阳	62	77.09	−2.33	79.41	70.39
21	浙江杭州	66	76.61	0.31	76.29	57.97

（续表）

排名	城 市	2019年项目数量	2019年总指数	较2018年总指数差异	2018年总指数	2017年总指数
22	贵州遵义	114	76.43	−0.74	77.17	65.79
23	湖南湘西	50	75.98	0.05	75.92	67.31
24	福建宁德	63	75.97	6.06	69.91	65.20
25	贵州六盘水	50	75.93	3.85	72.08	44.07
26	河南洛阳	57	75.86	5.34	70.52	53.95
27	浙江丽水	62	75.85	−3.07	78.92	72.40
28	山西晋中	50	75.81	0.54	75.26	76.76
29	内蒙古赤峰	56	75.29	−1.97	77.26	56.48
30	新疆乌鲁木齐	64	75.18	1.64	73.54	54.59
31	四川成都	55	74.99	0.10	74.90	84.67
32	浙江温州	83	74.90	−0.26	75.16	54.95
33	河南驻马店	69	74.70	−4.05	78.75	62.52
34	山东青岛	74	74.27	−1.67	75.94	72.47
35	山西临汾	58	73.67	−7.08	80.75	72.37
36	河南南阳	71	73.58	5.10	68.48	51.76
37	福建泉州	66	73.54	−2.08	75.62	76.05
38	四川宜宾	62	72.90	−1.87	74.77	67.20
39	河南信阳	52	72.43	−4.79	77.22	58.46
40	福建漳州	60	72.08	−3.29	75.37	70.12
41	浙江台州	67	70.93	−6.84	77.77	62.08
42	湖北武汉	67	70.41	−0.99	71.40	73.19
43	江西赣州	95	70.34	−2.19	72.53	65.61
44	北京	70	67.49	−7.43	74.92	52.25
45	贵州黔南	53	66.16	−12.00	78.16	54.51
46	海南海口	52	57.86	−13.10	70.96	42.96

通过和2018年的PPP市场透明度指数进行对比可以发现，部分地级以上城市2019年总指数较2018年是大幅上升的，尤其是新疆阿克苏，其2019年总指数较2018年上升了15.39，紧随其后的是广东东莞，较2018年上升了13.62。不过，同时也可以发现，很多地级以上城市2019年总指数较2018年有所降低，尤其是贵州黔南和海南海口，2019年总指数较2018年下降最多，分别下降了13.10和12。

5.2.2 与全国平均水平比较

此外，从46个城市的透明度总指数分布图来看，在大力推广PPP模式的过程中，大多数城市PPP市场透明度指数的差异并不是很明显，但也应该注意到部分城市的PPP市场透明度指数远低于其他城市，如北京、贵州黔南和海南海口的指数均低于70，尤其是海南海口的指数低于60。如图5－1所示，可将这46个城市的PPP市场透明度总指数的分布分成两个梯队：第一梯队城市的PPP市场透明度情况均领先于全国平均水平，即包括新疆阿克苏到贵州遵义在内的22个城市；第二梯队城市的PPP市场透明度情况则落后于全国平均水平，即包括湖南湘西到海南海口在内的24个城市。由于这里的分析对象都是开展PPP项目数量相对较多的城市，因此业务不熟悉不应该成为第二梯队城市PPP市场透明度指数不高的“借口”，而是说明部分城市确实需要加强PPP信息公开相关工作力度，避免出现整个PPP市场只重视规模而忽视规范化管理的问题。

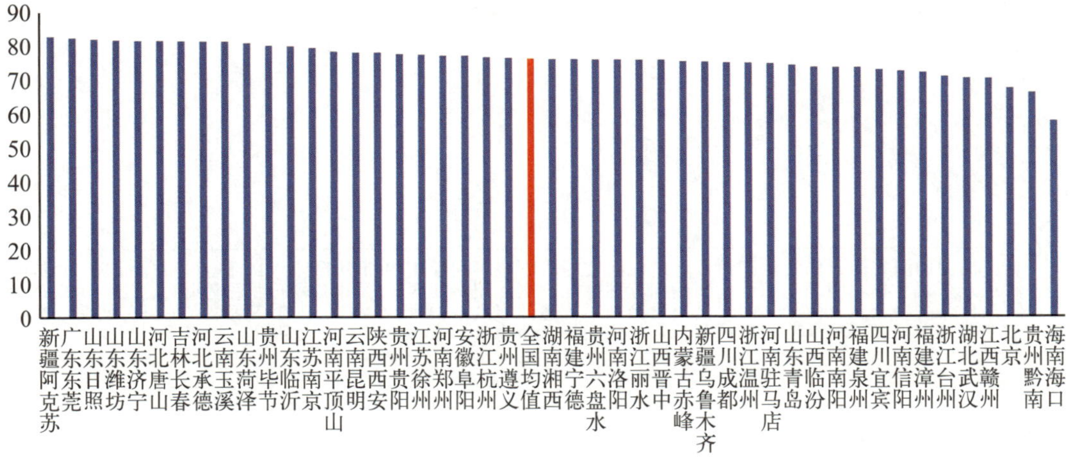

图5－1 2019年部分城市PPP市场透明度总指数分布

5.2.3 各城市即时公开和适时公开结果分析

图5-2和图5-3则分别展示了这46个城市的即时公开透明度指数和适时公开透明度指数的结果分布。通过图5-2可以看出，2019年即时公开透明度指数的平均结果要明显高于2017年，且与2018年的即时公开透明度指数相比差异不大：2019年即时公开透明度指数平均为78.6，2018年即时公开透明度指数平均为77.95，而2017年即时公开透明度指数平均为58.67。同时，通过图5-3可以观察到，2019年很多城市的适时公开透明度指数和2018年的适时公开透明度指数差异不大。此外，还可以发现从新疆阿克苏到贵州遵义在内的大部分城市2019年即时公开透明度指数和适时公开透明度指数都高于2018年，而从湖南湘西到海南海口在内的大部分城市2019年即时公开透明度指数和适时公开透明度指数都低于2018年，说明2019年PPP项目信息透明度工作做得好的城市在即时公开和适时公开方面做得都好，但是也有很多城市在即时公开和适时公开方面均在"走下坡路"。

在即时公开上，2019年较2018年进步幅度位居前三的城市为新疆阿克苏、广东东莞和江苏南京，其中，新疆阿克苏由2018年的67.11上升到2019年的85.02，广东东莞由2018年的70.25上升到2019年的84.61，江苏南京由2018年的73.37上升到2019年的83.41；退步最多的城市分别为浙江台州、贵州黔南和海南海口。在适时公

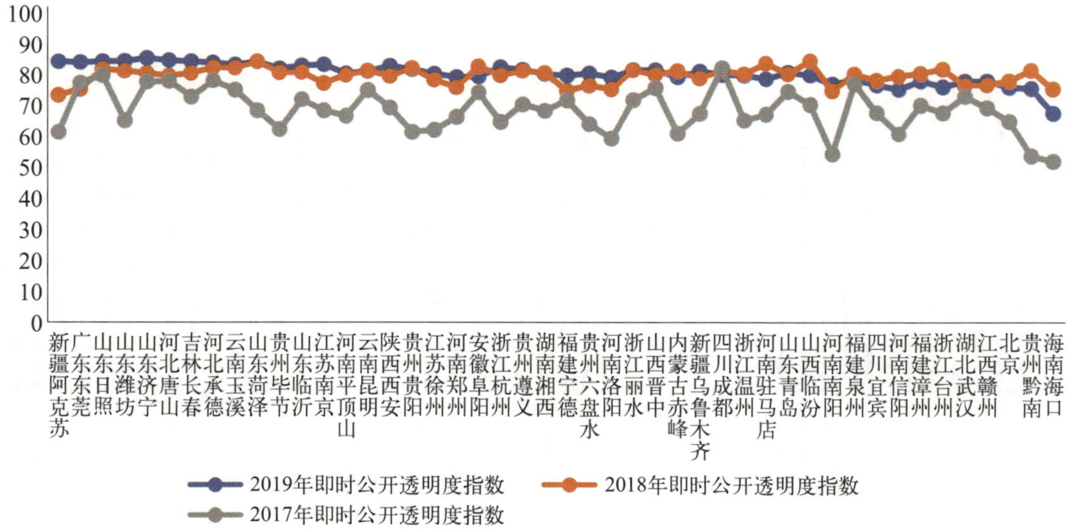

图5-2 2017—2019年部分城市PPP项目即时公开透明度指数分布

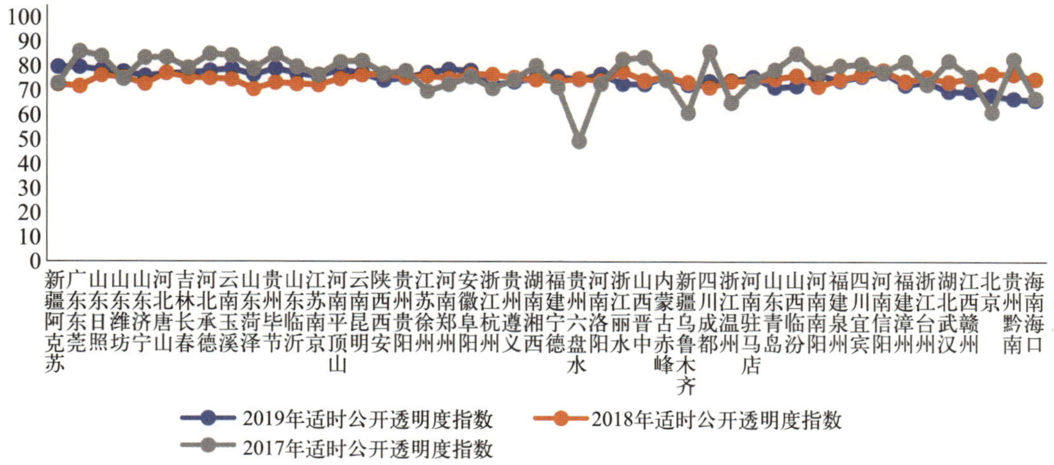

图 5-3　2017—2019 年部分城市 PPP 项目适时公开透明度指数分布

开上，2019年较2018年进步幅度位居前三的城市为新疆阿克苏、广东东莞和山东菏泽；退步最多的城市分别为北京、贵州黔南和海南海口。而且通过图5-4也可以发现，总体而言，2019年的即时公开透明度指数高于适时公开透明度指数，说明各城市在PPP项目信息适时公开方面的工作还有待进一步加强。

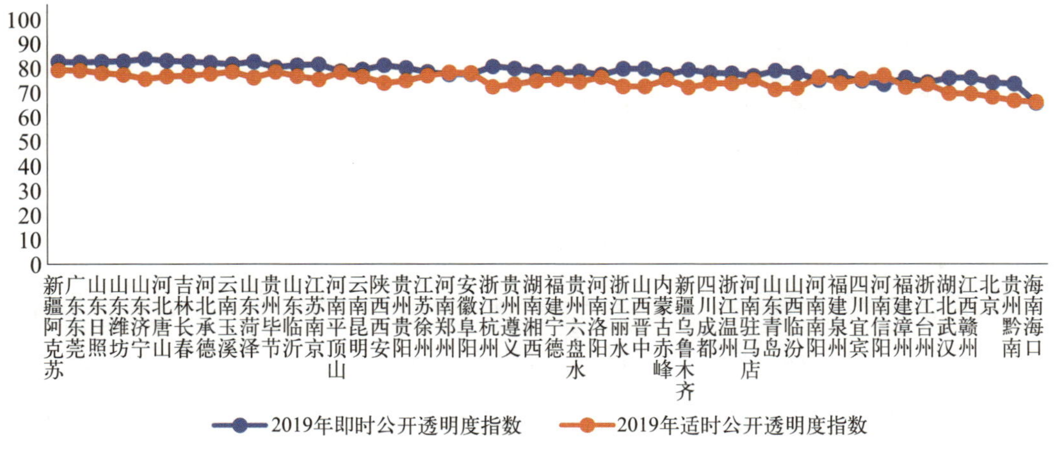

图 5-4　2019 年部分城市 PPP 项目即时公开和适时公开透明度指数分布

5.2.4　分阶段的各城市透明度结果分析

这些城市PPP项目不同阶段的分指数结果如图5-5和图5-6所示。图5-5展示了各个城市的即时公开透明度指数在识别阶段、准备阶段、采购阶段和执行阶段的情况对比，从中可以很明显地得出如下结论：在即时公开部分，各个城市的识别阶段和准备阶段信息公开工作做得比较好，指数普遍高于其他各阶段。出现这一结果的现实原因可能在于：识别阶段、准备阶段基本信息的完善有助于吸引社会资本方的参与，直接影响到PPP项目的招标结果，因而大多数项目的主管部门会较为重视识别阶段和准备阶段即时公开的信息填报，其平均指数分别达到89.59和83.07。而采购阶段和执行阶段的信息透明度指数平均分别为74.01和70.79，处在四个阶段公开情况的中下水平，且执行阶段、准备阶段的即时公开透明度指数的跳跃性很大。同时，也应该注意到，部分城市准备阶段的即时公开透明度指数是低于采购阶段和执行阶段的，尤其是海南海口，其准备阶段的即时公开透明度指数只有23.53，反映出该城市在PPP项目准备阶段的即时公开上还有待进一步提高。

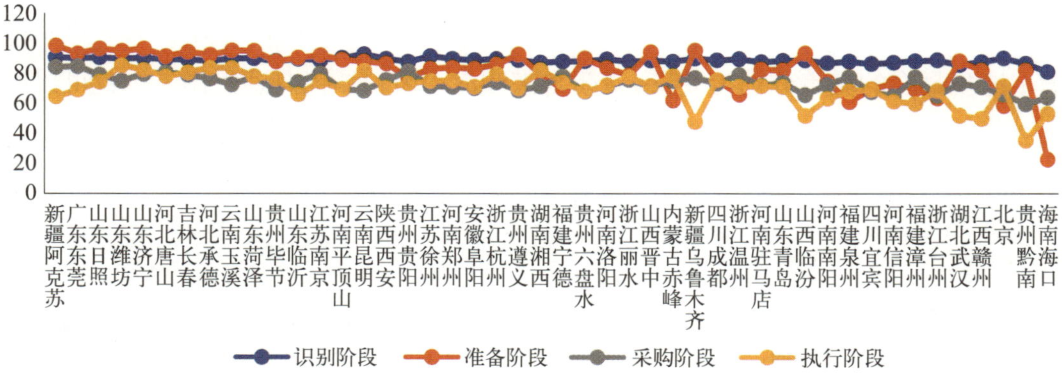

图5-5　2019年部分城市PPP项目即时公开透明度指数各阶段分布

对于适时公开透明度指数的情况（见图5-6），在适时公开部分所包含的识别阶段、准备阶段和采购阶段中，明显处于最低位的是各个城市的识别阶段信息公开情况，其平均指数为44.72，而适时公开的准备阶段的信息公开工作则做得较好，平均指数达到96.29。出现这种情况可能是因为在适时公开的识别阶段，包括物有所值评价报告、财政承受能力论证报告、可行性研究报告等重要的报告附件，这些报告信息的披露情况经过课题组的严格考察，发现存在问题的报告数量很多，甚至会出现"虚假"披露的情况。因此，物有所值评价报告、财政承受能力论证报告、可行性研究报告的不规范导致识别阶段的适时公开透明度指数在识别、准备、采购三阶段中排名最低。同时，这46个城市之间三个阶段的适时公开透明度指数没有发生很大的跳跃。

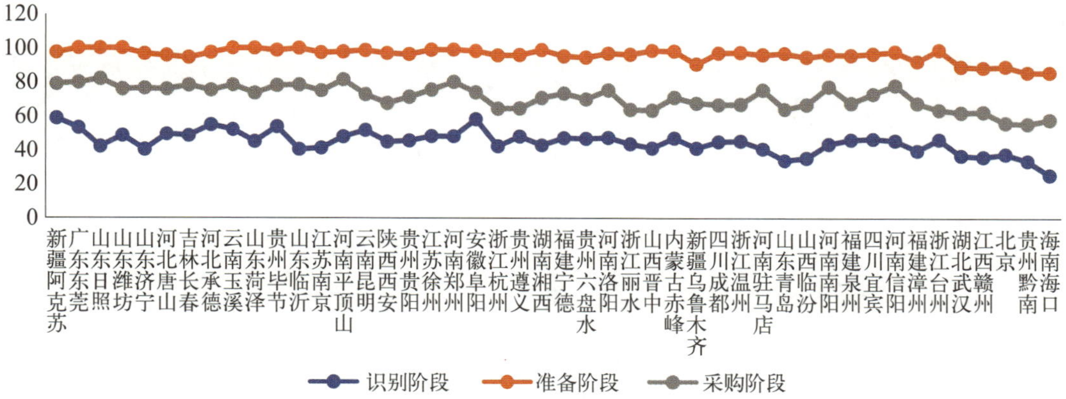

图5-6　2019年部分城市PPP项目适时公开透明度指数各阶段分布

如此鲜明的对比也可以警示各个地方相关部门应该重视“两评”的工作质量和信息公开工作，同时也提醒中央主管部门不能放松对“两评”的规范要求，由于问题普遍存在，所以有必要针对这些重点工作提出更详细、更具有可操作性的政策指引。

5.3　主要城市“两评一案”结果

本节将延续省级分析的内容，对重点城市“两评一案”的透明度结果进行分析。从表5-3可以看出，广东东莞、贵州毕节、云南玉溪和河南平顶山在“两评一案”报告信息披露上的工作成绩值得肯定，特别是广东东莞和河南平顶山的物有所值评价报告和财政承受能力论证报告的排名均是第一位，在这两项的信息披露上均取得了满分的成绩，根据前文的定义，即没有信息披露不全，更没有“虚假”披露行为。但是河南平顶山的PPP市场透明度总指数并没有特别靠前，原因在于对其他一些需要公布的指标，未能及时上报到系统中，尤其是在实施方案的信息公开上。

表5-3　“两评一案”城市的结果排序

排名	适时公开透明度指数	物有所值评价报告	财政承受能力论证报告	实施方案
1	新疆阿克苏	广东东莞	广东东莞	新疆阿克苏
2	广东东莞	河南平顶山	河南平顶山	安徽阜阳

（续表）

排名	适时公开透明度指数	物有所值评价报告	财政承受能力论证报告	实施方案
3	云南玉溪	山东日照	贵州毕节	江苏南京
4	贵州毕节	贵州毕节	云南玉溪	河北承德
5	河南平顶山	云南玉溪	山东潍坊	江苏徐州
6	河南郑州	山东菏泽	山东菏泽	吉林长春
7	山东日照	内蒙古赤峰	内蒙古赤峰	北京
8	安徽阜阳	山东临沂	山东临沂	浙江丽水
9	河北承德	山东潍坊	河南郑州	河北唐山
10	山东潍坊	云南昆明	云南昆明	福建泉州
11	河南信阳	河南郑州	湖南湘西	新疆乌鲁木齐
12	江苏徐州	新疆阿克苏	新疆阿克苏	海南海口
13	吉林长春	河南信阳	山东日照	河南驻马店
14	山东临沂	山西晋中	河南信阳	河南南阳
15	云南昆明	湖南湘西	山西晋中	河南洛阳
16	河北唐山	江苏徐州	四川宜宾	湖北武汉
17	河南洛阳	陕西西安	福建宁德	浙江杭州
18	河南南阳	河北承德	河北承德	贵州六盘水
19	山东菏泽	福建宁德	陕西西安	浙江台州
20	四川宜宾	山东济宁	河南洛阳	浙江温州
21	福建宁德	河南洛阳	安徽阜阳	贵州贵阳
22	山东济宁	安徽阜阳	山东济宁	四川宜宾
23	内蒙古赤峰	江苏南京	河南南阳	河南郑州
24	江苏南京	四川宜宾	江苏南京	四川成都
25	河南驻马店	浙江温州	浙江温州	河南信阳
26	贵州贵阳	浙江台州	浙江台州	贵州遵义
27	湖南湘西	福建泉州	福建泉州	江西赣州
28	贵州六盘水	贵州遵义	贵州遵义	山东青岛
29	福建泉州	河南南阳	四川成都	贵州黔南
30	浙江温州	河北唐山	河北唐山	陕西西安

（续表）

排名	适时公开透明度指数	物有所值评价报告	财政承受能力论证报告	实施方案
31	陕西西安	贵州贵阳	贵州贵阳	贵州毕节
32	四川成都	贵州六盘水	浙江杭州	河南平顶山
33	浙江台州	浙江丽水	贵州六盘水	内蒙古赤峰
34	贵州遵义	四川成都	浙江丽水	福建漳州
35	浙江丽水	河南驻马店	江苏徐州	福建宁德
36	山西晋中	吉林长春	河南驻马店	广东东莞
37	浙江杭州	山西临汾	吉林长春	山东菏泽
38	福建漳州	福建漳州	山西临汾	云南昆明
39	新疆乌鲁木齐	浙江杭州	福建漳州	云南玉溪
40	山西临汾	新疆乌鲁木齐	新疆乌鲁木齐	湖南湘西
41	山东青岛	湖北武汉	湖北武汉	山西临汾
42	湖北武汉	江西赣州	山东青岛	山西晋中
43	江西赣州	山东青岛	江西赣州	山东济宁
44	北京	贵州黔南	贵州黔南	山东潍坊
45	贵州黔南	北京	北京	山东临沂
46	海南海口	海南海口	海南海口	山东日照

此外，内蒙古赤峰在物有所值评价报告和财政承受能力论证报告方面均排在靠前的位置，但是适时公开透明度指数却排名倒数，主要归因于实施方案方面做得很差。海南海口和北京在物有所值评价报告和财政承受能力论证报告方面均排在垫底的位置，在实施方案方面做得还可以。

5.4 总指数跨期变化的原因分析

财政部印发的《关于规范政府和社会资本合作（PPP）综合信息平台项目库管理的通知》（财办金〔2017〕92号）提出，未按规定开展“两个论证”的PPP项目应该予以清退，具体包括：已进入采购阶段但未开展物有所值评价或财政承受能力论证的（2015年4月7日前进入采购阶段但未开展财政承受能力论证以及2015年12月18日前进入采购阶段但未开展物有所值评价的项目除外）；虽已开展物有所值评价和财政承受能力论证，但评价方法和程序不符合规定的。此外，随着大量PPP项目进入执行阶段，即时公开中需要公开社会资本方的信息、项目建设进度情况、项目质量符合性检查情况、社会资本或项目公司的年度运营情况及运营绩效达标情况以及中期评估报告等信息，适时公开中需要公开融资额度、融资主要条件及融资交割情况，这部分信息的公开比较难做，执行阶段信息公开难度的增加可能会阻碍2019年总指数的提高。正如第3章所分析的，2019年PPP市场透明度指数相较于2018年的变化并不大，可能是因为进入执行阶段的项目数占比大幅增加导致2019年PPP项目信息透明度降低，以及部分项目退库导致2019年PPP项目信息透明度增加双重因素复合作用的结果。

在本节，我们通过城市层面的数据来进一步分析这一问题。首先，图5-7展示了2019年较2018年执行阶段项目数量占比差异与2019年较2018年PPP市场透明度总指数差异的关系。从图5-7可以发现，2019年较2018年执行阶段项目数量占比差异与2019年较2018年PPP市场透明度总指数差异之间存在负相关关系，说明2019年较2018年执行阶段项目数量占比越多，2019年较2018年PPP市场透明度总指数越

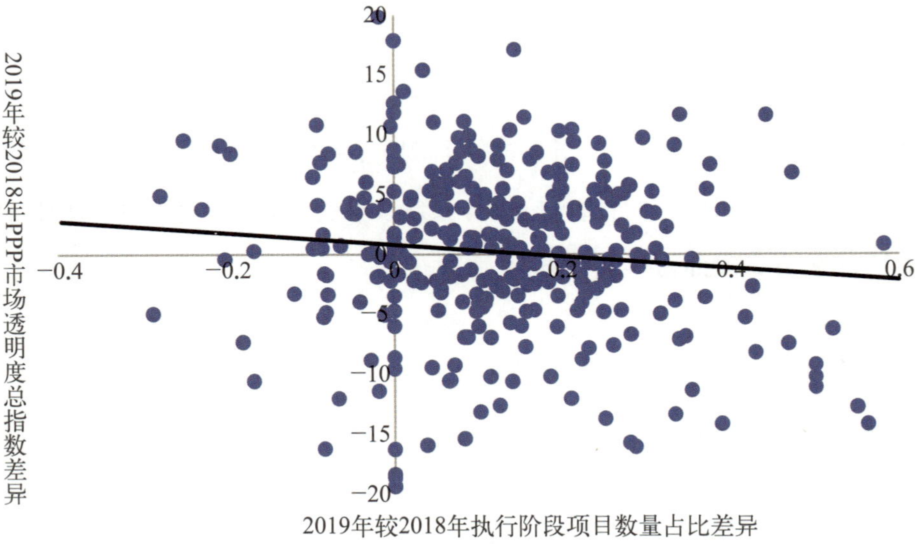

图5-7　2019年较2018年执行阶段项目数量占比差异与2019年较2018年PPP市场透明度总指数差异的相关性

低，这可能是因为更多项目进入执行阶段，适时公开工作比即时公开工作要难做，所以拉低了一些2019年项目的信息透明度指数。

此外，从图5-8可以发现，2019年退库项目数量占比与2019年较2018年PPP市场透明度总指数差异之间存在正相关关系，说明2019年各级财政部门对管理库入库项目集中清理工作又取得了进展，退库项目数量占比越多的地区，PPP市场透明度指数提高越多。

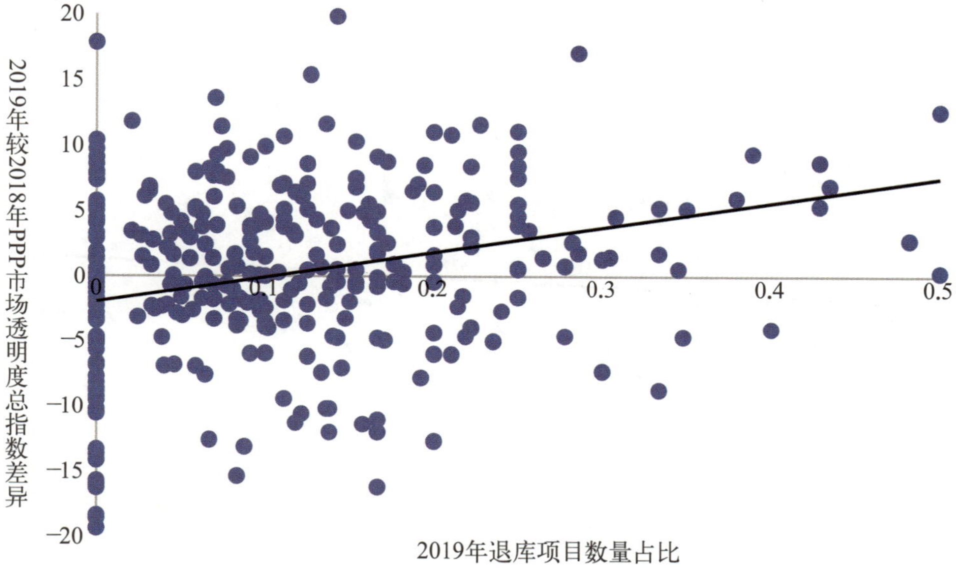

图5-8 2019年退库项目数量占比与2019年较2018年PPP市场透明度总指数差异的相关性

5.5 总指数与经济财政的相关性

本节以《2017中国城市统计年鉴》中统计的城市为研究对象，共289个地级以上城市，具体包括4个直辖市、15个副省会城市、17个省会城市和253个地级市，采用定量分析的方法，以289个地级以上城市2019年PPP市场透明度总指数为基础，画出了2019年PPP市场透明度总指数与2017年财政缺口的散点图（见图5-9），其中横轴为财政收支缺口的情况，纵轴为2019年PPP市场透明度总指数。选定2017年289个城市层面的数据作为研究对象主要基于以下的考虑：首先，这289个城市涵盖了全国90%的人口规模，基本可以代表全国的情况；其次，选定2017年的人均GDP、财政收入、财政支出的数据，可以避免内生性的问题，而且从《2017中国城市统计年鉴》获得的数据也可以确保其权威性。

通过图5-9可以发现，2019年PPP市场透明度指数与2017年财政收支缺口存在正相关关系，财政收支缺口越大，2019年PPP市场透明度指数越大。这可能是因为财政收支缺口越大的地区，更需要通过PPP来融资，从而更有压力将其做得更规范，以吸引社会资本方，从而透明度指数就更高。通过图5-10可以发现GDP增长率与2019年PPP市场透明度指数负相关，即经济增长越慢的地区，PPP市场透明度指数越高。

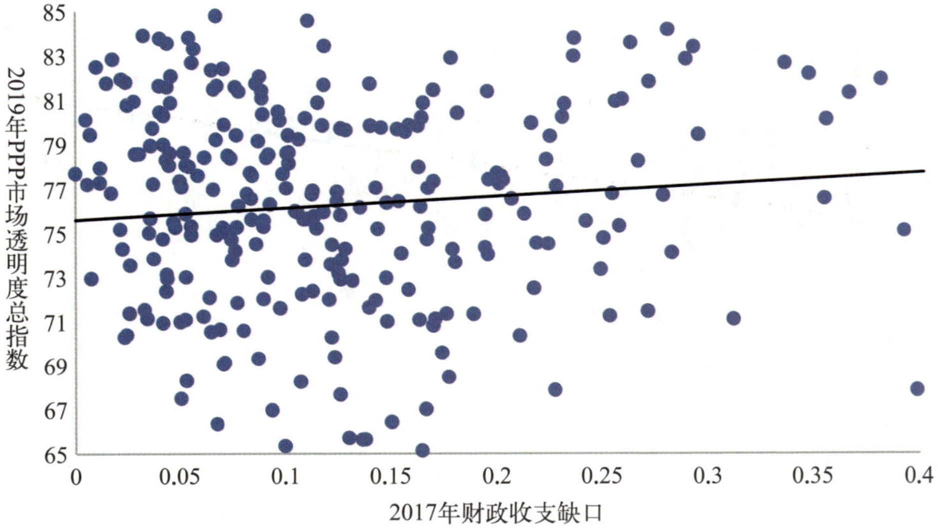

图5-9　2017年财政收支缺口与2019年PPP市场透明度指数相关性

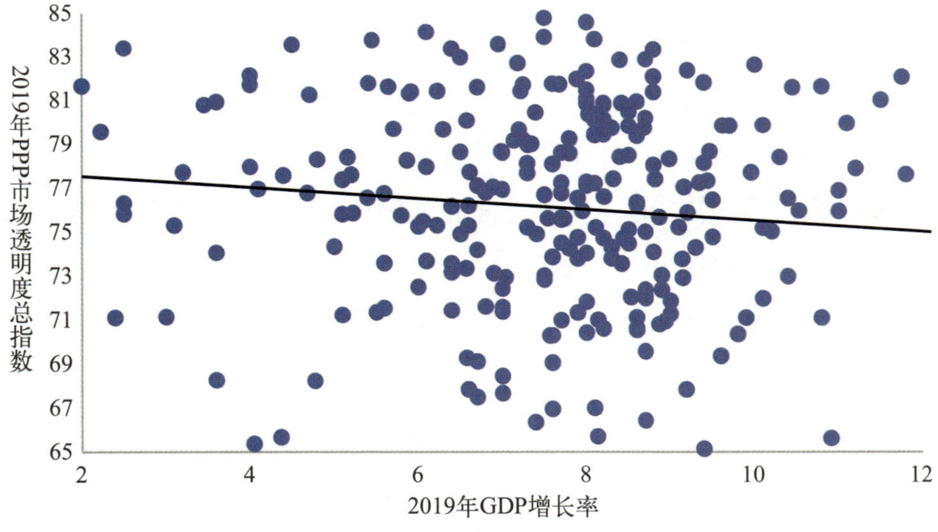

图5-10　2019年GDP增长率与2019年PPP市场透明度指数相关性

6

PPP中介机构信息公开现状评估

6.1 中介机构透明度评估意义

PPP项目反映了政府和社会资本方的长期合作关系，项目质量也需要接受长期考验，因而各方对PPP项目各类专业性咨询服务的需求和要求均远高于传统项目，聘请专业的中介咨询机构已成为国外政府实施PPP项目的通用做法。为了提高项目开发以及实施的质量和效率，我国财政部也在多个文件中提出，要在PPP项目中引进专业中介提供技术服务，以完善项目设计、优化项目方案。例如，2014年，《政府和社会资本合作模式操作指南（试行）》（财金〔2014〕113号）提出要积极发挥第三方专业机构的作用。2015年，财政部在《关于进一步做好政府和社会资本合作项目示范工作的通知》（财金〔2015〕57号）中进一步提出，要选择一批能力较强的专业中介机构，为示范项目实施提供技术支持。

具体来说，PPP项目中关联主体众多且关系复杂，在PPP项目的识别、准备、采购、执行和移交等过程中，往往会用到财务、法律、金融等多方面的专业知识，政府官员在具体实施的过程中往往捉襟见肘，很难具备项目所需的全部技能。中介机构则不然，他们在各自的领域内具备核心竞争力，实践经验丰富，可以帮助政府设计物有所值评价报告和可行性研究报告，从而提高政府与社会资本方的谈判能力。

然而，在我国PPP项目"井喷式"发展的同时，相关咨询服务需求的激增带动了很多公司转行做PPP中介机构，导致我国PPP中介机构能力参差不齐，甚至有些PPP中介机构根本不具备相应的专业技能。为此，相关监管部门也非常重视PPP中介机构的监督管理，制定了《PPP咨询机构库管理暂行办法》（财金〔2017〕8号）等管理办法，对PPP中介机构提交的信息进行核查和予以公开，向全社会开放入库中介机构信息查询功能，主动接受服务对象和社会各界人士的监督，促进PPP项目咨询服务质量提升，推进我国PPP中介市场秩序的规范化。

为了考察我国PPP中介机构信息公开的现状，促进中介机构加大信息公开力度，从而更好地维护PPP市场可持续发展的良好市场环境，参考前文关于PPP项目信息透明度指数的编制，我们在本章也编制了一套PPP中介机构信息透明度指数，对PPP中介机构信息公开的现状进行了评估。[①]不过，考虑到PPP中介机构信息公开的指标体系、评估对象与PPP项目信息透明度指数之间存在巨大的差异，因此，我们并没有将两者编入同一个指数体系当中，而是单独对PPP中介机构的信息公开现状进行指数编制和分析。

6.2 指标体系构建与指数计算

在汇报PPP中介机构信息透明度指数的结果之前，我们首先来简要介绍PPP中介机构信息公开评估的指标体系和指数计算的方法。

6.2.1 指标体系设计的原则和依据

（1）指标体系设计的原则。由于中介机构信息内容涵盖的多层次性，指标体系也必须由多层次结构组成，才能反映出各层次的特征。因此，参考前文关于PPP项目信息透明度指数编制的方法，课题组对PPP中介机构信息透明度指数的编制和信息公开现状的评估也划分了几个不同的层级。具体而言，参考PPP相关信息公开管理办法的精神和PPP综合信息平台中的中介库现状，课题组将PPP中介机构信息透明度的指标体系分为总指数、二级指标（具体包括机构基本信息、机构承担的PPP项目信息以及机构网站信息）以及底层具体指标三个层次。

（2）指标体系设计依据与数据来源。根据主管部门财政部政府和社会资本合作中心的规定，PPP中介机构的信息均要在财政部政府和社会资本合作中心举办的PPP综合信息平台的"机构库信息公开"系统中进行公布。考虑到数据来源的一致性，课题组选择该数据库系统中的具体字段作为评估依据和主要数据来源，具体包括

① 需要再次说明的是，这里评估的依然是中介机构信息公开情况的评估，并不是信息公开内容质量的评估，更不涉及PPP中介机构总体经营规范性或业务规模、市场占有率等的评估。

机构基本信息、机构承担的PPP项目信息两部分内容。此外，为了进一步丰富指标体系，考虑到PPP中介机构并不太多，课题组还逐个检索登录中介机构的官方网站查阅相关公开信息，以评估其网站中是否披露与PPP有关的信息，从而构成中介机构网站信息这个二级指标。

（3）评估对象。结合PPP主管部门的政策意见以及考虑到实际可操作性，课题组将分析对象界定为在PPP综合信息平台中“机构库信息公开”系统中入库且在PPP综合信息平台中公示的中介机构，共计357家。

（4）数据采集。课题组以政府和社会资本合作中心网站可获取数据为基础①，同时登录各家中介机构官方网站获取指标，并对其进行归类。经过课题组的整理，指标体系共包含29② 个指标字段，课题组对其进行了逐个提取，包括网站直接阅读提取和复制粘贴提取等方式。

6.2.2 PPP中介机构信息公开评估指标体系

根据上述原则和方法，PPP中介机构信息透明度指数最终的指标体系层级如图6-1所示，PPP中介机构信息公开评估指标体系包括总指数，机构基本信息、项目信息、机构网站信息三个二级分指数，以及再下一层级的具体指标。

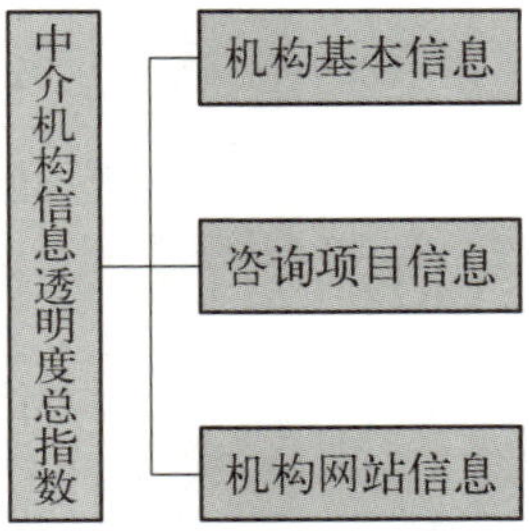

图6-1 PPP中介机构信息透明度指数层级图

PPP中介机构信息公开评估的具体指标如表6-1所示。在这些具体指标的评估得分上，课题组采取简单化原则。对于大部分指标，有信息公布，则得分为1，否则就得分为零。但对于个别信息含量较为丰富的指标，课题组也设计了0.5分这一中间得

① 本章数据全部来自课题组的手工收集。
② 与2018年的评估相比，增加了咨询项目的示范级别这一指标。

分的情形。具体而言，对于“机构网站”这个指标，如果在政府和社会资本合作中心网站上有公布网址，则得分为1分；如果通过百度等检索手段可以检索到公司网址，则得分为0.5分；既未在政府和社会资本合作中心网站上公布公司网址，也无法检索到，则得0分。此外，对于机构网站上的新闻，如果没有新闻，则为0分；有新闻但最近三条新闻时间间隔超过30天，则为0.5分；间隔时间不超过30天，则为1分。如此设计这些指标的得分，是为了有更好的区分度。

表6-1 PPP中介机构信息透明度评价指标体系

二级指标	具体指标
机构基本信息	公司名称
	机构简介
	经营范围
	注册成立时间
	成立年份
	通讯地址
	邮政编码
	机构网站
	业绩统计
	委托方评价
	核心高管
	机构荣誉
	机构资质
	历史退库记录
咨询项目信息	项目名称
	项目阶段
	所属地区
	所属行业
	投资总额
	示范级别

（续表）

二 级 指 标	具 体 指 标
咨询项目信息	咨询服务业业绩类别
	咨询机构项目经理
	项目经理PPP从业经历
	咨询服务委托方名称
	咨询服务合同签字页
网站信息	网站高管
	网站资质
	业务项目
	公司最近新闻

6.2.3 指数合成计算方法

在多指标综合评价中，权重确定直接影响评价的结果。考虑到与上一年评估结果的可比性，课题组对指数合成采取的办法与上一年一致。具体地，在具体指标合成为二级指标过程中，课题组选择了变异系数法进行合成。该方法的基本思路是根据各个指标在所有评价对象上观测值的变异程度大小，对其进行赋权。也就是说，如果一项指标的变异系数较大，那么说明这个指标在衡量评估对象总体的差异方面具有较大的解释力，则对这个指标就应该赋予较大的权重。

具体地，利用变异系数法确定各指标权重，首先要计算各指标的变异系数，该值反映了各指标的绝对变异程度：

$$CV_i = \frac{S_i}{\bar{x}_i}\ ,\ i = 1, 2, 3, \cdots, n$$

其中，S_i为各指标标准差，$\bar{x}_i$为各指标均值。然后，对各个指标变异系数进行归一化处理，计算各指标权重：

$$q_i = \frac{CV_i}{\sum_{i=1}^{n} CV_i}\ ,\ i = 1, 2, 3, \cdots, n$$

最后，将二级指标再合成为总指数。此时，课题组则选择了最为简单的简单平均法：机构基本信息、咨询项目信息和机构网站信息的权重各占1/3。

6.3 中介机构信息透明度指数分析

6.3.1 指数基本特征

表6-2是PPP中介机构信息透明度指数的基本描述性统计，从中我们可以看出，357个中介机构的透明度指数平均为75.2，接近前文所讨论的PPP项目透明度全国平均指数（详见第3章）。具体到三个二级分指数上，从表6-2中也可以看出，PPP中介机构参与的PPP项目的信息公开做得较好，分指数为90.89；在PPP综合信息平台中披露的中介机构基本信息次之，分指数为76.09；课题组从PPP中介机构官网上自行设计指标并采集的机构网站信息的分指数最低，仅为58.63。从时间前后对比看，2019年中介机构信息透明度指数与2018年基本相当，变化不大；从分项指标看，2019年中介机构基本信息披露工作优于2018年，但咨询项目信息和机构网站信息公开工作有一定的下滑；从政策角度看，咨询项目信息改善空间并不大，但机构网站信息公开工作未来需要进一步加强。

表6-2 指数描述统计

变 量	2018年			2019年		
	观测值	均 值	标准差	观测值	均 值	标准差
总指数得分	352	75.76	20.56	357	75.20	17.25
机构基本信息	352	70.42	28.49	357	76.09	22.41
咨询项目信息	352	94.57	14.67	357	90.89	20.06
机构网站信息	352	62.30	41.02	357	58.63	39.00

图6-2则进一步给出了PPP中介机构透明度总指数和三个二级分指数的直方分布图，从中可以看出PPP中介机构的项目信息和机构基本信息大部分公布较好，而机

构网站信息的公布则存在两极分化的现象，有一部分机构网站信息公开较好，但确实也有一些机构网站信息公开情况较差，这一结果也就导致表6-2中显示的网站信息公开分指数标准差较大。

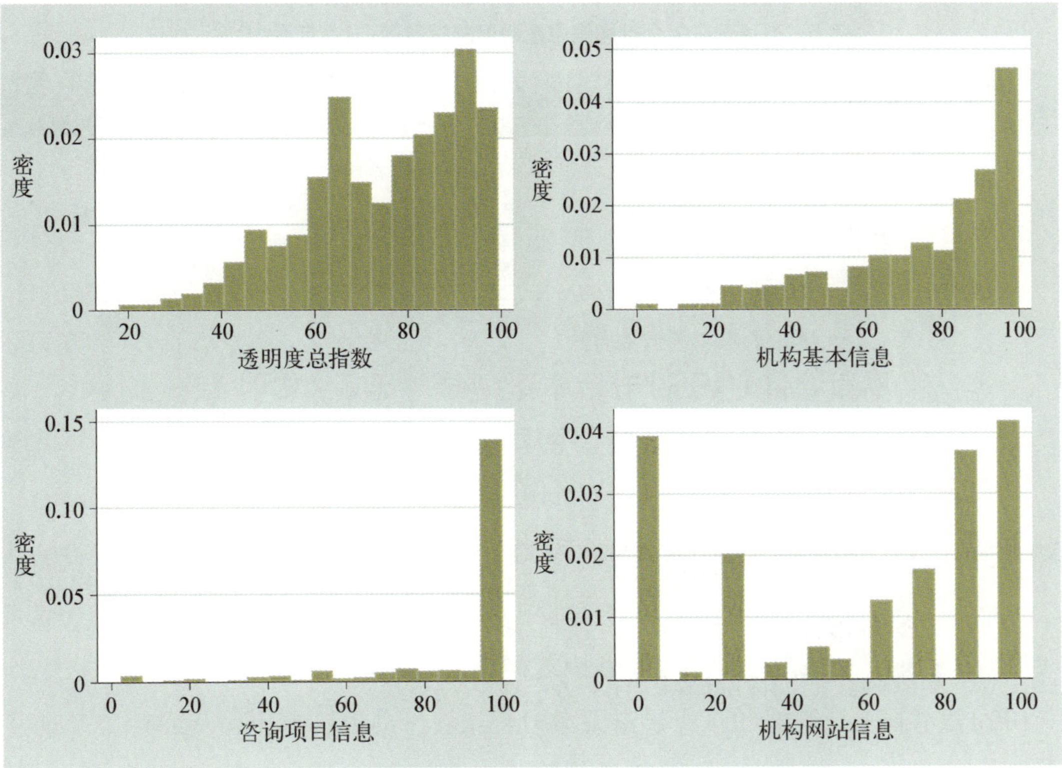

图6-2 PPP中介机构信息透明度总指数及分指数直方图

表6-3则给出了PPP中介机构透明度总指数排名前10位和后10位的中介机构具体名单。华春建设工程项目管理有限责任公司、安徽省招标集团股份有限公司、天津房友工程咨询有限公司三个公司信息公开工作非常好，在课题组设计的29个中介机构信息公开指标中，接近满分。但从表6-3也能看出，确有一些中介机构信息公开工作不太到位，信息透明度总指数仅为18～40，相关监管部门有必要督促这些中介机构加大信息公开的力度，特别是机构网站信息。与上一年对比看，最好的前10名变化并不大，换句话说，上一年度排前10名的机构大多数今年仍在前10名。中国远东国际招标有限公司由于机构网站信息公开有了很大改进，今年进入榜单前十，位列第五；上海济邦投资咨询有限公司今年进入榜单前十，提升了13位。最差的后10名

与上一年相比变化略大些，不过依旧是那些上一年排名靠后的公司。山东德邻企业管理咨询有限公司和城和城智库（北京）咨询有限公司并不在上一年的评估样本内，因而排名变化并不适用于这两个中介机构。

表6-3 PPP中介机构信息透明度总指数前10名与后10名

排名	机构名称	总指数	较上一年排名变化
1	华春建设工程项目管理有限责任公司	99.48	+2
2	安徽省招标集团股份有限公司	99.48	0
3	天津房友工程咨询有限公司	99.48	+1
4	中天运会计师事务所（特殊普通合伙）	99.35	+6
5	中国远东国际招标有限公司	99.35	+51
6	中招国际招标有限公司	99.03	−1
7	中工武大设计研究有限公司	98.90	−1
8	北京中交建设工程咨询有限公司	98.77	−1
9	上海济邦投资咨询有限公司	98.06	+13
10	中德华建（北京）国际工程技术有限公司	97.93	+3
……			
348	新疆联信方略企业管理咨询有限责任公司	39.72	−16
349	山东德邻企业管理咨询有限公司	37.90	0
350	武汉开元地产信息开发有限公司	36.72	−11
351	天津倚天工程咨询有限公司	34.84	−40
352	北京财科智合管理咨询有限责任公司	33.12	−13
353	贵州中建政研投资管理有限公司	32.12	−7
354	菏泽江天资产评估事务所	31.62	−6
355	北京光环时代国际咨询有限公司	29.96	−15
356	城和城智库（北京）咨询有限公司	24.32	0
357	新疆承泰建业工程管理咨询有限公司	18.13	−40

6.3.2 PPP中介信息公开与业务量相关关系

在图6-3当中，我们绘制了PPP中介机构信息透明度指数与其参与的PPP项目数量之间的关系。不出意料，结论与上一年高度一致。从中可以明显地看出，参与的PPP项目数量越多，PPP中介机构信息透明度指数就越高。从逻辑和实践上讲，参与PPP项目数量与中介机构信息公开存在相互促进的关系。一方面，参与项目数量越多，说明公司规模越大，管理越规范，从而更加重视自身的信息公开工作，信息透明度指数就越高；另一方面，中介机构信息公开工作做得越好，也就越能吸引更多的客户，从而参与更多的PPP项目。这两方面的原因共同作用，使得PPP中介机构信息透明度指数与中介机构参与的PPP项目数量之间呈现显著的正相关关系。

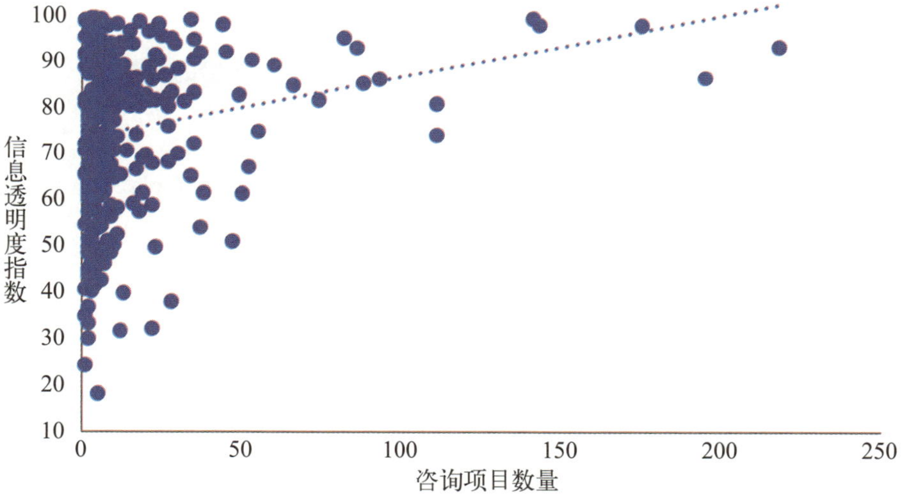

图6-3 PPP中介机构信息透明度总指数与咨询项目数量的关系

6.3.3 PPP中介机构信息公开与公司资历相关关系

如前文所述，PPP中介机构信息透明度与中介机构业务能力高度正相关，这里我们进一步分析中介机构信息透明度与中介机构资历的关系。从图6-4可以看出，中介机构经营时间越久，其信息公开工作的确也就做得越好，中介机构“年龄”与中介机构信息透明度指数之间存在高度显著的正相关关系。这一发现与上一年的结果也非常类似。当然这只是一个平均意义上的统计规律，新成立的PPP中介机构，信息公开工作并非全都一无是处，从图6-4也可以看到，也有新成立的PPP中介机构信息透明度指数可以达到80甚至90以上。

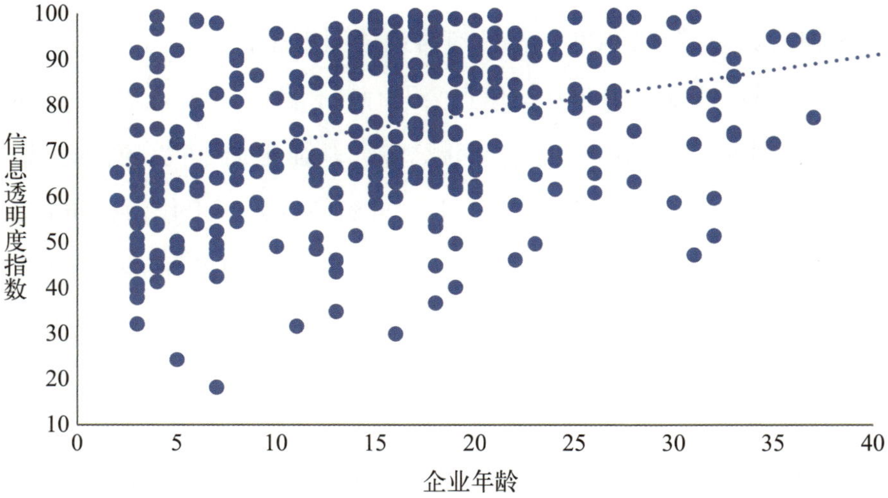

图6-4　PPP中介机构信息透明度指数与企业年龄的关系

7

总结与展望

7.1 报告总结

PPP是Public-Private Partnerships的英文首字母缩写，译为政府和社会资本合作。当前，中国的PPP模式已经不仅仅是政府的一种市场化投融资手段，更是一次全面的、系统的公共服务供给市场化社会化改革举措，因而各界对PPP的发展都寄予厚望，希望PPP能起到引领财政体制机制改革、助力公共事业全面深化改革的作用。在这一背景下，PPP项目的规范化管理就显得尤为重要，其中PPP项目及时、完善的信息公开又是PPP项目规范化管理的基础。2017年以来，财政部连续发布的多份文件都涉及了PPP项目的信息公开工作，特别是2017年初发布的《政府和社会资本合作(PPP)综合信息平台信息公开管理暂行办法》(财金〔2017〕1号)，详细规定了PPP项目信息公开的各方面要求。进入2018年后，PPP项目的退库清理成为PPP管理的重心之一，2 000多个不符合管理规范的PPP项目被清理退库，同时也有不少新增项目加入PPP管理库中。进入2019年后，伴随着更多的PPP项目进入执行阶段，如何有效推动PPP项目适时公开信息的管理工作显得愈发重要。同时，公众对提高PPP项目信息质量的呼声也越来越高。2020年3月31日，财政部发布《政府与社会资本合作项目绩效管理操作指引》，全方位建立了完整的PPP绩效考核体系，明确了责任主体，将信息真实、公开、透明、质量纳入具体的考核细则。

在此背景下，上海财经大学PPP研究中心课题组继过去连续两年对截至年底的PPP项目信息公开工作进行评估后，又对截至2019年12月31日的中国PPP项目的最新信息公开状况进行了详细的评估。具体而言，课题组对2019年底财政部PPP管理库的9 398个项目的信息公开工作进行了详细评估，编制了一套“2019中国PPP市场透明度指数”。该指数囊括75个指标字段，并分为即时公开透明度指数、适时公开透明度指数，以及识别阶段、准备阶段、采购阶段和执行阶段等各阶段的透明度分指数。

课题组采用层次分析法和专家打分法相结合的方法对指数进行合成：对于分指数下面的具体指标，按照专家对其重要程度的判定，设置不同的分值；而在分指数合成总指数当中，则采用同类指数编制过程中常用的层次分析法，以保证指数编制方法的可靠性。最终，通过对指数具体结果的统计分析，课题组得到以下几个主要发现：

第一，2019年全国PPP市场透明度总指数为76.19，较2018年略有提高。截至2019年12月31日，全国PPP市场透明度总指数为76.19（满分100，下同），与2018年的75.25相比提高了1左右。其中即时公开透明度指数为79.14，相比2018年（77.61）提高了1.5，而适时公开透明度指数为71.57，与2018年（71.55）几乎持平。进一步对PPP项目的异质性分析表明，PPP项目透明度指数没有明显的行业差异，示范项目和非示范项目的透明度指数也差别不大；项目发起时间则显著影响了项目透明度指数，项目发起时间越晚，项目越为透明。

第二，2019年PPP市场透明度指数相比2018年产生跨期差异的重要原因在于评估对象的变动。首先，进入执行阶段项目数占比大幅增加导致2019年PPP项目透明度降低。其次，通过分解退出效应、存量效应和进入效应来看，透明度指数较差的项目被退库，继续在库的项目改进了自己的信息公开工作，再加上新增项目比存量项目指数也要稍高一些，这些因素共同推动了2019年PPP市场透明度指数的提升。

第三，不同省份PPP市场透明度指数差异有所扩大，梯队层次明显。大多数省份的透明度指数集中在70～80之间，形成第二梯队。排名前5位的省份PPP市场透明度指数超过了80，构成了第一梯队。排在末尾的6个省份PPP市场透明度指数不足70，属于第三梯队。就具体排名而言，透明度排名第一的是甘肃（81.97），排名第二的是河北（81.29），排名第三的是吉林（80.52），排名第四的是山东（80.2），排名第五的是云南（80.17）。对比2018年的排行榜可以发现，PPP项目信息透明度工作进步最大的省份是江苏（77.69）和广东（77.20），两省在全国的排名较2018年均上升了17位，在2019年榜单中分列第九位和第十二位。

第四，超过半数的城市PPP市场透明度指数较2018年有所提高，剩余城市PPP市场透明度指数有所下降。课题组挑选了46个PPP项目数量较多（入管理库的项目超50个）的城市，对其PPP信息公开工作进行了分析。通过和2018年的PPP市场透明度指数对比可以发现，部分地级以上城市2019年的指数较2018年是大幅上升的，尤其是新疆阿克苏，其2019年总指数较2018年上升了15.39，紧随其后的是广东东莞，较2018年上升了13.62。不过，同时也可以发现，很多地级以上城市2019年的PPP市场透明度指数较2018年有所降低，尤其是贵州黔南和海南海口，2019年的总指数较2018年下降最多，分别下降了13.10和12。2019年PPP市场透明度指数排在前5位的城市为：新疆阿克苏（82.81）、广东东莞（82.48）、山东日照（82.06）、山东潍坊（81.79）和山东济宁（81.62）。

第五，PPP中介机构信息公开指数跨期差异不大，中介机构透明度指数得分与其资历、业务量正相关。课题组分析了PPP中介机构的信息公开现状，主要得到以下几个发现：中介机构信息透明度指数平均为75.20，而在二级指数中，中介机构参与的项目信息公开得分较高，但部分中介机构网站主动公开相关信息的工作不理想，与2018年相比意愿进一步降低。进一步的分析还发现，中介机构的信息透明度指数与中介机构参与的PPP项目数量和中介机构存续年龄具有明显的正相关关系。

7.2 政策建议

根据本报告的分析，我们可以看到，与2018年相比，2019年中国PPP市场信息公开工作进一步稳中有进。信息公开工作的完善为PPP市场的规范发展提供了重要保障，也对财政体制机制的改革起到了牵引作用。当然，在调查研究中，我们也注意到了一些PPP市场信息公开方面存在的问题。因此，针对这些问题，我们提出以下几条政策建议，以期PPP信息公开工作能进一步完善，提高PPP市场的信息透明度，进而推动中国PPP项目的规范管理。

第一，增加PPP项目信息公开的时效性考核。根据PPP项目的经营、管理规律，财政部对PPP项目的信息公开工作按照“即时公开”和“适时公开”两种类型进行分类管理，这是一个非常重要的创新举措，对PPP项目信息公开工作的有序开展很有价值。我们在PPP市场透明度指数编制过程中，也特别分开编制了即时公开和适时公开的透明度指数。不过，在研究过程中，我们也发现了一些可以改进的地方。我们认为，对于适时公开的信息，除了要考核其最终是否公开了该信息，最好还要记录、考核其公开该信息的时间节点。例如，有些信息是要求在进入执行阶段后6个月内公开，由于没有记录信息公开的具体时点，因而我们最终只能一刀切地考察2019年6月底进入执行阶段的所有项目，看其在2019年底是否公开了这些信息，但我们并不知道这些信息公开是否够即时。例如，有的项目可能在2019年初就进入了执行阶段，但其在2019年底才公开这些信息，超过了“进入执行阶段6个月内公开”的要求，但由于观察不到信息公开的时间节点，因而我们无法作出判断。再如，有的信息要求在该事项发生后次年4月30日之前进行公开，对此也应该要求项目公布该事项发生的具体时间和信息公开的具体时间。具体而言，可以考虑在PPP综合信息平台的后台中增加记录信息公开时间的信息，页面展示中则可以考虑以亮灯的形式提示这些项目的某些信息已经超过多少天还没有及时公开。例如，超过最后截止日30天还没公开为黄灯，超过60天还没公开则为红灯，等等。

第二，完善“不适用”信息和临时性重大事项信息公开的操作规范。PPP项目涵盖了跨度很大的不同行业和领域，在合作方式、回报机制等方面也存在很大的区别，因此，有些信息可能对一些项目适用，对另外一些项目就不适用。在指数编制中，对这些不完全适用于所有项目的信息，课题组没有将其纳入指数编制的指标范围内，因为该信息如果是空白，则课题组不知道该信息是不适用于该项目，还是适用于该项目但没有公布这一信息。其实对于该类信息，如果不适用于某项目，可以要求其特别注明“该信息不适用于本项目”或类似表述。这样处理后，我们就可以辨别所有项目在该类信息上究竟是不适用，还是适用但未公开。此外，对于临时性重大事项信息公开的管理，也应该有类似的要求。例如，对于“重大违约及履约担保的提取情况、对公众投诉的处理情况”等临时性重大事项的信息公开，应该要求如果没有发生该类事项，应该特别注明“截至目前，本项目没有发生重大违约及履约担保的提取、公众投诉等需要披露的事项”或其他类似表述。这一方法在上市公司、商业银行等机构的信息披露管理规范中是非常常见的。

第三，进一步完善即时公开、适时公开信息的分类管理。正如前文所述，将PPP项目的信息公开分为即时公开和适时公开是非常重要的举措。不过根据课题组的调查走访和专家座谈，我们发现对于什么信息应该即时公开、什么信息应该适时公开的分类标准，仍有进一步探讨改进的空间。例如，部分目前要求适时公开的信息其实可以进一步提高要求，改为即时公开；而另外一些资料整理工作较费时的即时公开的信息，也可以考虑改为适时公开。具体如何进一步完善这一分类管理的标准，我们建议主管部门广泛征求项目公司代表、中介咨询机构代表和学界代表的专业意见。

第四，加大对进入执行阶段后PPP项目信息公开的督察力度。通过前文的分析，我们可以看到进入执行阶段后的PPP项目信息公开工作很不理想，不如识别阶段和准备阶段的项目。究其原因就是执行阶段的项目缺少了“不公开不能入库”的工作抓手，因此，要推动执行阶段项目的信息公开，就必须探寻更多有效的监管路径。可以考虑将执行阶段的PPP项目的信息公开纳入绩效管理中，并与下一步的财政补贴、税收优惠等挂钩，从而督促有关部门和项目责任方增加对执行阶段项目信息公开的重视。

第五，加强PPP项目重点信息公开的监督检查力度。根据前文的分析，我们可以发现不同阶段的信息公开执行情况有较大差异。例如，在适时公开的信息中，识别阶段的物有所值评价报告、财政承受能力论证报告等公布情况相对于其他信息的公开情况不够理想，因而应该加强对这些信息的监督检查力度。通过随机抽查等方式，对这些报告的披露进展进行敦促。此外，对于执行阶段等信息，要完善制度的具体抓手，敦促有关责任主体主动公开、即时公开相关信息。例如，可以通过合同约定等方式，将项目公司在执行阶段的信息披露工作与政府付费等相挂钩，推动PPP项目信息公开工作。最后，为了防止虚假上传的现象，可以考虑通过关键词识别的方式进行自动化甄别。比如上传附件中不包含某些关键词的，不得上传。

第六，进一步明确PPP信息公开的责任主体和分工。自2017年3月1日开始施行《政府和社会资本合作（PPP）综合信息平台信息公开管理暂行办法》以来，PPP信息公开工作取得的积极成效有目共睹，这个在我们近三年的评估结果中一目了然。当然正如前文的指数结果所展示的，在PPP的信息公开中也存在一些难题尚待解决。具体而言，PPP信息公开的责任主体不够明晰会给PPP信息披露带来一系列系统性的问题。根据财金〔2017〕1号文第四条有关规定“地方各级财政部门会同同级政府有关部门推进、指导、协调、监督本行行政区域范围内的PPP项目信息公开工作，结合当地实际具体展开工作”。在具体实施过程中，财政部门需要协调水利局、交通局、体育局以及各方社会资本和第三方咨询机构收集汇总资料，而信息公开工作对财政部门以外的同级部门的约束力有限，往往会造成地方财政系统不能及时更新数据。这样的现象在财力较强的地方可能会得到缓解，因为信息公开进度不匹配，政府可以选择延迟付费的方式来惩罚相关部门。但这样的掣肘手段在财力单薄的地方难以实现，可能本身的条件就难以吸引到优质的社会资本，这样的做法会起到雪上加霜的效果。因此，还需要进一步明确责任主体和建设配套的激励机制。

第七，加强对PPP中介机构信息公开力度的推动。PPP项目是一种长期合作关系，项目质量会长期经受考验，对项目问题解决方案和项目协议的要求远远高于传统项目，聘请咨询公司已成为国外政府实施PPP项目的惯例。因此，在PPP项目的规范运行与管理中，PPP中介机构发挥着重要作用。通过第6章的讨论，我们发现PPP中介机构的信息公开工作还有很多有待加强的地方。这主要体现在两方面：一方面，要加大PPP中介机构自身的信息公开力度，在PPP中介信息平台上增加更多字段信息的要求，例如，增加PPP中介机构人员数量、人员结构、主要团队等信息；另一方面，在PPP项目运行过程中，也要加大对相关中介机构参与度、尽职度、主要参与的项目类型、中介机构分类等信息的公开力度。此外，可以对中介机构参与的项目中后期被退库的比例等信息进行公示，以及对其在服务某级地方政府时是否同时服务了与该政府有合作关系的社会资本方等信息（避免商业伦理冲突）进行公示，从而对PPP中介机构形成一种压力，推动其参与PPP项目时更加谨慎。

7.3 未来展望

以上是我们报告的全部内容。总的来说，在2017—2018年指数编制和分析的基础上，我们通过编制指数的方式，对截至2019年底的中国PPP项目的信息公开情况进行了详细的分析。报告保持了指标体系和指数编制方法的连续性，但也得到一些新的发现。然而，虽然精益求精，但我们相信在指标体系设置、指数编制方法和指数结果具体分析等方面，本报告依然存在很多不足之处，未来至少在以下几个方面可以进一步改进：

第一，指标体系可以进一步完善。正如报告中所阐述的，由于相关信息缺失等原因，PPP市场透明度指数被人为分成了即时公开指数和适时公开指数，而随着PPP综合信息平台的进一步完善，特别是如果各指标公布时间节点这样的信息也能准确得到记录的话，未来有望将即时公开和适时公开合而为一，从而使得PPP市场透明度指数的指标体系更加完善。除了评估相关信息是否披露外，还可以进一步评估披露的及时性等。此外，随着PPP事业的进一步深入发展，将会有越来越多的项目进入执行甚至移交阶段，而处于这些阶段的信息公开工作也会越来越重要，因而指标体系的重心也可以适当后移。

第二，信息质量可以纳入评估范围。正如前文我们提及过的，本报告仅评估PPP项目的信息公开工作，不评估这些信息所代表的具体工作的质量。例如，我们仅仅评估了PPP物有所值评价报告、财政承受能力论证报告是否得到披露，而不对物有所值评价报告、财政承受能力论证报告具体内容的优劣、科学与否等作出判断。但我们知道这些信息都是非常重要的，因而未来这些重点报告的具体内容也可以考虑纳入专门的评估分析中，以考察各地区、各方在PPP规范化管理方面的工作业绩。

附件一　专家判定矩阵调查表

受亚洲开发银行的委托，上海财经大学PPP研究中心承担了《2019中国PPP市场透明度评估报告》的研究工作。报告将通过编制指数的方式，全面反映我国PPP市场透明度工作的成绩和不足。在指数编制过程中，不同具体指标之间包含的信息量和重要程度差异很大，因此，课题组想通过专家问卷调查的方式，确定PPP项目信息透明度各影响因素的相对权重（层次图如图3-1所示）。

为此，课题组根据层次分析法（AHP）的形式设计如下调查表。这种方法是在同一个层次对影响因素的重要性进行两两比较。衡量尺度划分为9个等级，其中9、7、5、3、1的数值分别对应绝对重要、十分重要、比较重要、稍微重要、同样重要，而8、6、4、2表示重要程度介于相邻的两个等级之间。

在下面的表格中，靠左边的等级单元格表示左列因素重要于右列因素，靠右边的等级单元格表示右列因素重要于左列因素。请根据您的看法，在相应的单元格画"√"即可。您的判断对我们科学严谨地编制PPP市场透明度指数至关重要。

真诚感谢您的帮助！

上海财经大学课题组

2020年1月8日

下列各组两两比较要素，对于"透明度总指数"的相对重要性如何？																		
重要性比较																		
适时公开	9	8	7	6	5	4	3	2	1	2	3	4	5	6	7	8	9	即时公开

下列各组两两比较要素，对于"适时公开"的相对重要性如何？																		
重要性比较																		
识别阶段	9	8	7	6	5	4	3	2	1	2	3	4	5	6	7	8	9	准备阶段
识别阶段	9	8	7	6	5	4	3	2	1	2	3	4	5	6	7	8	9	采购阶段
准备阶段	9	8	7	6	5	4	3	2	1	2	3	4	5	6	7	8	9	采购阶段

下列各组两两比较要素，对于"即时公开"的相对重要性如何？																		
重要性比较																		
识别阶段	9	8	7	6	5	4	3	2	1	2	3	4	5	6	7	8	9	准备阶段
识别阶段	9	8	7	6	5	4	3	2	1	2	3	4	5	6	7	8	9	采购阶段
识别阶段	9	8	7	6	5	4	3	2	1	2	3	4	5	6	7	8	9	执行阶段
准备阶段	9	8	7	6	5	4	3	2	1	2	3	4	5	6	7	8	9	采购阶段
准备阶段	9	8	7	6	5	4	3	2	1	2	3	4	5	6	7	8	9	执行阶段
采购阶段	9	8	7	6	5	4	3	2	1	2	3	4	5	6	7	8	9	执行阶段

附件二　PPP综合信息平台信息公开管理暂行办法

关于印发《政府和社会资本合作(PPP)综合信息平台信息公开管理暂行办法》的通知

（财金〔2017〕1号）

各省、自治区、直辖市、计划单列市财政厅(局)，新疆生产建设兵团财务局，财政部驻各省、自治区、直辖市、计划单列市财政监察专员办事处：

为进一步贯彻落实《国务院办公厅转发财政部 发展改革委 人民银行关于在公共服务领域推广运用政府和社会资本合作模式指导意见的通知》》(国办发〔2015〕42号)有关要求，加强和规范政府和社会资本合作(PPP)项目信息公开工作，促进PPP项目各参与方诚实守信、严格履约，保障公众知情权，推动PPP市场公平竞争、规范发展，我们研究起草了《政府和社会资本合作(PPP)综合信息平台信息公开管理暂行办法》，现印发你们，请遵照执行。

财政部

2017年1月23日

政府和社会资本合作(PPP)综合信息平台信息公开管理暂行办法

第一章　总　则

第一条　为加强和规范政府和社会资本合作(PPP)信息公开工作，促进PPP项目各参与方诚实守信、严格履约，保障公众知情权，推动PPP市场公平竞争、规范发展，依据《中华人民共和国预算法》、《中华人民共和国政府采购法》和《国务院办公厅转发财政部 发展改革委 人民银行关于在公共服务领域推广政府和社会资本合作模式指导意见的通知》（国办发〔2015〕42号）等有关规定，制定本办法。

第二条　中华人民共和国境内已纳入PPP综合信息平台的PPP项目信息公开，适用本办法。

第三条　PPP项目信息公开遵循客观、公正、及时、便利的原则。

第四条　地方各级财政部门（以下简称“财政部门”）会同同级政府有关部门推进、指导、协调、监督本行政区域范围内的PPP项目信息公开工作，结合当地实际具体开展以下工作：

（一）收集、整理PPP项目信息；

（二）在PPP综合信息平台录入、维护和更新PPP项目信息；

（三）组织编制本级政府PPP项目信息公开年度工作报告；

（四）根据法律法规规定和实际需要，在其他渠道同时公开PPP项目信息；

（五）与PPP项目信息公开有关的其他工作。

政府有关部门、项目实施机构、社会资本或PPP项目公司等PPP项目参与主体应真实、完整、准确、及时地提供PPP项目信息。

第二章　信息公开的内容

第五条　项目识别阶段应当公开的PPP项目信息包括：

（一）项目实施方案概要，包含：项目基本情况（含项目合作范围、合作期限、项目产出说明和绩效标准等基本信息）、风险分配框架、运作方式、交易结构（含投融资结构、回报机制、相关配套安排）、合同体系、监管架构、采购方式选择；

（二）经财政部门和行业主管部门审核通过的物有所值评价报告，包含：定性评价的指标及权重、评分标准、评分结果；定量评价测算的主要指标、方法、过程和结果（含PSC值、PPP值）等（如有）；物有所值评价通过与否的结论；

（三）经财政部门审核通过的财政承受能力论证报告，包含：本项目各年度财政支出责任数额及累计支出责任总额，本级政府本年度全部已实施和拟实施的PPP项目各年度财政支出责任数额总和及其占各年度一般公共预算支出比例情况；财政承受能力论证的测算依据、主要因素和指标等；财政承受能力论证通过与否的结论；

（四）其他基础资料，包括：新建或改扩建项目建议书及批复文件、可行性研究报告（含规划许可证、选址意见书、土地预审意见、环境影响评价报告等支撑性文件）及批复文件、设计文件及批复文件（如有）；存量公共资产建设、运营维护的历史资料以及第三方出具的资产评估报告，以及存量资产或权益转让时所可能涉及到的员工安置方案、债权债务处置方案、土地处置方案等（如有）。

第六条　项目准备阶段应当公开的PPP项目信息包括：

（一）政府方授权文件，包括对实施机构、PPP项目合同的政府方签约主体、政府方出资代表（如有）等的授权；

（二）经审核通过的项目实施方案（含同级人民政府对实施方案的批复文件），包含：项目基本情况（含项目合作范围、合作期限、项目产出说明和绩效标准等基本信息），风险分配框架，运作方式，交易结构（含投融资结构、回报机制、相关配套安排），合同体系及核心边界条件；监管架构；采购方式选择；

（三）按经审核通过的项目实施方案验证的物有所值评价报告（如有）；

（四）按经审核通过的项目实施方案验证的财政承受能力论证报告（如有）。

第七条　项目采购阶段的信息公开应遵照政府采购等相关规定执行，应当公开的PPP项目信息包括：

（一）项目资格预审公告（含资格预审申请文件）及补充公告（如有）；

（二）项目采购文件，包括竞争者须知、PPP项目合同草案、评审办法（含评审小组组成、评审专家人数及产生方式、评审细则等）；

（三）补遗文件（如有）；

（四）资格预审评审及响应文件评审结论性意见；

（五）资格预审专家、评审专家名单、确认谈判工作组成员名单；

（六）预中标、成交结果公告；

（七）中标、成交结果公告及中标通知书；

（八）项目采购阶段更新、调整的政府方授权文件（如有），包括对实施机构、PPP项目合同的政府方签约主体、政府方出资代表（如有）等的授权；

（九）同级人民政府同意签署PPP项目合同的批复文件，以及已签署的PPP项目合同，并列示主要产出说明及绩效指标、回报机制、调价机制等核心条款。

第八条 项目执行阶段应当公开的PPP项目信息包括：

（一）项目公司（如有）设立登记、股东认缴资本金及资本金实缴到位情况、增减资情况（如有）、项目公司资质情况（如有）；

（二）项目融资机构名称、项目融资金额、融资结构及融资交割情况；

（三）项目施工许可证、建设进度、质量及造价等与PPP项目合同有关约定的对照审查情况；

（四）社会资本或项目公司的运营情况（特别是出现重大经营或财务风险，可能严重影响到社会资本或项目公司正常运营的情况）及运营绩效达标情况；

（五）项目公司绩效监测报告、中期评估报告、项目重大变更或终止情况、项目定价及历次调价情况；

（六）项目公司财务报告，包括项目收费情况，项目获得的政府补贴情况，项目公司资产负债情况等内容；

（七）项目公司成本监审、PPP项目合同的变更或补充协议签订情况；

（八）重大违约及履约担保的提取情况，对公众投诉的处理情况等；

（九）本级政府或其职能部门作出的对项目可能产生重大影响的规定、决定等；

（十）项目或项目直接相关方（主要是PPP项目合同的签约各方）重大纠纷、诉讼或仲裁事项，但根据相关司法程序要求不得公开的除外；

（十一）本级PPP项目目录、本级PPP项目示范试点库及项目变化情况、本级人大批准的政府对PPP项目的财政预算、执行及决算情况等。

第九条 项目移交阶段应当公开的PPP项目信息包括：

（一）移交工作组的组成、移交程序、移交标准等移交方案；

（二）移交资产或设施或权益清单、移交资产或权益评估报告（如适用）、性能测试方案，以及移交项目资产或设施上各类担保或权益限制的解除情况；

（三）项目设施移交标准达标检测结果；

（四）项目后评价报告（含对项目产出、成本效益、监管成效、可持续性、PPP模式应用等进行绩效评价），以及项目后续运作方式。

第三章 信息公开的方式

第十条 PPP项目信息公开的方式包括即时公开和适时公开。

第十一条 即时公开是指财政部门会同有关部门和项目实施机构等依据PPP项目所处的不同阶段及对应的录入时间要求，在PPP综合信息平台录入本办法规定的相关信息时即自动公开。即时公开的内容及要求详见本办法附件。

第十二条 适时公开是指在录入本办法规定的相关信息时不自动公开，而是由财政部门会同有关部门选择在项目进入特定阶段或达成特定条件后再行公开。除本办法另有规定外，项目识别、准备、采购阶段的信息，由财政部门会同有关部门选择在项目进入执行阶段后6个月内的任一时点予以公开；项目执行阶段的信息，由财政部门会同相关部门选择在该信息对应事项确定或完成后次年的4月30日前的任一时点予以公开。前述期限届满后未选择公开的信息将转为自动公开。适时公开的内容及要求详见本办法附件。

第十三条 依照本办法公开的PPP项目信息可在财政部政府和社会资本合作中心官方网站（www.cpppc.org）上公开查询。其中PPP项目政府采购信息应当在省级以上人民政府财政部门指定的政府采购信息发布媒体上同步发布。

第四章 监督管理

第十四条 财政部对全国PPP项目信息公开情况进行评价和监督，省级财政部门负责对本省PPP项目信息公开工作进行监督管理。下级财政部门未按照本办法规定真实、完整、准确、及时录入应公开PPP项目信息的，上级财政部门应责令其限期改正；逾期拒不改正或情节严重的，予以通报批评。

第十五条 政府有关部门、项目实施机构、社会资本或PPP项目公司等PPP项目信息提供方应当对其所提供信息的真实性、完整性、准确性、及时性负责。一经发现所提供信息不真实、不完整、不准确、不及时的，PPP项目信息提供方应主动及时予以修正、补充或采取其他有效补救措施。如经财政部门或利益相关方提供相关材料证实PPP项目信息提供方未按照规定提供信息或存在其他不当情形的，财政部门可以责令其限期改正；无正当理由拒不改正的，财政部门可将该项目从项目库中清退。被清退的项目自清退之日起一年内不得重新纳入PPP综合信息平台。

第十六条　财政部门应会同政府有关部门在每年2月28日前完成上一年度本级政府实施的PPP项目信息公开年度工作报告，报送省级财政部门，并由省级财政部门在每年3月31日前汇总上报至财政部。报告内容应包括：

（一）即时和适时公开PPP项目信息的情况；

（二）PPP项目信息公开工作存在的主要问题及改进情况；

（三）其他需要报告的事项。

第十七条　财政部门工作人员在PPP项目信息公开监督管理工作中存在滥用职权、玩忽职守、徇私舞弊等违法违纪行为的，按照《公务员法》、《行政监察法》、《财政违法行为处罚处分条例》等国家有关规定追究相应责任；涉嫌犯罪的，移送司法机关处理。

第十八条　公民、法人或者其他组织可以通过PPP综合信息平台对PPP项目信息公开情况提供反馈意见，相关信息提供方应及时予以核实处理。

第五章　附　则

第十九条　PPP综合信息平台是指依据《关于规范政府和社会资本合作（PPP）综合信息平台运行的通知》（财金〔2015〕166号）由财政部建立的全国PPP综合信息管理和发布平台，包含项目库、机构库、资料库三部分。

第二十条　PPP项目信息公开涉及国家秘密、商业秘密、个人隐私、知识产权，可能会危及国家安全、公共安全、经济安全和社会稳定或损害公民、法人或其他组织的合法权益的，依照相关法律法规处理。

第二十一条　本办法自2017年3月1日起施行。

PPP项目信息公开要求

项目所处阶段	公开内容	公开方式	公开的时点	信息提供方
项目识别	项目概况、项目合作范围、合作期限、项目运作方式、采购社会资本方式的选择	即时公开	实施方案编制完成之日起10个工作日内	项目发起方

（续表）

项目所处阶段	公　开　内　容	公开方式	公开的时点	信息提供方
项目识别	交易结构（含投融资结构、回报机制、相关配套安排）、项目产出说明和绩效标准、风险分配框架、合同体系、监管体系	适时公开	进入项目执行阶段后6个月内	项目发起方
	物有所值定性评价指标及权重、评分标准、评分结果	即时公开	报告定稿之日起10个工作日内	
	物有所值评价通过与否的评价结论（含财政部门会同行业部门对报告的审核意见）	即时公开	实施方案批复文件下发后10个工作日内	
	审核通过的物有所值评价报告（含财政部门对报告的批复文件）	适时公开	进入项目执行阶段后6个月内	
	本项目以及年度全部已实施和拟实施的PPP项目财政支出责任数额及年度预算安排情况，以及每一年度全部PPP项目从预算中安排的支出责任占一般公共预算支出比例情况	即时公开	实施方案批复文件下发后10个工作日内	
	财政承受能力论证的测算依据、主要因素和指标	即时公开	报告定稿之日起10个工作日内	
	通过财政承受能力论证与否的结论	即时公开	实施方案批复文件下发后10个工作日内	
	审核通过的财政承受能力论证报告（含财政部门对报告的批复文件）	适时公开	进入项目执行阶段后6个月内	
	新建或改扩建项目建议书及批复文件	适时公开	进入项目执行阶段后6个月内	实施机构
	可行性研究报告（含全套支撑性文件）及批复文件，设计文件及批复文件（如适用）	适时公开	进入项目执行阶段后6个月内	实施机构
	存量公共资产或权益的资产评估报告，以及存量资产或权益转让时所可能涉及到的各类方案等（如适用）	适时公开	进入项目执行阶段后6个月内	实施机构

（续表）

项目所处阶段	公 开 内 容	公开方式	公开的时点	信息提供方
项目准备	政府方授权文件，包括对实施机构、PPP项目合同的政府方签约主体、政府方出资代表（如适用）等的授权	即时公开	授权后10个工作日内	项目所在地本级政府
	项目概况、项目合作范围、合作期限、项目运作方式、采购社会资本方式的选择	即时公开	进入采购程序后10个工作日内	实施机构
	交易结构（含投融资结构、回报机制、相关配套安排）、项目产出说明和绩效标准、风险分配框架、核心边界条件、合同体系、监管体系	适时公开	进入项目执行阶段后6个月内	实施机构
	政府对实施方案的审核批复文件	即时公开	批复文件下发后10个工作日内	实施机构
	审核通过的项目实施方案及修正案	适时公开	进入项目执行阶段后6个月内	实施机构
项目采购	项目资格预审公告（含资格预审申请文件）	即时公开	资格预审公告发布后10个工作日内	实施机构
	项目采购文件、补遗文件（如有）	适时公开	进入项目执行阶段后6个月内	实施机构
	资格预审评审报告及响应文件评审报告中专家组评审结论性意见，附资格预审专家和评审专家名单	适时公开	进入项目执行阶段后6个月内	采购监管机构
	确认谈判工作组成员名单	适时公开	进入项目执行阶段后6个月内	实施机构
	预中标及成交结果公告；中标、成交结果公告及中标通知书	即时公开	依法律规定及采购文件约定	实施机构、采购监管机构
	已签署的PPP项目合同	适时公开	进入项目执行阶段后6个月内	实施机构
	PPP项目合同核心条款，应包括主要产出说明、绩效指标回报机制、调价机制	即时公开	项目合同经人民政府审核通过后10个工作日内	实施机构、项目公司

（续表）

项目所处阶段	公　开　内　容	公开方式	公开的时点	信息提供方
项目采购	本项目政府支出责任确认文件或更新调整文件（如适用），以及同级人大（或人大常委会）将本项目财政支出责任纳入跨年度预算的批复文件（如适用）	适时公开	进入项目执行阶段后6个月内	实施机构
	项目采购阶段调整、更新的政府方授权文件（如有）	即时公开	项目合同经人民政府审核通过后10个工作日内的附件依据相关法律规定公开	实施机构
项目执行	项目公司设立登记、股东认缴及实缴资本金情况、增减资（如适用）	即时公开	设立时及资本金到位后10个工作日内	项目公司
	融资额度、融资主要条件及融资交割情况	适时公开	对应事项确定或完成后次年的4月30日前	项目公司
	项目施工许可证、建设进度、质量及造价等与PPP项目合同的符合性审查情况	即时公开	依据PPP项目合同约定；如PPP项目合同未约定时，则在对应活动结束后次年的4月30日前予以公开	实施机构、项目公司
	社会资本或项目公司的年度运营情况及运营绩效达标情况	即时公开	依据PPP项目合同约定；如PPP项目合同未约定时，则在对应活动结束后次年的4月30日前予以公开	项目公司
	项目公司绩效监测报告、中期评估报告、项目重大变更或终止情况、项目定价及历次调价情况	即时公开	依据PPP项目合同约定；如PPP项目合同未约定时，则在对应活动结束后次年的4月30日前予以公开	实施机构
	项目公司成本监审、所有的PPP合同修订协议或补充协议	适时公开	对应活动结束后次年的4月30日前	实施机构项目公司
	项目公司财务报告相关内容，包括项目收费情况，项目获得的政府补贴情况，项目公司资产负债情况等	适时公开	对应活动结束后次年的4月30日前	项目公司
	重大违约及履约担保的提取情况，对公众投诉的处理情况等	即时公开	发生之日起10个工作日内	实施机构
	本级政府或其职能部门作出的对项目可能产生重大影响的规定、决定等	即时公开	规定及决定 下发后10个工作日	实施机构

（续表）

项目所处阶段	公开内容	公开方式	公开的时点	信息提供方
项目执行	项目或项目直接相关方重大纠纷、涉诉或涉仲情况	即时公开	除本办法另有规定外，发生后10个工作日内	项目公司
	本级PPP项目目录、本级PPP项目示范试点库及项目变化情况、本级人大批准的政府对PPP项目的财政预算、执行及决算情况等	即时公开	依法律规定（如有）公开或每季度公开	
项目移交	移交工作组的组成、移交程序、移交标准等移交方案	即时公开	移交方案确定后10个工作日内	实施机构
	移交资产或设施或权益清单、移交资产或权益评估报告（如适用）、性能测试方案	即时公开	清单或报告定稿或测试完成后10个工作日内	实施机构
	移交项目资产或设施上各类担保或权益限制的解除情况（如适用）	即时公开	对应解除完成后10个工作日内	实施机构、项目公司
	项目设施移交标准达标检测结果	即时公开	达标检测结果出具后10个工作日内	实施机构
	项目后评价报告，以及项目后续运作方式	即时公开	后评估报告定稿或项目后续运作方式确定后10个工作日内	实施机构

附件三　PPP信息公开和规范管理制度目录

序号	发布时间	文件号	文件	发布者
1	2013.12.19	财政部74号令	《政府采购非招标采购方式管理办法》	财政部
2	2014.09.23	财金〔2014〕76号	《关于推广运用政府和社会资本合作模式有关问题的通知》	财政部
3	2014.11.29	财金〔2014〕113号	《关于印发政府和社会资本合作模式操作指南（试行）的通知》	财政部
4	2014.11.30	财金〔2014〕112号	《关于政府和社会资本合作示范项目实施有关问题的通知》	财政部
5	2014.12.30	财金〔2014〕156号	《关于规范政府和社会资本合作合同管理工作的通知》	财政部
6	2014.12.31	财金〔2014〕215号	《关于印发〈政府和社会合作项目政府采购管理办法〉的通知》	财政部
7	2014.12.31	财金〔2014〕214号	《关于印发〈政府采购竞争性磋商采购方式管理暂行办法〉的通知》	财政部
8	2015.02.13	财建〔2015〕29号	《关于推进市政公共领域开展政府和社会资本合作项目推介工作的通知》	财政部 住建部
9	2015.03.10	发改投资〔2015〕445号	《关于推进开发性金融支持政府和社会资本合作有关工作的通知》	国家发改委
10	2015.04.07	财金〔2015〕21号	《关于印发〈政府和社会合作项目财政承受能力论证指引〉的通知》	财政部
11	2015.05.19	国办发〔2015〕42号	《国务院办公厅转发财政部发展改革委人民银行关于在公共服务领域推广政府和社会资本合作模式指导意见的通知》	国务院办公厅

（续表）

序号	发布时间	文件号	文件	发布者
12	2015.06.25	财金〔2015〕57号	《关于进一步做好政府和社会资本合作项目示范工作的通知》	财政部
13	2015.12.18	财金〔2015〕166号	《关于规范政府和社会资本合作（PPP）综合信息平台运行的通知》	财政部
14	2015.12.18	财金〔2015〕167号	《关于印发〈PPP物有所值评价指引（试行）〉的通知》	财政部
15	2016.01		《中华人民共和国政府和社会资本合作法（征求意见稿）》	财政部
16	2016.05.28	财金〔2016〕32	关于进一步共同做好政府和社会资本合作（PPP）有关工作的通知》	国家发改委 财政部
17	2016.10.20	财金〔2016〕92号	《关于印发〈政府和社会资本合作项目财政管理暂行办法〉的通知》	财政部
18	2016.12.21	发改投资〔2016〕2698号	《关于推进传统基础设施领域政府和社会资本合作（PPP）项目资产证券化相关工作的通知》	国家发改委
19	2016.12.30	财金〔2016〕144号	《财政部政府和社会资本合作（PPP）专家库管理办法》	财政部
20	2017.01.23	财金〔2017〕1号	《关于印发〈政府和社会资本合作（PPP）综合信息平台信息公开管理暂行办法〉的通知》	财政部
21	2017.03.22	财金〔2017〕8号	《关于印发〈政府和社会资本合作（PPP）咨询机构库管理暂行办法〉的通知》	财政部
22	2017.10.19		《政府和社会资本合作（PPP）项目资产支持证券挂牌条件确认指南和信息披露指南》	上海证券交易所
23	2017.11.10	财办金〔2017〕92号	《关于规范政府和社会资本合作（PPP）综合信息平台项目库管理的通知》	财政部
24	2019.03.07	财金〔2019〕10号	《财政部关于推进政府和社会资本合作规范发展的实施意见》	财政部
25	2020.03.16	财金〔2020〕13号	《政府和社会资本合作（PPP）项目绩效管理操作指引》	财政部

附件四　项目数大于20的城市PPP市场透明度排名

排名	城　　市	2019年项目数量	即时公开透明度指数	适时公开透明度指数	透明度总指数
1	安徽宣城	34	85.19	83.57	84.56
2	云南德宏	20	89.76	74.45	83.79
3	河北石家庄	37	85.25	81.48	83.78
4	山东滨州	25	88.73	75.95	83.75
5	吉林四平	20	87.02	78.09	83.54
6	新疆和田	20	87.74	76.91	83.52
7	山东淄博	28	88.78	73.51	82.82
8	新疆阿克苏	66	85.02	79.36	82.81
9	山东德州	44	86.27	77.07	82.68
10	云南临沧	25	85.42	78.21	82.61
11	广东东莞	108	84.61	79.15	82.48
12	云南大理	38	87.73	74.05	82.39
13	云南昭通	21	85.61	77.23	82.34
14	山东聊城	29	87.56	74.12	82.32
15	新疆昌吉	31	82.86	80.86	82.08
16	山东日照	56	85.07	77.35	82.06

（续表）

排名	城　　市	2019年 项目数量	即时公开 透明度指数	适时公开 透明度指数	透明度总指数
17	山东济南	46	85.65	76.15	81.94
18	山东潍坊	93	85.33	76.26	81.79
19	山东烟台	39	84.42	77.57	81.75
20	河北沧州	46	83.53	78.87	81.71
21	河北邢台	39	86.79	73.73	81.70
22	云南红河	46	84.58	77.10	81.66
23	河北保定	37	81.88	81.29	81.65
24	山东济宁	82	86.87	73.42	81.62
25	河北唐山	52	85.68	75.16	81.58
26	吉林长春	50	85.19	75.63	81.46
27	新疆博州	48	84.40	76.79	81.43
28	河北承德	56	84.35	76.82	81.41
29	云南玉溪	57	83.42	78.25	81.41
30	甘肃兰州	22	83.94	77.36	81.38
31	湖南永州	23	83.54	77.95	81.36
32	湖南株洲	30	83.70	76.91	81.05
33	云南保山	31	85.14	74.51	80.99
34	江苏泰州	28	83.06	77.61	80.94
35	内蒙古巴彦淖尔	25	84.34	75.54	80.91
36	福建莆田	28	83.52	76.67	80.85
37	山东菏泽	74	85.00	74.34	80.85
38	湖南益阳	29	83.74	76.27	80.83
39	辽宁朝阳	23	83.57	76.45	80.79
40	山东威海	27	84.02	75.63	80.75
41	内蒙锡林郭勒	30	86.96	70.98	80.72
42	湖南湘潭	21	83.45	75.76	80.45

（续表）

排名	城　市	2019年项目数量	即时公开透明度指数	适时公开透明度指数	透明度总指数
43	河南新乡	44	79.49	81.66	80.34
44	贵州毕节	65	81.29	78.21	80.09
45	云南丽江	20	85.80	71.15	80.09
46	河北邯郸	36	83.00	75.50	80.07
47	山东临沂	76	82.79	75.34	79.88
48	云南曲靖	42	83.64	73.94	79.86
49	四川泸州	27	85.86	70.34	79.81
50	广西玉林	31	79.10	80.75	79.74
51	湖南长沙	43	82.68	75.10	79.72
52	安徽池州	21	78.46	81.61	79.69
53	河南商丘	36	83.89	73.04	79.66
54	河北衡水	32	83.09	74.23	79.64
55	江苏南京	90	83.41	73.22	79.43
56	广西南宁	29	80.51	77.70	79.41
57	内蒙古呼伦贝尔	34	83.90	72.39	79.41
58	安徽六安	41	80.58	77.44	79.35
59	湖南常德	38	84.14	71.54	79.23
60	江苏淮安	41	82.18	74.53	79.20
61	贵州黔西南	34	84.32	70.88	79.08
62	辽宁大连	34	82.28	73.71	78.94
63	广东阳江	26	81.56	74.01	78.62
64	湖北荆门	33	82.28	72.82	78.59
65	广东广州	24	82.87	71.88	78.59
66	河南平顶山	59	78.66	77.97	78.39
67	安徽合肥	20	78.53	77.94	78.30
68	广东河源	24	83.07	70.82	78.29

（续表）

排名	城　市	2019年项目数量	即时公开透明度指数	适时公开透明度指数	透明度总指数
69	广东梅州	23	81.45	73.21	78.23
70	安徽蚌埠	30	77.65	78.90	78.13
71	云南昆明	54	79.86	75.26	78.06
72	陕西西安	83	82.72	70.78	78.06
73	河南许昌	29	77.48	78.86	78.02
74	山东东营	33	80.59	73.83	77.95
75	云南普洱	26	79.10	75.94	77.87
76	云南楚雄	44	80.09	74.35	77.85
77	吉林吉林	23	80.75	72.93	77.70
78	陕西汉中	29	80.15	73.82	77.68
79	贵州贵阳	51	80.90	72.46	77.61
80	广东肇庆	27	78.87	75.57	77.58
81	四川南充	35	79.71	73.79	77.40
82	陕西渭南	31	80.83	72.01	77.39
83	江苏徐州	58	78.38	75.77	77.36
84	新疆伊犁	24	80.14	72.98	77.34
85	浙江嘉兴	22	81.89	70.05	77.27
86	安徽亳州	34	77.52	76.74	77.21
87	河南郑州	56	76.62	77.82	77.09
88	安徽阜阳	62	76.94	77.32	77.09
89	安徽宿州	42	77.81	75.80	77.03
90	湖北宜昌	37	78.76	74.14	76.96
91	云南文山	28	81.09	70.45	76.94
92	河南开封	34	76.83	77.06	76.92
93	安徽滁州	36	78.27	74.69	76.88
94	贵州铜仁	26	79.95	72.05	76.87

（续表）

排名	城　　市	2019 年项目数量	即时公开透明度指数	适时公开透明度指数	透明度总指数
95	浙江宁波	49	79.30	72.89	76.80
96	湖南邵阳	22	76.81	76.66	76.75
97	陕西铜川	21	80.29	71.03	76.68
98	浙江杭州	66	81.91	68.31	76.61
99	河南安阳	45	78.96	72.80	76.56
100	广西崇左	24	80.72	69.96	76.52
101	贵州遵义	114	80.60	69.91	76.43
102	江西宜春	48	81.19	68.99	76.43
103	安徽安庆	48	75.90	77.06	76.35
104	山西长治	37	80.78	69.27	76.29
105	广东汕头	29	81.09	68.63	76.23
106	河南周口	47	78.80	72.07	76.18
107	山西吕梁	49	83.20	65.12	76.15
108	湖南湘西	50	78.32	72.31	75.98
109	福建宁德	63	77.57	73.46	75.97
110	贵州六盘水	50	78.68	71.62	75.93
111	河南洛阳	57	76.50	74.87	75.86
112	浙江丽水	62	80.46	68.63	75.85
113	甘肃酒泉	20	82.13	65.93	75.82
114	山西晋中	50	80.43	68.57	75.81
115	河南濮阳	42	76.45	74.68	75.76
116	浙江湖州	45	79.80	69.18	75.66
117	广东湛江	26	76.52	74.24	75.63
118	湖南郴州	38	76.01	74.83	75.55
119	河南焦作	31	75.01	76.25	75.49
120	湖南岳阳	25	77.34	72.10	75.30

（续表）

排名	城　市	2019年项目数量	即时公开透明度指数	适时公开透明度指数	透明度总指数
121	内蒙古赤峰	56	76.57	73.30	75.29
122	江西南昌	20	78.72	69.84	75.26
123	江苏盐城	26	76.36	73.50	75.25
124	山西朔州	23	80.84	66.48	75.24
125	湖北黄冈	27	80.64	66.69	75.20
126	江西萍乡	30	81.51	65.33	75.20
127	新疆乌鲁木齐	64	79.76	68.02	75.18
128	湖北十堰	23	78.18	70.46	75.17
129	四川巴中	44	76.09	73.52	75.09
130	河南三门峡	23	74.85	75.25	75.01
131	四川成都	55	77.84	70.55	74.99
132	浙江温州	83	77.48	70.86	74.90
133	广东江门	40	80.57	65.62	74.74
134	安徽铜陵	21	79.66	66.95	74.71
135	河南驻马店	69	75.71	73.13	74.70
136	江苏宿迁	43	77.57	69.72	74.51
137	贵州安顺	28	72.82	77.14	74.50
138	四川乐山	32	75.86	72.30	74.47
139	山西大同	29	77.92	68.70	74.33
140	山东青岛	74	79.21	66.56	74.27
141	广东韶关	25	76.36	70.95	74.25
142	四川广元	36	74.64	73.22	74.09
143	湖南怀化	23	74.60	73.11	74.01
144	江苏扬州	27	77.04	68.85	73.85
145	湖南衡阳	25	80.85	62.73	73.78
146	福建龙岩	26	72.70	75.46	73.78

（续表）

排名	城　市	2019 年项目数量	即时公开透明度指数	适时公开透明度指数	透明度总指数
147	江西九江	23	81.72	61.34	73.77
148	贵州黔东南	49	77.90	67.06	73.68
149	山西临汾	58	77.65	67.46	73.67
150	福建南平	26	73.61	73.53	73.58
151	河南南阳	71	72.83	74.74	73.58
152	福建泉州	66	75.25	70.88	73.54
153	山西忻州	37	78.86	64.68	73.33
154	广东惠州	44	73.74	72.14	73.12
155	四川凉山	44	75.59	69.14	73.08
156	安徽马鞍山	20	74.24	71.11	73.02
157	宁夏银川	25	75.52	69.05	72.99
158	湖南娄底	33	74.86	69.99	72.96
159	浙江绍兴	31	74.96	69.79	72.94
160	四川宜宾	62	72.38	73.71	72.90
161	湖北孝感	31	75.87	68.07	72.83
162	河南信阳	52	70.07	76.12	72.43
163	湖北咸宁	34	79.19	61.69	72.36
164	福建福州	48	71.96	72.98	72.36
165	重庆	43	77.48	64.01	72.23
166	福建漳州	60	74.60	68.15	72.08
167	福建三明	22	74.89	67.55	72.03
168	浙江衢州	40	76.37	65.07	71.96
169	湖北黄石	23	77.31	63.31	71.85
170	内蒙古鄂尔多斯	33	78.68	60.35	71.53
171	四川达州	28	72.63	69.28	71.32
172	辽宁沈阳	26	75.47	64.36	71.14

（续表）

排名	城　市	2019年项目数量	即时公开透明度指数	适时公开透明度指数	透明度总指数
173	湖北荆州	29	79.12	58.29	71.00
174	山西太原	34	78.12	59.83	70.98
175	浙江台州	67	71.44	70.14	70.93
176	江西吉安	23	75.83	62.97	70.81
177	湖北恩施	35	74.52	64.56	70.63
178	湖北武汉	67	74.45	64.09	70.41
179	江西赣州	95	74.46	63.89	70.34
180	四川内江	25	67.73	74.27	70.28
181	江西抚州	36	76.76	58.29	69.56
182	四川绵阳	30	69.43	69.23	69.35
183	湖北襄阳	44	71.46	65.88	69.28
184	新疆巴音	30	76.15	58.39	69.22
185	广西柳州	27	71.42	65.53	69.12
186	山西运城	34	74.68	58.71	68.45
187	天津	49	74.70	58.24	68.28
188	新疆哈密	27	76.06	54.52	67.66
189	北京	70	71.29	61.56	67.49
190	四川广安	20	72.90	57.76	66.99
191	黑龙江哈尔滨	30	70.94	60.71	66.95
192	四川遂宁	22	68.93	62.48	66.42
193	贵州黔南	53	70.55	59.30	66.16
194	四川自贡	23	67.59	62.79	65.72
195	广东清远	23	77.89	46.52	65.66
196	江西上饶	38	72.17	54.12	65.13
197	浙江金华	39	67.77	51.02	61.24
198	海南海口	52	57.54	58.35	57.86

后　记

这份《2019中国PPP市场透明度报告》是由上海财经大学PPP研究中心课题组通力合作、共同撰写的。课题组负责人为上海财经大学公共经济与管理学院党委书记方芳副教授，课题组核心成员包括上海财经大学公共经济与管理学院的宗庆庆副教授和沈言言博士研究生。课题组在2017—2018年连续两年PPP市场透明度指数编制的基础上，对截至2019年底的中国PPP市场的信息公开状况进行调查、分析和评估。评估过程中，课题组既延续保持了指标体系和指数编制的稳定性，从而保证了2019年PPP市场透明度与2017年和2018年的评估结果可比，同时也对比分析了2019年PPP项目信息公开与前两年的情况变化。课题组希望能够通过准确、客观地反映中国PPP市场的信息公开状况，为中国PPP事业的健康持续发展尽绵薄之力。

本研究项目的顺利完成，得益于各方的大力支持与帮助。首先，亚洲开发银行、上海财经大学公共财政研究院、上海财经大学公共经济与管理学院克服种种困难，对本课题给予立项支持，为本课题的顺利开展提供了宝贵的经费资助。此外，财政部政府和社会资本合作中心为本课题的顺利开展给予了宝贵的支持。最后，上海财经大学公共经济与管理学院、上海财经大学科研处等机构也为本课题的顺利推进提供了保障。上海济邦投资咨询有限公司董事长张燎、云南城投华东与华南事业部财务总监陆志祥、北京中泽融信管理咨询公司董事总经理赵仕坤、联合国贸易和发展会议经济事务官员梁国勇、国新集团上海分公司总经理田晖、中国建设银行上海分行副行长周涛、上海财经大学经济学院院长周亚虹教授、上海财经大学公共财政研究院执行院长刘小川教授、上海财经大学公共财政研究院副院长兼PPP研究中心主任范子英教授等专家也对本课题的顺利开展提出了很多宝贵的意见。对这些机构和专家的宝贵支持,在此一并谢过,但需要再次说明的是,本报告是由课题组独立开展的,仅代表课题组的学术观点,并不代表上述机构的官方观点。

最后,陈力拓、陈潇、丁沁娴、高嘉雯、龚志强、黄立朋、黄翔、梁雅雯、盛玲玉、石佳、向希悦、徐兆培、薛宗岳、颜姝慧、俞九九、曾敬、张晓莹、周芸芹、朱君毅等上海财经大学的研究生和本科生参与了本项目数据收集和整理工作,在此一并致谢。

课题组再次对各方给予的支持和帮助表示最诚挚的谢意,同时也欢迎各界专家和从业者对课题组的工作提出宝贵的意见和建议,以期未来编制的PPP市场透明度指数更加科学严谨。具体可与课题组成员联系:

宗庆庆老师(邮箱:zong.qingqing@mail.sufe.edu.cn)